D1035162

WITHDRAWN

Shelley's Poetic Thoughts

Shelley's Poetic Thoughts

Richard Cronin

St. Martin's Press   New York

St. Martin's Press, Inc., '75 Fifth Avenue, New York, NY 10010
Printed in Hong Kong
First published in the United States of America in 1981
ISBN 0–312–71664–8

Library of Congress Cataloging in Publication Data

Cronin, Richard.
  Shelley's poetic thoughts.

  Includes bibliographical references and index.
  1. Shelley, Percy Bysshe, 1792–1822—Criticism
and interpretation. I. Title.
PR5438.C7   1980   821'.7   80–18441
ISBN 0–312–71664–8

To my wife

Contents

Preface

A number of books on Shelley have appeared in the last thirty years. This relieves me of the need to justify my interest in a once-neglected poet, but obliges me to explain my behaviour in adding to the already considerable bulk of commentary on Shelley's poems.

Shelley's recent critics may be divided, in a rough and ready manner, into three groups. The business of the first has been to demonstrate the coherence and precision of Shelley's thought as it is revealed in the poems and prose writings. Shelley's knowledge of science, first brought to notice by Whitehead's outlandish suggestion that Shelley had he lived might have proved a Newton among chemists, has been discussed by Carl Grabo, by Peter Butter, by Desmond King-Hele and by G. M. Matthews;[1] his philosophical thought by Grabo, by C. E. Pulos, by J. A. Notopolous, by Neville Rogers, and by Earl Wasserman;[2] and his political thought has been the special concern of K. N. Cameron.[3] Shelley's symbolism, and his myth-making and myth-adapting have also been given close attention. Yeats began this line of inquiry, and it has been pursued by Peter Butter, by Neville Rogers and by Harold Bloom. E. B. Hungerford, Earl Wasserman and Stuart Curran take a more historical interest in Shelley's manipulation of existing mythologies.[4] The third critical approach is to examine the relationship between Shelley's life and his work. This approach is pursued by Newman White in the standard biography of Shelley, by Richard Holmes in his more recent biography, and by a number of critics: Carlos Baker, K. N. Cameron, A. M. D. Hughes, Desmond King-Hele, James Rieger and Judith Chernaik.[5]

The poems have been discussed in relation to their thought, in relation to their symbolism and mythology, and in relation to the man who wrote them. There are good reasons why these approaches should have been pursued. The demonstration that

Shelley's thought is precise, coherent, and embraces both problems of philosophy and hard political realities is an appropriate response to Matthew Arnold's characterisation of Shelley as an ineffectual butterfly, and to the habit of reading Shelley's verse as though it were a meaningless rhapsody. That Shelley often understands natural phenomena with a scientific precision is a refutation of Leavis's charge that the weakness of Shelley's verse derives from the weakness of his grasp upon the actual. When Yeats, Butter and Bloom describe Shelley's technique of symbolism, and his capacity for myth-making, they establish him as one in a line of English poets stretching from Spenser to Yeats himself. The study of the relationship between the life and the works was also necessary if only because criticism of Shelley's poetry has often confined itself to the kind of vulgar, biographical interpretation that does equal violence to the life and to the poems.

Useful work has been done: from most of the critics who have done it I have learned, and to some of them, especially Earl Wasserman, I am deeply indebted. It is not a criticism of, but rather a compliment to, the existing work that my own approach is somewhat different. The concern of most of Shelley's critics has been with the inner meaning of the poems, with, to borrow a metaphor from linguistics, a deep structure of which the individual poem is only one transformation. The reader is led through the individual poem to a larger unity, whether it be a system of thought, a central myth or body of symbols, or a presiding personality. There is a tendency, though certainly not a uniform one,[6] for the study of the individual poem to be a means through which the critic's argument is·pursued, rather than the end at which the argument arrives. As a consequence comparatively little attention has been paid to the superficial matters that distinguish one poem from another. Little is said about genres, verse forms, about details of style. Not much is said to elucidate what Wordsworth could be supposed to have meant when he said of Shelley that, though he reprehended many of his principles, yet he was a better artist than any of his contemporaries.

This then will be, I hope in no sense other than I intend, a superficial book on Shelley, a book centrally concerned with Shelley's handling of language and poetic forms. But it would be foolish to attempt a purely formal appreciation of Shelley's poems for the poems resist such an approach. The best of them force the reader to understand Shelley's manner of saying by reference to what is said, and to understand what is said by reference to Shelley's manner of saying it. Coleridge distinguishes between 'poetic thoughts' and 'thoughts translated into the language of poetry'. Coleridge's phrase 'poetic thoughts' carries a useful ambiguity: it means both 'thoughts within poetry' and 'thoughts about poetry'. The phrase suggests the subject and the thesis of this book. It is not a book about Shelley's thought detached from the poems, neither is it about Shelley's poems devoid of the thought: it is a book about 'poetic thoughts'. It argues that Shelley's poems are successful only when his thought within the poem reveals itself through thought about the poem.

There is still no complete edition of Shelley's work, the authority of which has been generally accepted. I have therefore used the most widely available texts of the poems and prose; *Shelley's Poetical Works*, ed. Thomas Hutchinson, corrected by G. M. Matthews (London, 1970), and *Shelley's Prose: The Trumpet of a Prophecy*, edited by D. L. Clark (Albuquerque, New Mexico, 1954). I have made two exceptions to this. The poem entitled in Hutchinson *The Revolt of Islam* is a censored version of a poem originally entitled *Laon and Cythna*. Neville Rogers prints a text of the original poem, and I have corrected Hutchinson's text by reference to his.[7] The text of *The Triumph of Life* given by Hutchinson is impossibly bad, and I have therefore used G. M. Matthews's edition of the poem published in *Studia Neophilologica*, 32 (1960), pp. 271–309. Parts of chapters 1 and 2 are revised versions of articles that have appeared in the *Keats-Shelley Journal* and in *Essays in Criticism*. I am grateful to the editors of these journals for permission to re-print them.

I have incurred many debts in writing this book. I am aware that my debts to Shelley's earlier critics are only inadequately acknowledged in the notes, but I see no help for it. The most important debts one is conscious of only generally. In my discussion of eighteenth-century ideas about language I am indebted to C. K. Ogden's *Bentham's Theory of Fictions* and to S. K. Land's *From Signs to Propositions*. My understanding of the function of genre has been largely shaped by Ernst Gombrich's *Art and Illusion*, and my understanding of poetic influence by

W. J. Bate's *The Burden of the Past*. I owe more personal debts to my teachers Emrys Jones and John Buxton, and to my colleagues Ingrid Swanson, Peter Butter, Robert Cummings and Philip Drew.

Richard Cronin

1 Language and Genre

Language

Words and Ideas

In September 1800 Coleridge wrote to William Godwin recommending him to write a book on language that would 'destroy the old antithesis of Words and Things: elevating as it were Words into Things and living Things too'.[1] It is a pity that Godwin never pursued the suggestion, for Coleridge was, in effect, asking him to express systematically an attitude to language that, Coleridge believed, distinguished the poetry written by himself and Wordsworth from the poetry of the eighteenth century.

In the autumn of 1800 Coleridge was in a state of intellectual excitement provoked by his belief that he had extricated himself from the confines of Hartleian materialism by recognising the mind as an active rather than a passive principle. His liberation from the similarly restrictive confines of eighteenth-century aesthetics had come earlier, in 1789. In *Biographia Literaria* Coleridge describes how, when still a schoolboy, he had taken the first step in his education as a poet by realising the deficiencies of the school of Pope. The poetry of that school, he came to think, was 'characterised not so much by poetic thoughts as by thoughts *translated* into the language of poetry', and could be defined as 'translations of prose thoughts into poetic language'.[2] There is an evident correspondence between the 'old antithesis of Words and Things' that in 1800 Coleridge called upon Godwin to overthrow, and the antithesis between thought and language that he detected and regretted in the most characteristic poetry of the eighteenth century, a correspondence even more evident if one remembers that in the terminology of John Locke, the great progenitor of eighteenth-century thought, a 'thing' is classed as an 'idea'.

1

In Book 3 of *An Essay Concerning Human Understanding* Locke established a linguistic model that dominated the discussion of language throughout the eighteenth century. Locke discusses language in order to dispense with it. His attempt is to distinguish genuine philosophical dispute from disputes about words of the kind that he imagined the scholastics to have confused with philosophical argument. The means he adopts is to insist resolutely on 'the old antithesis between Words and Things'. This is the principle that distinguishes his own work from that of the scholastic philosophers, and the vantage-point from which he can ridicule all disputes that seem to him merely verbal. To use a word that does not signify a specific idea is to talk nonsense; to argue about words rather than about the ideas they signify is to be monkishly absurd.

To Locke's example can be traced the impatience common to many British empiricists, even Hume, with all verbal disputes. But by the end of the eighteenth century there was an increasing willingness to accept that philosophical questions inevitably engaged questions about language, and that the two could scarcely be disentangled. Philosophy either reached its conclusions in defiance of language, in which case the philosopher might lament the lack of, or try to construct, a language compatible with his conclusions, or it would seek answers to its questions from within language, answers inherent in the structure of ordinary language. Godwin announced his doctrine of necessity, and then lamented that it was impossible for a man speaking or writing English to adhere to that doctrine,[3] and Jeremy Bentham seriously considered the construction of a new language free from the defects of ordinary English. Horne Tooke, on the other hand, sought to prove the truth of materialism by demonstrating that all abstract nouns were originally words which described sensible experience. Philosophy for Godwin or Bentham was a project undertaken in defiance of language, but for Horne Tooke philosophy ought to be reduced to a study of language. Locke's *Essay* ought, Tooke claims, to have been entitled 'A *Grammaticall* Essay on *Words* or *Language*',[4] a suggestion that would surely have outraged Locke himself. But for both groups the study of language became a vital concern, for both shared a belief much stronger than Locke's that the processes of language and the processes of thought are intimately connected.

Godwin, Bentham and Tooke in their different ways all share

the interest in language that had developed increasingly during the latter half of the eighteenth century. In particular a new interest had developed in the origin of language, a problem studied by Adam Smith in Britain, by Condillac in France, and by Herder in Germany. The speculations of each of these thinkers tended to integrate thought with its expression, to challenge 'the old antithesis of Words and Things'. Advances in thought might be considered inevitably to precipitate advances in language; or the development of thought and language might be conceived as indistinguishable; or development of thought might be considered an effect of development in language.[5]

Locke distinguished words from ideas, but by the end of the eighteenth century the two were collapsing together, and, as Coleridge's letter to Godwin indicates, the poets were alive to these developments. Pope could write:

True wit is nature to advantage dress'd:
What oft was thought, but ne'er so well express'd.

This is a neoclassical commonplace but the priority of thought over expression and the distinction between the two were notions sanctioned not only by the classical rhetoricians, but by Locke and the modern philosophers.[6] Contrast Pope's couplet with Shelley's celebration in *Prometheus Unbound* of Prometheus's gift to man of language:

He gave man speech, and speech created thought,
Which is the measure of the universe. (II, iv, 72–3)

One of Shelley's reviewers complained that this was to put the cart before the horse,[7] but the reviewer was exposing his ignorance of the new theorists of language. Shelley might have cited some of the most impressive thinkers of the later eighteenth century as his authorities. Condillac writes 'les progrès de l'esprit humain dépendent presque entièrement de l'addresse avec laquelle nous nous servons du langage'.[8] Bentham insists that 'the correction, extension and improvement of thought' is 'and that to a prodigious degree, a consequence' of 'speech'.[9]

If speech created thought, then, in a real sense, we create the world through speaking it:

> Language is a perpetual Orphic song
> Which rules with Daedal harmony a throng
> Of thoughts and forms, which else senseless and shapeless
>   were. (*Prometheus Unbound*, IV, 415–17)

The chaotic stream of impressions which is our consciousness achieves meaning only through the order that language imposes on it. The primal act of creation, as Genesis records, was the utterance of a sentence: 'And God said, Let there be light: and there was light'. In speaking a sentence God transformed chaos into an ordered universe. This is the true sense in which the Word is God.

For Pope then the poet's task was only to express gracefully pre-established and generally accepted thoughts. But for Shelley a poet's speech, not by a loose metaphor but as matter of fact, was an act of divine creation. He quoted approvingly 'the bold and true word of Tasso': '*non c'è in mondo chi merita nome di creatore, che Dio ed il Poeta*'.[10]

The new attitude to language encouraged, as Shelley's quotation from Tasso indicates, a restoration of poetry to the status claimed for it by the poets of the Renaissance. The Romantic poets made claims for their profession more extravagant than any put forward by Pope. And yet their confidence was precarious. When in Act IV of *Prometheus Unbound* Shelley describes language as an Orphic song his tone is celebratory, but he is describing a redeemed world which, we must imagine, is given meaning by a redeemed language. That the English of the early nineteenth century was not such a language is a major theme in the work of the greatest British philosopher contemporary with the Romantics, Jeremy Bentham. If speech created thought then the limits of thought are defined by the limits of language. The grammar and vocabulary of the language are also the grammar and vocabulary of the mind. For Bentham this situation was a cause not for celebration but for dismay.

Bentham's attack on language is massive and far-reaching. It leads him quite naturally into an attack on poetry, for poetry is the most purely verbal of all human activities. Language, according to Bentham, is a pernicious instrument because it accredits real existence to 'fictions'. It allows its speaker to assert propositions which cannot be validated because they refer to nothing outside themselves. The poet is a worthless individual because he upholds the fictitious in language:

> Between poetry and truth there is a natural opposition: false morals, fictitious nature. The poet always stands in need of something false. When he pretends to lay his foundations on truth, the ornament of his superstructure is fictitious: his business consists in stimulating our passions, and exciting our prejudices. Truth, exactitude of every kind, is fatal to poetry.[11]

Given that the Romantic poets were fond of making extravagant claims for the value of poetry, the extent to which they assimilated Bentham's attack is surprising. A Benthamite distrust of the fictitious and irrational in poetry was an aspect of the despair to which Wordsworth was reduced by his flirtation with radical philosophers.

> Then I said,
> Go to the Poets: they will speak to thee
> More perfectly of purer creatures, yet
> If Reason be nobility in man,
> Can aught be more ignoble than the man
> Whom they describe, would fasten if they may
> Upon our love by sympathies of truth.[12]

Wordsworth recovered from this scepticism, but it is apparent in Byron when he writes: 'I hate things all fiction . . . and pure invention is but the talent of a liar'.[13] It encouraged a peculiarly schizoid notion of the status of the poet. Shelley, the author of what to the modern reader seems an intemperate celebration of the importance of poetry, could also write: 'I consider poetry very subordinate to moral and political science'.[14]

Bentham was interested in the emotive power of language; how it misleads, confuses, and encourages acceptance of a range of conventional values. It perpetuates moral conventions by imposing a moral value on a word like 'lust', which, Bentham claims, ought only to signify a motive.[15] Latent in language is a rhetoric which works covertly to secure approval for established social institutions:

Amongst the instruments of delusion employed for reconciling the people to the dominion of the one and the few, is the device of employing for the designations of persons, and classes of persons, instead of the ordinary and appropriate denominations, the names of so many abstract, fictitious entities, contrived for the purpose. [16]

He offers such examples as the habit of referring to the king as 'the crown', the effect of which is that 'in the stead of the more or less obnoxious individual or individuals, the object presented is a creature of the fancy, by the idea of which, as in poetry, the imagination is tickled'. [17]

Bentham's analysis concludes inevitably in an attack on poetry, because the obstructions to clear thought that he describes result from the affective power of words, the poet's great resource. He charges language with covertly marshalling support for established morality, and the established institutions which impose it. He asserts a connection between language and conservatism. And Shelley agreed. In *Laon and Cythna* the evil god rules with the aid of Fear, Hatred and Tyranny:

> His spirit is their power, and they, his slaves,
> In air, and light, and thought, and language dwell . . . (388–9)

Language is one of the means by which the evil god maintains his power, and in *Laon and Cythna* the dominion of the evil god is closely associated with the power of those two conservative institutions, the monarchy and the church. In *Swellfoot the Tyrant* a chorus of priests speak of: 'emperors, kings, and priests, and lords/Who rule by viziers, sceptres, bank-notes, words . . .' (II, ii, 7–8). I do not believe that this means only that the officers rule by written and spoken orders, nor only that they control the press, but that they control language; that language, because it is a conservative force, is one of the means by which established authority maintains its power.

Speech created thought. Language is constitutive of the reality that it signifies. In Act IV of *Prometheus Unbound* this led Shelley to celebrate the ordering power of language, an Orphic song. But this is proper cause for celebration only if language imposes on the chaos of our impressions a redeemed order, and to claim that the ordinary English of Shelley's day imposed such an order on experience was patently false. Bentham implies, on the contrary, that language seeks to impose on experience an Ahrimanic order, the order sought by the conservative evil god of Shelley's Zoroastrian universe. The effort to be a radical poet, Bentham implies, is an aspiration towards a contradiction in terms. Since poets depend on the affective power of words, and since it is that affective power in which the conservative force of language resides, the radical poet is condemned to protect what he detests.

For Bentham the solution was clear: a new language must be constructed free from the defects of ordinary English. This is not a practicable solution for a poet, and yet Shelley entertained it. When Cythna in *Laon and Cythna* seeks to establish a true moral system in opposition to the corrupt morality of her society, she devises a new language in which to conduct her enquiry:

And in the sand would I make signs to range
These woofs, as they were woven, of my thought;
Clear, elemental shapes, whose smallest change
A subtler language within language wrought... (3109–12)

For Cythna this is a reasonable solution of the difficulty; for the reader of the poem it is less satisfactory. One of the reasons that Blake chose to invent rather than to inherit his mythology may well have been that in this way he could achieve some of the advantages of an invented language, but this stratagem has not pleased all his readers. If we disregard the extraordinary man-oeuvres of Cythna and of Blake, then the pursuit of a new language free from the inherited associations that enrich and obscure ordinary language must remain for the poet an impossible dream. Shelley prays for its fulfilment in *Ode to Liberty*:

Oh, that the words which make the thoughts obscure
    From which they spring, as clouds of glimmering dew
From a white lake blot Heaven's blue portraiture,
    Were stripped of their thin masks and various hue
And frowns and smiles and splendours not their own,
    Till in the nakedness of false and true
    They stand before their Lord, each to receive its due!
                                                    (234–40)

Shelley is thinking of the original purity of the language instituted by Adam when he named the contents of his empire, and dreaming that this language might be restored after a last judgement of words (just as Eden will be restored after a last judgement of men), so that words will be stripped of their accreted associations and walk naked once again within a grammatical paradise. But his use of a fanciful myth suggests that he regards this notion as no more than an idle dream. Nor is it clear whether the primeval purity of the language to which he aspires would leave the writing of poetry possible.

The radical poet then had a choice; to write a poetry that tries to work beneath, and in defiance of, the words of which it is composed, or to achieve an awareness of the conservative force of language and engage in a self-conscious struggle against it. Of the occasions when Shelley made the first choice, when he produced poetry which gives every appearance of its writer having given up language as a bad job, the reader of his collected poems will have unpleasant memories. His successful poems are the results of his making the second choice. Shelley's struggles with language take many forms only one of which I shall discuss at this point.

The first canto of *Laon and Cythna* contains an emblem rather than an example of a characteristic Shelleyan technique. A despondent revolutionary witnesses an aerial combat between an eagle and a snake, which ends when the snake is dropped, wounded, into the sea. The snake swims to shore where it is comforted by a woman, another witness of the battle. She asks the young man to accompany her and the snake on a voyage. His reaction is chivalrous:

> Shall this fair woman all alone,
> Over the sea with that fierce Serpent go?
> His head is on her heart, and who can know
> How soon he may devour his feeble prey? (318–21)

For all that he is a revolutionary, the young man is a conventional thinker. He accepts what he has been taught, that the snake is a noxious, treacherous, evil animal. He agrees to accompany the lady only to protect her from the snake. On the voyage, the lady explains to him the origin of the combat he has witnessed. The eagle's proper form is as a 'blood-red Comet', the snake is properly 'the Morning Star': the eagle is the spirit of evil, the snake the spirit of good. After being defeated by the spirit of evil, the star was transformed into a snake by his adversary:

> for his immortal foe,
> He changed from starry shape, beauteous and mild,
> To a dire snake, with man and beast unreconciled. (367–9)

The Bible and *Paradise Lost* are inverted. The history of Lucifer, the morning star, once the most beautiful angel in heaven, who was transformed into a serpent as a punishment for seducing Adam and Eve, is ascribed to the spirit of good. It is a not very sophisticated example of a typical Shelleyan manoeuvre. He steals the mythology of his opponents, and forces it to express his own subversive humanist ethic. Like his hero Prometheus he steals fire from heaven and puts it at the service of man. More interesting is the young man's initially hostile reaction to the snake. Although he would claim to be a revolutionary, he is still in thrall to the conservatism inherent in his language. He presumes the snake to be evil. His revolutionary education is completed only when the lady explains to him that the eagle, popularly associated with nobility and empire, is in truth the spirit of evil incarnate, and that the snake, popularly associated with treacherous guile and rebellion, is the form in which he has been taught to perceive the spirit of good. The young man is taught that his perceptions are controlled by his language. There is no escape from this predicament. Even the lady, a fully emancipated revolutionary, sees the spirit of good as a snake. Her only recourse is to worship it and love it in spite of her perception. Only in the temple of the spirit, Shelley's heaven, to which she conducts the young man, does the snake assume his true form. Only if language were naked, as in *Ode to Liberty* Shelley dreamed it might be, could one escape from its distortions. Given language as it is, the radical poet, like the snake-loving lady, must accept that his ideals will be distorted by the words in which they are expressed. His poems must educate their readers, as the lady educates the young man, by struggling against those distortions.

It is possible to argue that the episode from *Laon and Cythna* is an example as well as an emblem of this technique, for it attempts to interchange the connotative significances of the words 'eagle' and 'snake'. But the exercise is conducted for the most part on a conceptual level. In *Epipsychidion* a similar manoeuvre is woven into the fabric of the poem's language. After an ecstatic address to Emily, and a spiritualised account of his own love life, Shelley turns to assail the prejudices of monogamists:

> I never was attached to that great sect,
> Whose doctrine is, that each one should select
> Out of the crowd a mistress or a friend,
> And all the rest, though fair and wise, commend
> To cold oblivion, though it is in the code
> Of modern morals... (149–54)

Such sentiments are an affront to the conventional belief in the sanctity of marriage, and Shelley encourages rather than fights against the conventional shocked reactions. His verse assumes a Byronic tone, a rakish jauntiness, that runs the risk of confirming the reader in his opinion of the moral inferiority of the promiscuous. But as with the young man's initial hostility to the snake, the conventional reaction is accepted only so that it may be superseded. Shelley invites Emily to accompany him to a paradisial island, an island hidden in mist:

> And from the sea there rise, and from the sky
> There fall, clear exhalations, soft and bright,
> Veil after veil, each hiding some delight,
> Which Sun or Moon or zephyr draw aside,
> Till the isle's beauty, like a naked bride
> Glowing at once with love and loveliness,
> Blushes and trembles at its own excess... (470–6)

Shelley's rejection of the conventional notion of marriage, and the posture of Byronic cynicism which that rejection forced him to assume, were necessary in order to achieve this passage, in which the vocabulary of marriage reappears, shorn of its disagreeable associations, but still connoting innocence, wonder and erotic expectancy. The earlier passage is an attempt to burn away from a word like 'bride' those connotations which Shelley found unacceptable, to disrobe the word, reducing it to a state of Edenic nakedness so that it might become fit to express his own ethic of love.

The ethic latent in a particular vocabulary is rejected in order that Shelley may reintroduce the vocabulary shorn of the ethic. In *Epipsychidion* the whole poem is necessary to achieve the manoeuvre. In *Prometheus Unbound* it is completed in one and a half lines. Man after the fall of Jupiter is free: 'Exempt from awe, worship, degree, the king/Over himself. . . (III, iv, 196–7). Line 196 appears to constitute a complete list of exemptions. The final privilege accorded to man, exemption from 'the king' establishes Shelley's absolute opposition to all monarchical sentiment. But even as the reader apprehends this, he turns the line and finds the word 'king' snatched from a list of the oppressions that existed in the old world, and transformed into a word celebrating the happy freedom of man in the new world, where he is 'king over himself'. The complete process occurs in the time it takes the reader to correct his misreading of Shelley's syntax.

The same technique in *Letter to Maria Gisborne* is used with splendid comic impudence. Shelley recalls, and accepts, the charges made against him by moralistic reviewers: 'So I, a thing whom moralists call worm . . .' (5). But in the next line the worm becomes a silkworm, and Shelley turns the insult into a delicate compliment to his poetry, 'fine threads of rare and subtle thought', and to the butterfly-like immortality that his poems will earn him.

Perhaps the most sustained example of this technique is Shelley's prose masterpiece, *An Address to the People on the Death of the Princess Charlotte*. Without her consent, and for no cogent reason, this lady had been selected by the radicals as the standard-bearer of their hopes. As a consequence her death was received by some of them, including Byron, with fulsome displays of grief. Shelley's pamphlet is designed to expose the immoral sentimentality of this reaction. He argues that a demonstration of public grief would be more appropriate were it a reaction to the deaths of three labourers, Brandreth, Ludlam and Turner, who had been inveigled into treasonable activity by an *agent provocateur* in the pay of the government, and then executed for their crime. The princess died a natural death, an end that one day awaits us all; they were executed, suffered a death that no man has the right to impose on his fellows. Her death is a proper cause for private mourning; their deaths, because they expose the chicanery of the government, the iniquity of the judiciary, and the desperation to which the abject

poverty of the most numerous section of the population reduces
ordinary men, are a proper cause for public mourning.

> Mourn then, People of England. Clothe yourselves in solemn
> black. Let the bells be tolled. Think of mortality and change.
> Shroud yourselves in solitude and the gloom of sacred sorrow.
> Spare no symbol of universal grief. Weep – mourn – lament.
> Fill the great City – fill the boundless fields with lamentation
> and the echo of groans. A beautiful Princess is dead: she who
> should have been the Queen of her beloved nation, and whose
> posterity should have ruled it forever. She loved the domestic
> affections, and cherished arts which adorn, and valour which
> defends. She was amiable and would have become wise, but
> she was young, and in the flower of youth the despoiler came.
> LIBERTY is dead.

A pun is maintained throughout the paragraph until, finally, the
splendid vocabulary of monarchical compliment is snatched
from the individual, the real sadness of whose fate it only
obscures, and awarded to the principle, liberty, to which it is appropriate. In the final sentence of the pamphlet the disentangle-
ment of the vocabulary of royalty, and the sentiments of awe,
love and obedience which it inspires, from the obsolete insti-
tution of kingship and its outmoded paraphernalia, is complete:

> Let us follow the corpse of British liberty slowly and
> reverentially to its tomb: and if some glorious Phantom should
> appear and make its throne of broken swords and sceptres and
> royal crowns trampled in the dust, let us say that the Spirit of
> Liberty has arisen from its grave, and left all that was gross and
> mortal there, and kneel down and worship it as our Queen.

Shelley's struggle against monarchical sentiment results in a
struggle against language. He succeeds by annexing the emotive
vocabulary of royalty, and placing it at the service of what he
considers a more valid ethical and political ideal. And yet his
procedure is paradoxical. The new ideal is supported by exactly
the same appeal to emotional prejudice that sustained the old.
This paradox is reflected in the Romantic conception of the poet
as permanent opposition, Blake's notion that the poet must join
the devil's party. It also helps to explain the Romantic preoccu-

pation with concepts of cyclical or dialectical progression. The transformation of Orc into Urizen is embodied in the nature of language itself. The poet, in struggling against one prejudice, helps to create another.

In struggling against the emotive power of language, the radical poet can succeed only in diverting, not in destroying that power. He will therefore be forced into troublesome paradoxes. Shelley celebrates republicanism in the language of monarchy, and uses, in attacking marriage, a nuptial vocabulary. His predicament derives from a recognition that 'speech created thought', and yet in struggling to adjust his language, the poet attempts to make thought direct speech. There are easy escapes from these paradoxes available. The poet may relax into the belief that he can say only what his language will have him say, that poetry is not the expression of an individual's meaning, but a discharge of 'collected lightning'. [18] This may be acceptable if, like Shelley in *A Defence of Poetry*, the radical poet can persuade himself that the spirit working within his language is a spirit of reform to which even those poets averse to change must minister, 'for it is less their spirit than the spirit of the age'. But such confidence is precarious. Bentham warns that the spirit of English in the early nineteenth century would be better represented by the massively reactionary chariot, that, in *The Triumph of Life* drags even the reformer Rousseau in its wake. The alternative is to reject language with contempt. Wordsworth asserts that words are only 'under-agents in their souls', and that in its essence poetry is non-verbal, a reflection to which he is provoked by the belief that some of the finest poets he has known have been illiterate peasants in a condition of near absolute inarticulacy. [19] A wholesale acceptance and a wholesale rejection of the given language have much the same effect on the poem; both encourage that arrogant carelessness with words that mars so much Romantic poetry. When Shelley chooses either of these courses, he fails. His successes are the result of a more energetic, if also more paradoxical, struggle with his native language.

Words and Propositions

Locke identified the word as the primary unit of meaning in

language: the third book of the *Essay* is entitled 'Of Words'. He
thinks of a word as a name; a language is a collection of names,
and a sentence is a selection of names. The import of a sentence is
an aggregate of the significances of the individual words that it
contains. During the eighteenth century this notion was first
modified and then replaced. The new assumption is expressed
most trenchantly by Bentham, who argues that 'by anything less
than a proposition, no communication can take place', and
claims that 'a word is to a *proposition* what a *letter* is to a word'.[20] If
the unit of meaning is the proposition rather than the word, then
words achieve meaning not through the correspondence of each
of them with a particular idea, but through their relations one
with another within the sentence. The sentence becomes not a
selection of words, but a system of words: the meaning of the
sentence is a product of the particular words chosen and of the
syntax that relates them.

The antithetical couplet reflects a tendency to locate meaning
in the word rather than in the proposition. Take Pope's version
of a classical commonplace: 'Good-nature and good-sense must
ever join;/To err is human, to forgive divine . . .'. The patterns of
parallel and contrast have the effect of emphasising the
significance of individual words, of, say, the word 'human' as
opposed to the word 'divine'. Pope's syntax is striking – it is
what makes the couplet memorable – but its function is odd.
The parallel construction in the second line expresses a relation
between erring and forgiving that is more complex than the
syntax suggests. Pope asks the critic first to recognise that a
tendency to error is a common human characteristic to which he
is himself liable, and secondly, the critic is advised, when he
detects error in a poet, to moderate the severity of his verdict by
remembering that in exercising forgiveness he is practising a
divine virtue. Pope's syntax elides two sequential arguments
into a simple statement: to elicit the sequence the reader must
attend to the value of the individual words rather than to their
syntactic connection. Pope's syntax is not active in establishing his meaning, but in lending his epigram a form of definitive finality. Syntax is rhetorical or decorative rather than
functional.

In contrast to this take a characteristic passage from Shelley
(*Prometheus Unbound*). Asia is describing the life enjoyed by
mankind under the reign of Saturn:

such the state
Of the earth's primal spirits beneath his sway,
As the calm joy of flowers and living leaves
Before the wind or sun has withered them
And semi-vital worms ... (II, iv, 34–8)

The passage is syntactically odd; it may even seem clumsy. The phrase 'And semi-vital worms' is coordinate with the phrases 'flowers' and 'living leaves', but it is separated from them by a clause describing the flowers and the leaves, so that it seems to be tacked clumsily to the end of a completed sentence. The syntax forces itself on the reader's attention by its inelegance in a manner that Pope would not have allowed, but it does so because the manner in which the sentence is organised in itself expresses Shelley's meaning. The description of the flowers and leaves is languidly beautiful; it works to assimilate the word used to describe Saturn's rule 'sway' to the peaceful movement of flowers in a breeze. It successfully encourages in the reader a nostalgia for a carefree vegetable existence which it is the function of the delayed phrase, 'semi-vital worms', to expose as regressive and unworthy of man. The sentence is experienced as a process, one that exactly corresponds to the sequence of events that Shelley is describing; man may at first bask in paradise, but inevitably he will come to feel that the life he lives there is degrading, unworthy of him, because it deprives him of knowledge, 'the birthright of his being'. The sentence works also to express Shelley's characteristic reaction to an inherited mythology. He suggests the conventional association between the Golden Age and Eden, and appears to accept their conventional value, but he does so in order to create a dramatic contrast between the traditional nostalgia for Eden and his own subversive contempt for it. He plays host to the mythology he inherits rather as Macbeth played host to Duncan. It would be untrue to argue from this passage that Shelley approved of Saturn's rule, and it would be inadequate to argue that he condemned it. The meaning of the sentence is its syntax; it means that Saturn's government was an apparent good that was exposed as evil.

The contrast between Pope's couplet and Shelley's lines indicates a difference between Augustan and Romantic verse of the first importance, and one that has not been sufficiently attended to. Put briefly, meaning in Augustan verse is aggregative, meaning in Romantic verse is propositional. A correct reading of individual sentences is possible only if the reader accepts this, but the notion has wider importance. Consider for example the dispute over whether the sun and the 'Shape all light' in Shelley's *The Triumph of Life* are forces of good or evil. In Romantic verse meaning exists in the relation between the various members of a description. Sometimes, as in Asia's description of life under Saturn, the members may appear, when isolated from one another, to be inconsistent. Asia first suggests that life under Saturn is good, and then she suggests that it is bad. The meaning of her proposition is the movement from one suggestion to the other. The character or value of the Golden Age does not exist as a fixed point of reference outside the temporal sequence of her words; she creates it as she describes it. This notion will control the extended readings of individual poems in the later chapters of this book.

Both Romantic sentences, and Romantic characters tend then to be propositional rather than aggregative. But there is also a sense in which a Romantic poem is best regarded as a single proposition which allows no judgement to be made of the meaning or of the success of any part of it separately from the whole. This of course is a precept to which Pope subscribed: "'Tis not a lip, or eye, we beauty call,/But the joint force and full result of all'. But it is a characteristic of the Romantic poem that it will contain parts which seem designed to shock the reader's aesthetic sense, that it will strenuously exemplify Coleridge's precept: 'a poem of any length neither can, nor ought to be, all poetry'. Some examples have entered into literary folklore: 'I measured it from side to side,/'Twas three feet long and two feet wide'. In a lyrical ballad like *The Thorn* this may not seem extraordinary, but the *Prelude* contains long passages that seem to be no more than loosely versified prose, and even an elaborately artificial poem like *Adonais* can include lines like the following:

> As long as skies are blue, or fields are green,
> Evening must usher night, night urge the morrow,
> Month follow month with woe, and year wake year to
> sorrow. (189–9)

In comparison with these examples a poem by Pope maintains a stable level of poetic excellence.

A normal reaction, and a reasonable one, would be to contrast Pope's craftsmanship with Romantic carelessness, or the Romantic surrender to an inspirational theory of composition. But it also seems to me true that Pope's continuous surface polish reflects a stronger tendency to accredit independent value to the part than is common among the Romantics. Blake, Wordsworth and Shelley in particular are prepared to use the most extraordinary means in pursuit of an end, or parts in the construction of a whole. Their defenders and their attackers have often failed to engage each other by not realising that this is the point at issue. An admiring critic of *Ode to the West Wind* might well expect his reader to take seriously the notorious line: 'I fall upon the thorns of life! I bleed!' His reader might well refuse to do so on the grounds that the line is self-evidently bad. But between the two positions there might not exist an unbridgeable gap of taste so much as a disagreement about the relation that ought to obtain between a part and a whole, a line and a poem. Shelley's admirer might deny that one ought to expect the excellence that he attributes to the whole poem to be manifest in each, or perhaps any, of its parts. To realise the point at issue is not to produce a solution, but it is necessary before significant argument can begin.

Metaphor

Locke's disapproval of 'figurative speeches' is well known. He admits that verbal ornaments 'can scarce pass for Faults' 'in discourses, where we seek rather Pleasure and Delight, than Information and Improvement', but he disapproves of their use for other purposes except when they function to preserve 'order and clearness':

> But yet, if we would speak of Things as they are, we must allow that all the Art of Rhetorick, besides Order and Clearness, all the artificial and figurative application of Words Eloquence hath invented, are for nothing else, but to insinuate wrong Ideas, move the Passions, and thereby mislead the Judgment, and so indeed are perfect cheat.[21]

This attack anticipates Bentham's strictures on language that I described earlier in the chapter, and yet it is crucially different. Locke considers these abuses of language the invention of 'Eloquence', and refers the reader who wishes to see them classified to 'the Books of Rhetorick'. Bentham on the other hand considered them integral with the language, and with the society that developed it. Locke could propose, as a solution to the difficulty, the use of a more chaste English; Bentham looked forward to the invention of a new language.

Locke's distrust of metaphor derives in the end from the notion, inescapable within the terms of his linguistic model, that in metaphor an idea is communicated by an inappropriate and therefore misleading sign. His hostility to metaphor is a product of the two aspects of his theory of language that I have already discussed; the notion that the word is separable from the thought that it signifies, and ought to be subordinated to it, and the notion that the word is the primary unit of meaning in language. It might be expected that, when these beliefs were no longer generally held, the status of metaphor and of the other figures of speech might be raised. But English Romanticism, we are often told, became a self-conscious movement in 1800 when Wordsworth published its manifesto, the preface to the second edition of *Lyrical Ballads*, and the preface contains an attack on figurative language as vehement as Locke's. Wordsworth defends his decision to write in the language of 'low and rustic people' because their language is free of the false artificiality characteristic of the elevated diction favoured by later eighteenth-century poets (I quote from the extended preface of 1802):

> Accordingly, such a language, arising out of repeated experi-
> ence and regular feelings, is a more permanent, and a far more
> philosophical language, than that which is frequently substi-
> tuted for it by Poets, who think that they are confirming
> honour upon themselves and their art, in proportion as they
> separate themselves from the sympathies of men, and indulge
> in arbitrary and capricious habits of expression, in order to
> furnish food for fickle tastes and fickle appetites, of their own
> creation. [22]

Wordsworth scorns 'arbitrary and capricious habits of expression', which include, it seems, most of the figurative devices of

eighteenth-century poetry, more comprehensively even than Locke. Locke allowed such devices in works designed to give 'Pleasure and Delight': he sanctioned their use in poetry. But Wordsworth resolutely refuses to admit that there is a necessary distinction between poetry and truth, and therefore figurative language in poetry becomes liable to the same objection that Locke brought against its use in works which attempt to speak of 'Things as they are'.

Nevertheless, Wordsworth manages to rescue metaphor as a device allowable in poetry. Figurative language may be employed when it is an inevitable constituent of impassioned speech:

> if the Poet's subject be judiciously chosen, it will naturally, and upon fit occasion, lead him to passions, the language of which, if reflected truly and judiciously, must necessarily be dignified and variegated, and alive with metaphors and figures. [23]

The word 'truly' here as elsewhere in Wordsworth's preface is confusing. Wordsworth seems unsure whether to claim that the poet who simply transcribes what men say when in the grip of passion will write a language 'alive with metaphors and figures', or whether the language will result from the poet's attempt to express in words the impassioned man's feelings. Nevertheless it seems clear that Wordsworth accepts figurative language only when it is integral rather than decorative: 'If words be not . . . an incarnation of the thought, but only a clothing for it, then surely will they prove an ill gift . . .'. [24]

Wordsworth is somewhat hesitant in assigning to metaphor a central place in the language of poetry, because he finds it difficult to demonstrate satisfactorily that metaphor need not be separable from meaning. Shelley finds this much easier. In the *Defence* he describes the language of primitive peoples:

> Their language is vitally metaphorical: that is, it marks the before unapprehended relations of things and perpetuates their apprehension until the words which represent them become through time, signs for portions or classes of thought instead of pictures of integral thoughts: and then, if no new poets should arise to create afresh the associations which have been thus disorganized, language will be dead to all the nobler purposes of human intercourse. [25]

Metaphor is the dynamo of language, the means by which it extends its semantic range; it enables a limited stock of words to express a much wider range of experience by indicating 'before unapprehended relations of things'. It is also the means by which men lend to their world a human organisation. The inevitable process by which metaphors, once vital, became dead, reverses this achievement. The apprehended relation, once signalled by, say, the use of the word 'impression' for an idea, is lost as the word loses its metaphorical status, and in consequence the humanly organised world degenerates into a dead universe of unrelated things. The role of metaphor within a language therefore both indicates and determines the health of the society that uses the language. Shelley identifies the poet as the chief preserver of the vitality of metaphor, and, in performing this task, the poet sustains and renovates the entire social structure. Shelley's notorious claim that poets are 'the unacknowledged legislators of the world' is already implicit in his notion of the function of metaphor.

Wordsworth and Shelley both rescue metaphor as a device which may be integral with the expression of meaning, but they do so by stripping metaphors of metaphorical status. Our delight in one of Pope's metaphors is determined in part by our awareness that the particular metaphor was chosen from a range of possible expressions: metaphor is 'a way of saying it'. But for Wordsworth and Shelley it is 'the way of saying it', or it is nothing at all. Shelley celebrates metaphor, but only by arguing that it can be a mode of direct expression, 'a picture of an integral thought'. The prototype of the poet as maker of metaphors becomes Wordsworth's Idiot Boy, whose only words are: 'The Cocks did crow to-whoo, to-whoo,/And the Sun did shine so cold'. The boy does not compare an owl to a cock, nor the moon to the sun: he sees the one as the other. Like Shelley's primitives he 'marks the before unapprehended relations of things'.

No-one could claim that most metaphors in Romantic poetry function quite differently from metaphors in Augustan poetry. Nevertheless there is a significantly different tendency. Leavis complains that in Shelley's poems the tenor and the vehicle of a metaphor are often confused. This is true, sometimes even when the comparison seems to be lucidly articulated. In *Ode to the West Wind* the approaching clouds are spread over the sky:

> Like the bright hair uplifted from the head
> Of some fierce Maenad, even from the dim verge
> Of the horizon to the zenith's height,
> The locks of the approaching storm. (20–3)

The simile seems to have been discarded only to reappear in the word 'locks', at which point one realises that 'hair' and 'locks' are both related to cloud through the literal meaning of the word 'cirrus'. The Maenad's hair is offered as a visual description of the clouds, but the poem is spoken by a poet, a type of Orpheus, and the west wind emerges in the fifth stanza of the ode as a metaphor for the creative energy that the poet must either harness, or be destroyed by, as Orpheus was destroyed by the Maenads. In the lines quoted, the clouds driven by the wind are compared with a Maenad, and yet within the whole poem it would be as true to say that Maenads are compared with wind-driven clouds. A Shelleyan metaphor is apt to stand on its head. Leavis objects to this, but in doing so he is denying that metaphor ought to become, what Shelley prizes it as, 'the picture of an integral thought'. Metaphor, for Shelley, is most powerful when it is not a comparison between one thing and another, but a single, whole apprehension which refuses analysis into its constituent parts. Indeed, as I shall argue later, Shelley suggests that the use of metaphors in which tenor and vehicle are clearly distinguished is an evidence of imaginative weakness.

A similar difficulty confronts the reader who encounters one of Shelley's sequences of comparisons. *To a Skylark*, for example, includes a series of stanzas in which the unseen singing bird is compared with one thing after another, as if Shelley, unable to devise a satisfactory simile, were attempting to compensate for his failure by offering a selection of his inadequate attempts. But for Shelley everything exists as it is perceived. The similes are not an attempt to acquaint the reader with the skylark's appearance by comparing the bird to a hidden Poet and to a 'high-born maiden', an effort foiled because Shelley cannot see the bird he is attempting to describe. The function of metaphor is not to compare one object or action with another, but to express the perceiver's apprehension of the object or action. The poet, listening to the bird's song, apprehends it now through one relation, now through another. The poem is an attempt to express, and through expression to discover, the manner in which the poet perceives the bird.

From Writer to Reader

For Locke a word achieves meaning if it represents an idea in the mind of its speaker: it communicates meaning if it allows the person who hears it to guess its speaker's idea. The diagram below represents Locke's model for any utterance:

(speaker's idea)→(word)→(listener's idea).

His emphasis is on the first two links of this chain; the speaker's idea and the word he uses to represent it. And yet Locke insists that the primary function of language is to communicate. His failure, then, to allow the listener an essential role in establishing the meaning of an utterance must derive from a reasonable confidence in the stable value of the word.

Locke argued that the proper use of a word depended on the speaker's knowledge of its definition. Only if the speaker possessed this knowledge would he be able to select accurately a word to represent a particular idea. His listener would understand him if he shared the speaker's knowledge of the word's definition. A Lockean conversation is a dialogue between two copies of a single dictionary in each of which every word used is defined as an idea.

During the eighteenth century the notion that a word relied for its meaning on its user's knowledge of its definition became difficult to maintain. The philosophers interested in the origin of language encountered the problem that considerable metaphysical sophistication is necessary to define the relation expressed by a preposition like 'of'. It became difficult to believe that a knowledge of its definition must have preceded the development and the use of the word; difficult also to believe that all those who used the word appropriately could, if challenged, define it.[26] One of the important results of Johnson's dictionary was its demonstration that many words, and those the commonest, signify a bewilderingly complex range of ideas. Dugald Stewart writes:

When I consult Johnson's Dictionary, I find many words of which he has enumerated forty, fifty, or even sixty different significations; and, after all the pains he has taken to distinguish these from each other, I am frequently at a loss how to avail myself of his definitions. Yet, when a word of this kind occurs to me in a book, or even when I hear it pronounced in the rapidity of discourse, I at once select. without the slightest effort of conscious thought, the precise meaning which it was intended to convey. [27]

Locke's theory seems unable to account for this. To him multiple significations of a single word seemed a troublesome defect of language, but Johnson's dictionary revealed that such words were central in language; they could not be avoided, and yet their use caused surprisingly few problems. To Stewart the solution was clear: the precise meaning of such words was established by 'the general import of the sentence'. Instead of a speaker communicating an idea by selecting the word which conventionally signified that idea, his choice being dependent on his knowledge of the word's definition, Stewart recognised that the significance of a particular word could be, and often was, established by the context in which the word appeared.

It is difficult to express both briefly and clearly the change in the vocabulary of poetry that is illuminated by this development in the theory of language. What I take to be apparent is a lessening of the poet's confidence in the stable value of the word. Pope and Wordsworth both make use of key words of disconcerting vagueness; for example, 'nature' in *An Essay on Criticism* and in *An Essay on Man*, and 'power' in the *Prelude*. And yet a reader puzzled by Pope's use of the word 'nature' would be assisted if he consulted a good historical dictionary whereas a reader who sought the same help when puzzling over Wordsworth's use of the word 'power' would be disappointed. What this suggests is that Pope relies on a knowledge of a word's meaning shared between himself and his reader far more confidently than Wordsworth. Wordsworth expects his reader to take his whole poem as a huge context within which his word achieves significance. The Romantic poet characteristically makes massive demands on the reader's interpretative energy, demands with which no reader can fully comply.

The difference is clearer if we compare Pope's technique of

allusion with Romantic symbolism or Romantic mythology. Allusion is a technique that very obviously assumes a culture common between the poet and his readers, a technique that leans on shared knowledge. Romantic poets, of course, use the same technique, but not nearly so pervasively. As a consequence critical explorations of the sources of Romantic poems often have a doubtful status; they seem unsure whether the identification of a poem's sources helps to establish its meaning, or whether such discoveries are a study of the poem's genetics. It is also characteristic of some Romantic poets to fight against allusion. A character like Moneta in *The Fall of Hyperion* not to mention the characters in Blake's prophetic books seems to be named in order to prevent the reader from fully understanding the character through any established common associations. The poet tries to present the poem as the sole context within which he is to be understood. Shelley's Demogorgon is a similar case, but in Shelley the technique is most fully developed in *The Triumph of Life* in which all three of the mythological characters are unnamed, and spoken of only as 'shapes'. Such characters achieve meaning as the word 'power' achieves meaning in the *Prelude*, through their context.

Locke emphasised the location of meaning in the relation between the speaker's ideas and his words. By the end of the eighteenth century, more emphasis was placed on the relation between the words and their receiver. Dugald Stewart writes:

> We speak of *communicating*, by means of words, our ideas and our feelings to others; and we seldom reflect sufficiently on the latitude with which this metaphorical phrase ought to be understood. Even in conversing on the plainest and most familiar subjects, however full and circumstantial our subjects may be, the words which we employ, if examined with accuracy, will be found to do nothing more than to suggest *hints* to our hearers, leaving by far the principal part of interpretation to be performed by the Mind itself.[28]

Communication is a dicier business for Stewart than it was for Locke; language hints. Similarly the Romantic poet seems less confident than his eighteenth-century predecessors in the adequacy of his words, his poem, to mediate between himself and his audience. [29] Wordsworth felt this doubt acutely. He fears that his 'language may frequently have suffered from those arbitrary connections of feelings and ideas, from which no man can altogether protect himself'. [30]

One result of this scepticism was the tendency to exalt the poet independently of his achieved poems: 'the most glorious poetry that has ever been communicated to the world is probably a feeble shadow of the original conceptions of the poet'. [31] Another result was the willingness to allow the reader a place in the establishment of the poem's meaning. Shelley uses this notion to make a rational defence of the claim that poetry is infinite:

A great poem is a fountain for ever overflowing with the waters of wisdom and delight; and after one person and one age has exhausted all its divine effluence which their peculiar relations enable them to share, another and yet another succeeds, and new relations are ever developed, the source of an unforeseen and an unconceived delight. [32]

The delight that a poem gives its reader may be 'unforeseen' even by the poet.

The separation of the poet from the poem carried with it the consequence that in reading the poem the reader was liberated from the poet. Hence the writing of criticism that ignored the poet's manifest intentions; the satanic readings of *Paradise Lost* expounded by Blake and Shelley are notorious examples. Another result was the composition of poems which include the reader's response to the poem as a necessary constituent of its meaning. Blake's prophetic books, *Kubla Khan* and *Prometheus Unbound* are crucial examples of this technique. These poems might best be termed unstable allegories; that is, they are written in an allegoric or symbolic mode, and yet the poem refuses to define the application or the range of applications that its fiction ought to have. The poem accepts, indeed insists on, an area of indeterminacy in its meaning. It communicates, as Dugald Stewart suggests that all language communicates: 'the words which we employ . . . will be found to do nothing more than to suggest *hints* to our hearers, leaving by far the principal part of interpretation to be performed by the Mind itself'.

Genre

Neoclassicism and the Sublime

Romantic poetry, we are often told, is the outcome of the rejection of the neoclassical notion that the poet must submit to external disciplines, to rules, in favour of the notion that poetry is 'the spontaneous overflow of powerful feeling', an 'unpremeditated song'. There is an obvious contrast between Dryden's defence of the 'rules' for poetic composition, his insistence that they are founded on 'good sense, and sound reason', and that to flout them is inevitably to produce 'ridiculous mistakes and gross absurdities', and Shelley's praise of Byron's *Manfred*: 'The same freedom from common rules that marked the 3rd canto [of *Childe Harold*] and *Chillon* is visible here, and it was that which all your earlier productions, except *Lara*, wanted'. [33] That the contrast is commonplace ought not to obscure its partial truth, but it is oversimple. Augustan poetry is not written in passive obedience to the generic conventions approved by neoclassical critics. Mock-epic, the most distinctive generic innovation made by the Augustans, works after all by breaking generic rules.

It is helpful to recall that within the eighteenth century there developed side by side two incompatible literary theories, the neoclassical with its aim of codifying the proper forms for poetry, and the theory of the sublime which pressed towards the position that the problem of form in poetry is irrelevant. 1674, the year in which Boileau published both his translation of Horace, *L'Art Poétique*, and his *Traité du Sublime*, the treatise on Longinus from which the Greek critic's influence on poetic theory stems, is the obvious starting-point of this uneasy alliance. The major development in eighteenth-century aesthetic theory was the realisation that the two theories were incompatible. A critic like John Dennis might be both Aristotelian and Longinan, but by the end of the century the two traditions could be held together only by inconsistency, paradox, or by the development of a special dialectic.

The development of the theory of the sublime in the eighteenth century has been ably traced by Samuel Monk. [34] Monk describes, and celebrates, the process by which the theory freed itself from imprisonment within rhetoric. He finds that this process is completed when Kant at last succeeds in denying sublimity to the object, and locating it only in the perceiver's perception of the object. At this point the conflict between the theory of the sublime and the principles of neoclassicism becomes inescapable. The formal concerns of the neoclassical critic, his interest in genre and in decorum, could have no place within a theory that, as expounded by Kant, regarded aesthetic value as independent of any object.

Romanticism has traditionally been conceived, by Monk for example, as the final triumph of the sublime over the neoclassical, and there is much truth in this view. If, for example, the poet accepts Kant's belief that the sublime is a quality of the percipient rather than the perceived, then an obvious question presents itself. Should the sublime of poetry be located in the poet's perception of his subject, in which case poetry becomes a private phenomenon, or in the reader's perception of the poem, in which case the poem becomes a blank screen onto which the reader projects his own emotions? Wordsworth's note on his composition of *The Thorn* engages this question. Struck by the emotion aroused in him on seeing a thorn bush on a stormy day, he asked himself: 'Cannot I, by some invention, do as much to make this thorn permanently an impressive object as the storm has made it to my eyes at this moment?'. The association in the poem between the bush and the story of Martha Ray is designed to elicit the same response from the reader that the association of the bush and the storm had elicited from Wordsworth. The poem becomes a makeshift necessary only in the absence of an efficient telepathic communication between the poet and his public; aesthetic value exists only in the mind of the poet and of his reader, the poem is simply an attempt to coordinate the two.

The poet's purpose, Shelley asserts, is to communicate to his reader his 'original conceptions', but the made poem can never be more than their 'feeble shadow'. No value inheres in the poem as such: its importance is simply as a cable along which an electric current flows from poet to reader. The poem cannot embody the poet's conceptions, its success is simply a product of its efficiency as a conductor. Poetry, Shelley tells us:

arrests the vanishing apparitions which haunt the interlunations of life, and, veiling them, or in language or in form, sends them forth among mankind, bearing sweet news of kindred joy to those with whom their sisters abide – abide because there is no portal of expression from the caverns of the spirit which they inhabit into the universe of things. [35]

Poetry exists in the mind of the poet and of his reader, but only potentially in the poem. The poem is simply (Shelley's spectral metaphors make the word particularly appropriate) the medium. This notion of poetry is clearly the outcome of an epistemology more sophisticated than any that might be deduced from the canons of neoclassical criticism. The poem in itself is an unknowable as any object in itself to Hume. But despite the respectability of its intellectual pedigree it is likely to alarm any literary critic. It denies any objective criterion against which the poet's conception of his poem or the reader's reception of it might be judged or tested.

These notions had surprising influences on poets. Wordsworth's letter to Sara Hutchinson replying to her criticisms of *Resolution and Independence* is an interesting example. She had objected in particular to Wordsworth's presentation of the leech-gatherer. In his defence Wordsworth makes almost no reference to the poem: he refers instead to the situation out of which the poem arose. He insists:

> I cannot conceive a figure more impressive than that of an old man like this, the survivor of a wife and ten children, travelling alone among the mountains and all lonely places, carrying with him his own fortitude, and the necessities which an unjust state of society has forced upon him. [36]

Oddly, he demands that Sara respond to information, the death of the old man's family, that he has not given within the poem. Her technical objections are brushed aside. Wordsworth cares little whether the old man is described 'well or ill', nor even whether Sara is 'pleased or not with *this Poem*'. What he demands is that she recreate from the poem the conception out of which it arose, that she share 'my feelings in writing that Poem'. In comparison with the importance of this endeavour questions about his technical success in the composition of the poem seem to Wordsworth trivial.

Even odder are Wordsworth's *Essays upon Epitaphs*. Wordsworth begins by considering various epitaphs, including those of

Pope, and by attempting to deduce general rules for their composition. It is an endeavour of the kind that preoccupied neoclassical critics of the eighteenth century. But the essay reaches its climax in a passage that strikingly exemplifies the gulf between the two periods:

> In an obscure corner of a Country Churchyard I once espied, half-overgrown with Hemlock and Nettles, a very small Stone laid upon the ground, bearing nothing more than the name of the Deceased with the date of birth and death, importing that it was an Infant which had been born one day and died the following. I know not how the Reader may be in sympathy with me, but more awful thoughts of rights conferred, of hopes awakened, of remembrances stealing away or vanishing were imported to my mind by that Inscription there before my eyes than by any other that it has ever been my lot to meet with upon a Tomb-stone.[37]

Wordsworth arrives at the position that the perfect form for an epitaph is exemplified in an inscription of one name and two dates on a stone, and its perfection is demonstrated by the quality and intensity of Wordsworth's feelings on viewing it. This conclusion would seem to negate all poetic endeavour, and yet one of Wordsworth's major achievements is that in a few poems he manages to contrive the effect that inheres in the primal simplicity of the stone. *Michael* and *The Ruined Cottage* may be regarded as educations, preparing the reader, as Wordsworth's life prepared him, for a rich confrontation with the utter simplicity of a half-built wall or a broken-down cottage. The poem is an elaborate stratagem, finally successful when it can be dismissed, just as the reader is invited to dismiss all literary epitaphs in contemplating one, small, tersely inscribed stone. A characteristic Romantic mode is the poem that struggles towards a recognition of its own irrelevance. One remembers the emblem that fascinated Coleridge and Shelley; the poem is a snake eating its own tail, perfect only when it disappears.

It is obvious that such attitudes are incompatible with any respect for generic conventions or generic distinctions. Much of Wordsworth's Preface is taken up with a denial of the significance of one of the most basic of generic distinctions, that between poetry and prose. Compare Shelley's claim that Plato,

Cicero, Bacon and Jesus, along with other 'authors of revolutions in opinion' ought all to be considered poets.

Wordsworth defines poetry as 'the spontaneous overflow of powerful feeling'. He accepts that feeling must be disciplined by 'long and deep thought', but this discipline must not be a part of the poem's composition, for that would compromise its spontaneity; rather it must be a part of the poet's education. Poetry is defined in terms of the poet rather than of his poem: the poet's masterpiece is, so to speak, himself, and his poems are so many peepholes offering the reader glimpses of the real achievement, which is internal, inexpressible. If this is so then it follows that no one poem can adequately represent a poet's achievement; the whole of his work should be regarded as the most accurate exposition of the poem which is himself. So Wordsworth suggests that we regard his entire *oeuvre* as comprising a single structure, which he compares with a Gothic cathedral, within which the individual poem has only a provisional unity. Shelley, a man uncommitted to the notion that the individual human personality is essentially unique, considers even this limitation arbitrary, and refers his reader to 'that great poem which all poets, like the co-operating thoughts of one great mind, have built up since the beginning of the world'.[38] Since the Roman empire as well as *Paradise Lost* is regarded as an episode in this poem, it becomes, to all intents and purposes, coextensive with reality. Generic distinctions of course disappear in the immensity of these perspectives.

There is then, a sustained, even grandiose, Romantic rhetoric directed against literary conventions and genres. And yet, if we consider once again Wordsworth's *Essays upon Epitaphs* then it becomes clear that the conventions ushered so grandly out of the front door, slip round and re-enter from the back. Pages of conventional criticism, Johnsonian in its tone and in its techniques, are necessary before Wordsworth can reject all such argument as irrelevant, and come to rest in the contemplation of a few words on a stone which gain their effect through their not being, not attempting to be, literature. A conventional literary argument is necessary to prepare the reader to accompany Wordsworth in stepping beyond literature. The preface to *Lyrical Ballads* which seems to attack all generic distinction introduces a collection of poems that takes such distinctions for granted, *Lyrical Ballads with Pastoral and Other Poems*.

The notion that romanticism is the victory of the sublime over the neoclassical, of the psychological over the formal, must in the end be rejected. The case is rather that whereas in 1674 Boileau published *L'Art Poetique* and *Traité du Sublime*, but made no relation between them, in the theory of the Romantics generic and psychological theories are related.

Coleridge distinguishes the poem from poetry. He is content to define the poem much as a neoclassical critic might have done, but poetry is very different: 'What is poetry? is so very nearly the same question with, what is a poet? that the answer to the one is involved in the answer to the other'.[39] Coleridge's movement from poem to poetry is a movement from a formal critical theory to a psychological theory, or, as Abrams puts it: 'he begins with the product, but after a point, moves into the process'.[40] Poetry, unlike the poem, is not to be defined by reference to formal characteristics, but by reference to the poet's state of mind in composition. At this point Coleridge introduces his well-known description of the imagination, the defining quality of poetry, as 'the balance or reconciliation of opposite or discordant qualities'. Poetry is defined in opposition to the poem, but also as the synthesis which results from the reconciliation of the two. Coleridge ends his argument with an elaborate analogy: 'Finally, good sense is the body of poetic genius, fancy its drapery, motion its life, and imagination the soul that is every-where and in each'.[41] Imagination, here almost a synonym for 'poetry', both completes Coleridge's fourfold elemental scheme and synthesises the elements of which it is one. Coleridge struggles, through paradox, to reconcile formal and psychological definitions of poetry (in his terms to reconcile the 'poem' with 'poetry'). The notion of organic form is so important to him because it offers a means of expressing a reconciliation between formalism and spontaneity, the generic bias of the neoclassical critic and the psychological bias of the sublime critic. It is in this attempt that Coleridge reveals himself as the central theoretician of English romanticism.

Genre and History

Biographia Literaria is an exercise in literary theory, but it is also a kind of autobiography. The theoretical attempt to discover timeless truths is associated with an exercise in an essentially temporal literary form, autobiography. At the beginning of chapter IX Coleridge describes how he had confronted the question that the paradoxical form of his book suggests: 'I began to ask myself; is a system of philosophy, as different from mere history and historic classification, possible?' Coleridge eventually answered, yes, to this question, but he recognised that whether or not truth is a notion relative to time is a question both perplexing and crucial. It is a problem closely associated with the status of genre.

At the centre of Augustan literature is the work of the conservative satirists, Dryden, Pope and Swift. They were men who recognised the flux of history, but refused to accept that aesthetic and moral values shared in that flux. The latter belief made them neoclassicists, the former satirists. But by the end of the eighteenth century there was an increasing willingness to accept that aesthetic and moral values were relative to particular societies and cultures. Scott is the novelist of cultural relativism, Byron its poet, but the notion was widely diffused.

Peacock, a sharp-minded man, drives the relativist conclusion home to its logical conclusion in *The Four Ages of Poetry*; Homer is 'the mental rattle that awakened the attention of intellect in the infancy of society'.[42] For a nineteenth-century man to attend seriously to that rattle is an absurdity only surpassed by the activity of the modern poet whose business it is to construct rattles for the entertainment of an adult society. Poetry is the product of a barbarian civilisation and condemned in later times always to hanker after its origins. The joke is at the expense of Wordsworthian primitivism, but Peacock suggests a more serious problem when he asserts that the value of poetry, even at its best, is confined to the age in which it was produced. For Pope the eighteenth-century poet was a civilised man condemned to write for barbarians. For Peacock, he is a barbarian absurdly expecting the trinkets he produces to entertain the likes of Sir Humphrey Davy.

Shelley's most comprehensive statement of his aesthetic theory *A Defence of Poetry* was written in answer to Peacock's squib. Shelley refutes easily Peacock's two central positions: that the progress of society is inimical to the progress of poetry, and that poetry is irrelevant to the needs of the present age. But

Peacock's denial that the poetry of the past could have present value exercises all his ingenuity, and perhaps defeats it.

A Defence of Poetry has usually been regarded as confused. That it is inconsistent is, I think, difficult to deny, but it seems likely that its inconsistencies are controlled, and that they are evidence of the same dilemma that forced Coleridge into paradox, but expressed by a man whose philosophical allegiances led him to distrust the impression of inconsistency transcended that paradox is designed to give, and to prefer the dialogue, whether explicit or implicit, as a means of registering contradictions.

A genre, Shelley accepted, is a historical process, that is, a set of conventions subject to the flux of history. That was why it is possible for a poet to work with established genres, but it also followed that the value of a poem could not be located in the genre to which it belonged, for otherwise aesthetic value could not survive historical change. Shelley's notion of genre threatened the reduction of the status of every poem to that of a historical document. That is why, within *A Defence of Poetry*, an acceptance of generic conventions and a formal description of poetry is countered by a series of passages in which Shelley maintains that all generic distinction is idle.

The essay contains a history of poetry, correcting that written by Peacock, but sharing with him the assumption that a poem is the product of the society in which it was written, together with assertions that poetry is essentially outside both time and place. The corruption of Charles II's government is inextricably linked with the meanness of the literary achievements of the Restoration, and yet the philosophical schemes which Dante and Milton inherited from their societies, though they obscure, do not compromise their achievement. Both positions are maintained with a disconcerting extremism.

That Shelley was aware of his inconsistency is probable, for the essay contains a series of puns which embody the antagonism between its two theoretical stances. Shelley claims two advantages for Greek drama over modern drama; the Greeks assimilated within their drama 'religious institutions', and in abandoning the mask modern actors substitute a 'partial and inharmonious effect' for the possibility afforded by the mask of moulding 'the many expressions' appropriate to a dramatic character into 'one permanent and unchanging expression'.[43] Later we read:

The distorted notions of invisible things which Dante and his
rival Milton have idealized, are merely the mask and the
mantle in which these great poets walk through eternity
enveloped and disguised.[44]

The assimilation of religious institutions, the lack of which in
modern drama is a deficiency, is taken in Dante and Milton to be
a distortion, a disguise. The inconsistency between the two
passages is embodied in the word 'mask'. The mask worn by
Greek actors freed them from 'partial' or transient representations of character, but the 'mask' worn by Dante and Milton is
the temporal disguise in which they 'walk through eternity'.

A similar play on the word 'form' extends throughout the
essay. At one point we read:

The beauty of the internal nature cannot be so far concealed by
its accidental vesture, but that the spirit of the form shall
communicate itself to the very disguise.[45]

But later Shelley condemns those periods in which 'Tragedy
becomes a cold imitation of the form of the great masterpieces of
antiquity'.[46] The same word is used to signify both the 'internal
nature' of poetry, and the 'accidental vesture' that can only
disguise its essential character.

Poetry is defined as that which admits a very radical translation:

The grammatical forms which express the moods of time, and
the difference of persons, and the distinctions of place, are
convertible with respect to the highest poetry without injuring
it as poetry.[47]

But a poem is also defined as that which forbids translation:

Hence the vanity of translation: it were as wise to cast a violet
into a crucible that you might discover the formal principle of
its colour and odour, as seek to transfuse from one language
into another, the creations of a poet.[48]

The terms 'mask', 'form' and 'translation' act as pivotal words
through which Shelley expresses both a recognition that the

value of poetry is dependent on its external form and on its historical situation, and an assertion that its value is independent of time and place, and separable from its 'accidental vesture'.

Shelley's attempt to reconcile the temporal with the permanent value of poetry, or of a formal with an essential mode of appreciation, is tentative and unconvincing. It hinges on the prophetic role of the poet, whose sensitivity to the spirit of the age enables him in some sense to predict the future that will result from it, and whose poems are also one of the causes of the effect which is the future. In this way a poem may be said to have its being both in the age when it was written, and in the future which it predicts, and, to an extent, causes. The Homeric poems were 'the elements of that social system which is the column upon which all succeeding civilization has reposed'.[49] Homer, in understanding his own age, also predicted and caused the column that rose from it, Greek civilisation, and the building which developed from that column, Western civilisation. In their role as both cause and effect of Greek civilisation the Homeric poems had a value which is related to their present value by the continuing relationship between ourselves and Ancient Greece. Reading Homer is neither an exercise in free association, nor a sterile exercise in historical research because 'we are all Greeks'.[50] Unconvincing this may be, but Shelley's emphasis is on the dilemma rather than its resolution, and it is the dilemma that helps towards an understanding of his poetry.

Shelley and Genre

In Shelley's thought, in his poetry, and in his life, there is an ever-present drive towards a rejection of conventional controls, and yet he also recognised that controls, systems, conventions, are humanly necessary. Even 'Christian and chivalric systems of manners and religion' were admirable in that, when they were 'copied into the imaginations of men', they 'became as generals to the bewildered armies of their thoughts'.[51] A convention, like a general, may be an evil, but it is a necessary evil, for the alternative to convention is bewilderment. These contrary pulls resulted in a complex attitude to language, the system of conventions that 'generals' all thought, and to genres, the systems of convention that 'general' literature. Shelley's poetry may be described as the expression of these contrary pulls.

As language is the necessary precondition of thought, so genre is a precondition of literature. Without a genre the poet will lack an ordering principle with which to marshal the 'bewildered armies' of his poeticisms. But no poet is wholly free to create a genre, any more than a poet is free to create the language in which he writes. A genre is a convention, a system of tacit agreements between the poet and his reader. A private genre, like a private language, is therefore a contradiction in terms. A poet must work with the genres available to him; his area of choice is limited by his historical situation. Shelley recognised this as a truth with general application: 'it may be assumed as a maxim that no nation or religion can supersede any other without incorporating into itself a portion of that which it supersedes'. If true of politics and religion the maxim must also be true of poetry, and the truth it adumbrates is that no poet can escape the forms he inherits from his predecessors. This would be insignificant if a genre were only a 'mould', but even to consider the metaphor is to realise that a genre, like a mould, shapes what it contains, that the genre a poet chooses is not a container in which his meaning is encapsulated, but a part of his meaning. To accept that thought is controlled by the language within which it is conducted, is to accept also that the poet's meaning is controlled by the genre within which the poem is written. In Shelley's poems there is a recurring character who is celebrated for being 'himself alone'.[52] Such praise is pathos, for Shelley's poems are written out of a sober recognition that no such perfect autonomy is possible for the poet.

Shelley is typically Romantic in his expression of contradictory attitudes towards both language and genre; his peculiarity is in the extremism with which he pursues his inconsistencies. Of all Romantic poets Shelley was the most committed to the use of established genres: the relationships between *Prometheus Unbound* and *Prometheus Bound*, *Adonais* and the tradition of pastoral elegy, and *The Triumph of Life* and Petrarch's *Triumphs* are, in obvious ways, closer than those between other major Romantic poems and their models, and yet Shelley outdoes even Wordsworth in his contempt for rules and conventions, and he demands repeatedly that man free himself from his past. This seems to me a paradox crucial to Shelley's poetry. Far more than most poets Shelley needed 'generals' to marshal 'the bewildered armies of his thoughts', but he was also painfully conscious that the language might control its speaker rather than the speaker his language, that the genre might direct the poet rather than the poet the genre. At this stage one example of Shelley's dilemma must suffice.

An Address to the People on the Death of the Princess Charlotte closely follows the conventional structure of the classical oration, in particular of the funeral speech over the body of the dead hero. In the gradual emergence of its real theme, the execution of the three labourers, from its apparent theme, the death of the princess, and in its progressive ascent to a climax of grief and indignation which is also a covert incitement to the reader to engage in retaliatory action, it recalls the speech made by Shakespeare's Antony over the body of the dead Caesar. And yet Shelley's ethical stance is inconsistent with that implicit in classical celebratory or commemorative orations. The men he commemorates are more worthy of regard than other men, not because of their achievements, nor because of their high birth, but because their deaths are representative of the unjust relationship between the government and the governed. Shelley demands that his reader accept that the death of a princess is a private matter, whereas the deaths of the three labourers are a matter of public moment. He rejects an aristocratic theory of individual value in favour of a democratic or representative theory, and in doing so he attempts to change, and change radically, the ethical stance implicit in the genre within which he is working.

In attempting this displacement Shelley runs the same risk that attends the construction of a grandiose monument as a tomb for an unknown soldier. Such a monument attempts to replace the notion of the hero as extraordinary individual with the notion that the heroism of war is a virtue shared by many common soldiers, and is therefore best honoured in building a representative, unnamed tomb. And yet, in constructing a monument like that which marks the grave of a Wellington or a Napoleon, the unknown soldier loses his representative status, and becomes a hero who differs from Wellington and Napoleon only in being abstract. The form of the monument overpowers the democratic belief that directed its construction. The genre proves too strong for the poet.

Shelley ends his pamphlet by mourning the death, and piously expecting the resurrection of a princess called, not Charlotte, but Liberty. The question remains whether an aristocratic genre is successfully subverted to the service of a democratic ethic, or whether Liberty wins approval only in so far as she attains the status of a royal princess. In this pamphlet, the directness and fierceness of Shelley's irony successfully overcomes the ethic implicit in the genre he uses, but in the more delicate tonal variations of his poems, the issue is more doubtful.

In *Adonais* the 'one Spirit's plastic stress' creates by: 'Torturing th'unwilling dross that checks its flight/To its own likeness, as each mass may bear . . .' (384–5). This may serve as a metaphor for Shelley's activity in his major poems. The poem results from the struggle in which the poet engages to impose his own likeness on resistant materials, on a language and on genres developed for purposes other than his own. In Shelley's unsuccessful poems he either ignores the limitations inherent in his materials, or he surrenders to them. In his best poems he achieves a fine equipoise, and it is these poems that are discussed in the following chapters.

2 Realism and Fantasy

This chapter concerns *The Mask of Anarchy* and *The Witch of Atlas*, poems that apparently represent the north and south poles of Shelley's achievement. The one is a political ballad prompted by a brutal attack on a Manchester reform meeting by the local militia, an attack still remembered as the Peterloo Massacre;[1] the other is, in Shelley's words, a 'visionary rhyme' which tells 'no story false or true'. The one, according to Mary Shelley was 'written for the people',[2] the other she describes as the product of a Shelley seeking 'shelter' from painful reality in 'the airiest flights of fancy'.[3]

It is convenient to begin a discussion of Shelley's work by considering these poems for two reasons. They have proved more easily available to modern readers than Shelley's more ambitious poems,[4] and it seems best to begin a study of Shelley's work from what common ground is available. Secondly, the two poems are so obviously and widely different that to describe the techniques they have in common is to offer persuasive evidence that these techniques are characteristic of the whole of Shelley's mature poetry, and central to it.

The Mask of Anarchy

Mary Shelley contrasts the human realism of *The Mask of Anarchy* with the fanciful detachment from humanity of *The Witch of Atlas*. This opposition is too stiff to be useful. Brecht's remarks on the *Mask* helpfully refuse it.[5] They occur in one of Brecht's defences of his own style against the charge that it deviates from the narrow path of socialist realism. The obligation to write such apologies is surely the heaviest burden imposed on the Marxist poet, but Brecht's self-defence is jaunty enough. He argues cunningly that the mistakes of his critics is to confine the term realism to the mode developed by nineteenth-century bourgeois novelists like Balzac. Cervantes and Swift write in a different manner, and yet they too may properly be described as realists working within an alternative (non-bourgeois) tradition of realism. The representative of this alternative tradition that he chooses to discuss at length, and again his choice is artful, is *The Mask of Anarchy*, a poem that his critics would think twice before repudiating. He uses Shelley's ballad to support his claim that 'realism' need not prohibit 'fantasy'. Brecht suggests that fantasy may be a form of realism, that Shelley's poem, even though it does not describe the massacre that prompted it, even though it represents the forces of government through a stylised masquerade, even though its heroine is a girl called 'Hope' rather than an exemplary proletarian, is a realistic presentation of a class conflict.

But Brecht's remarks on *The Mask of Anarchy* are less interesting than the poem he wrote in imitation of it, *Der Anacronistische Zug oder Freiheit und Democracy*.[6] Brecht's poem is, in fact, modelled only on the first twenty-five stanzas of Shelley's poem, the description of the procession, but the imitation is close and perceptive. He fully realises Shelley's pun on the word 'mask': its primary meaning is 'masquerade' or 'procession' its secondary meaning is 'disguise'. Brecht translates the primary meaning in the poem's title, 'zug', but he also represents his masquers as postwar Nazis inefficiently disguised as Christian Democrats; some have patched over the hooks of their swastikas to form crosses, others, since the closure of the concentration camps, have begun to proclaim their belief in the rights of minorities. Brecht also understands Shelley's ironic vocabulary. His marchers all shout their belief in the new postwar virtues, freedom and democracy, but in their mouths the words invert their meanings and become translations of the Nazi slogans of the past. Shelley's masquers worship a skeleton who claims to represent '*God, and King, and Law*'. The skeleton presents himself as the summation of all the forces of social cohesion, but his name is Anarchy. The government justified the attack on the reform meeting on the grounds that stern action was necessary to forestall the threat of anarchic disturbances, but the meeting was orderly and peaceable, and the real forces of anarchy were the local militia who attacked it. Brecht, like Shelley, describes a world of double-talk, in which words stand on their heads obedient to the commands of their fascist trainer.

Brecht's handling of the ballad stanza is flexible. His first stanza is written in hope. After the war years, spring returns to Germany, green shoots begin to push through the rubble:

Frühling wurd's in deutschem land,
Über Asch und Trümerwand
Flog ein erstes Birkengrün
Probweis, delikat und kühn.[7]

The diction, the coinage '*birkengrün*', the green of the birch tree, for example, expresses the speaker's sensitivity to the vulnerable green shoots. The rhythm of the stanza delicately interplays with the ballad metre. Notice how the second line hovers between a backward and a forward reference, until the absence of a comma at its end directs it hopefully towards the future. The rhythmic movement follows the speaker's mind as he turns from the past, from the war, and looks towards a new beginning. But the hope is shortlived, the procession approaches, and the green shoots are crushed under the jackboots that the erstwhile Nazis have not bothered to remove. As the poem continues, the delicate rhythmic possibilities suggested in the first stanza are overpowered by the mechanical thump of the ballad line. The vocabulary, which in the first stanza was searching and suggestive, becomes brutal and direct:

Blut and Dreck in Wahlverwandschaft
Zug da durch die deutsche Landschaft
Rülpste, kotzte, stank und schrie:
Freiheit und Democracy.[8]

The change in the poem's technique imitates not only the sequence of events that the poem describes, a promise of spring, of a new beginning, that is violated by the resurrection of all the old evils, but also the emotions of its speaker, hope followed by an increasingly outraged indignation as he is disenchanted. It is a lyrical ballad.

The obvious difference between *The Mask of Anarchy* and Brecht's ballad is that Brecht's is a poem of disillusionment, a poem in which Hope is defeated, whereas in *The Mask of Anarchy* Hope, quite literally, is triumphant. But a more important distinction is that Brecht inhabits his ballad style, whereas

Shelley remains detached from his, self-consciously apeing the role of the popular balladeer. One of the effects of Brecht's first stanza is to deny any distinction between ballads and poems, the balladeer and the poet. Shelley's first stanza enforces such distinctions:

> As I lay asleep in Italy
> There came a voice from over the Sea,
> And with great power it forth led me
> To walk in the visions of Poesy. (1–4)

The dream framework is constructed with an utter lack of artifice (contrast the opening stanzas of *The Triumph of Life*), the expression is pointedly clumsy, 'forth led me', and self-consciously naïve, 'the visions of Poesy'. Shelley establishes the ballad style as a pose, he adopts the role of a simple balladeer. The personal allusion to his residence in Italy only stresses the distinction between the old Etonian and the role he has chosen. It is necessary to make this point because the character of the poem has been obscured by the kind of praise it has received. Leavis compares it with Blake's songs, and Richard Holmes suggests that its style is a gesture of 'triumphant solidarity with the underprivileged, oppressed and unrepresented, against the élite class in power'.[9] Leavis and Holmes both refuse to recognise what is sufficiently obvious, that Shelley, unlike Blake and unlike Brecht, patronises the popular style in which he writes. *The Mask of Anarchy* reveals Shelley as a popular poet no more than 'Pyramus and Thisbe' reveals Shakespeare as a popular dramatist.

Shelley sometimes uses a rough ballad style in writing political satire. The best example is a ballad called *The Devil's Walk* written in 1812 in imitation of Coleridge.[10] The poem contains some admirable fooling, this for example on the Prince of Wales's portliness:

> For he is fat,—his waistcoat gay,
> When strained upon a levee day,
> Scarce meets across his princely paunch;
> And pantaloons are like half-moons
>   Upon each brawny haunch. (71–5)

This, particularly the Lear-like description of the pantaloons, is funny, but the poem is noticeably less successful when it attempts to be serious, and turns from the Prince of Wales to the Peninsular War:

> The hell-hounds, Murder, Want and Woe,
> Forever hungering, flocked around;
> From Spain had Satan sought their food,
> 'Twas human woe and human blood! (124–7)

As the theme becomes serious the ballad form becomes an evident embarrassment: the reader struggles against a ludicrous temptation to pronounce 'food' and 'blood' as a full rhyme. The same image recurs in *The Mask of Anarchy*, in the description of the 'seven blood-hounds' who followed Castlereagh, but in the later poem its handling is assured:

> All were fat; and well they might
> Be in admirable plight,
> For one by one, and two by two,
> He tossed them human hearts to chew
> Which from his wide cloak he drew (9–13)

In *The Mask of Anarchy* Shelley is free, as he was not when writing *The Devil's Walk*, to exploit, even when being serious, the comic naivety of the ballad style. He gains assurance by assuming the style, by allowing his seriousness to be expressed over the balladeer's head rather than through his mouth.

In the description of the procession Shelley's effects are gained by the reader's awareness of two voices in the poem, the assumed voice of the naive balladeer, and the voice of the sophisticated poet who makes capital from the balladeer's innocence and clumsiness. Mary Shelley accurately noticed two divergent registers within the poem: 'The poem was written for the people, and is therefore in a more popular tone than usual: portions strike as abrupt and unpolished, but many stanzas are all his own'.[11] The reader of the poem ought to be aware both of the voice of the balladeer, and of Shelley manipulating that voice.

The most obvious characteristic of the syntax of the popular ballad is its avoidance of subordinate clauses: main clauses are simply juxtaposed or coordinated. Shelley imitates this: 'I met

Murder on the way—/He had a mask like Castlereagh—(5–6). But the naïvety that such a syntax implies is a pose that the reader is expected to penetrate. The balladeer introduces Murder in two unrelated propositions which fail to explain the significance of his mask, but the reader is expected to supply the missing connective. The balladeer is ignorant of the ambiguity in the phrase 'a mask like Castlereagh', for him it is only a way of saying that the mask worn by Murder looked like Castlereagh. But the reader is aware of the other possibility, that Murder and Castlereagh both wear masks, that Castlereagh's pursuit of peace is only a mask for his plan to stamp out violently all popular resistance to tyranny. The balladeer mentions Castlereagh's pets: 'Seven blood-hounds followed him'. From his point of view this is only a scrupulous notation of fact, the kind of irrelevantly precise detail characteristic of the popular ballad. But for the politically aware reader the reference is precise: K. N. Cameron notes the allusion to 'the seven nations that in 1815 agreed with Britain to put off the abolition of the universal slave trade'.[12]

The reader's awareness that the ballad style is assumed, playacted, sanctions those lines in which Shelley drops his mask and speaks in his own person:

Clothed with the Bible, as with light,
And the shadows of the night,
Like Sidmouth, next, Hypocrisy
On a crocodile rode by. (22–5)

The first couplet is sophisticated, self-consciously ironic, in a manner beyond the capacity of the balladeer, but the inconsistency is not offensive because the reader has been made aware that the balladeer's voice is a fiction, a pretence.

Shelley's fiction is most important in enabling him to present the forces of Anarchy throughout the first part of the poem as comic villains. Leigh Hunt was quick to notice the poem's comedy (the preface to his edition of the *Mask* is still in many ways the best critical account of it). He speaks of its 'union of ludicrousness with terror', and adds: 'His very strokes of humour, while they startle with their extravagance and even ghastliness, cut to the heart with pathos'.[13]

Take once again the description of the bloodhounds who follow Castlereagh:

For one by one, and two by two,
He tossed them human hearts to chew
Which from his wide cloak he drew. (11–13)

The first line poses as a popular ballad line-filler, a line there to make up the stanza, but its mock-innocence exposes the second line as incongruous, both shockingly and comically incongruous. The crucial word in the third line is 'wide'. If we accepted the *Mask* as a genuine popular ballad, then 'wide' would be simply a neutral adjective chosen from the balladeer's scanty stock of one-syllable modifiers. But to the sophisticated reader it has a much more precise significance. Castlereagh becomes the villain of a stage melodrama.

My point is that Shelley exploits both the strengths and the weaknesses of the popular ballad. Take, for example, the description of the Lord Chancellor, Eldon:

Next came Fraud, and he had on,
Like Eldon, an ermined gown;
His big tears, for he wept well,
Turned to mill-stones as they fell. (14–17)

One of the strengths of the ballad is its refusal of generalisation in favour of concrete detail. Shelley harnesses this strength in his use of abstract nouns: 'Fraud' ceases to be an empty personification and becomes a being on the same plane of reality as 'Eldon'. But in the same stanza Shelley also makes play with ballad clumsiness; the gauche colloquialism 'he had on' is used to expose the absurdity of Fraud's magnificent costume, and the rhythmic breakdown in the second line isolates Eldon for the reader's attention and throws a stress on 'ermined' which is easily interpreted by the knowing reader as a sneer. Again in this stanza the naïve words 'big' and 'well' are covertly active, 'big' suggesting that Eldon's is the kind of grief most fitly measured by the impressiveness of its symptoms, and 'well' suggesting that he is an artist in sorrow.

The odd compound of hatred and comedy that controls the first part of the poem is well illustrated in the stanza describing the effect of Eldon's tears:

And the little children, who
Round his feet played to and fro,

Thinking every tear a gem,
Had their brains knocked out by them. (18–21)

The first three lines might have been taken from the *Songs of Innocence*. They are violated by the stanza's last line, but it would be wrong to deny that an element of comedy is also present, the comedy of cartoon violence.
  In stanza VIII Anarchy is introduced:

Last came Anarchy: he rode
On a white horse, splashed with blood;
He was pale even to the lips,
Like Death in the Apocalypse. (30–3)

Much of the stanza's force derives from one word 'splashed'. Its effectiveness becomes clear if it is replaced by a more literary word like 'stained'. 'Splashed' is a word more appropriate to the balladeer, but Shelley exploits both its obscenity, its suggestion that blood is of no more significance than whitewash, and also its grotesque comedy. The description of the army following Anarchy relies for its effect on a similar rejection of literary vocabulary:

And a mighty troop around,
With their trampling shook the ground,
Waving each a bloody sword
For the service of their Lord. (42–5)

'Trampling' instead of 'marching', 'waving' instead of 'brandishing', 'bloody' instead of 'crimson'. The vocabulary mocks the heroic assertion in the phrase 'a mighty troop'.
  Towards the close of the description of the masquerade the irony becomes increasingly direct as Shelley prepares to move into his own voice. But even after the intervention of Hope, the techniques of the first part of the poem are operative:

My father Time is weak and gray
With waiting for a better day;
See how idiot-like he stands,
Fumbling with his palsied hands! (90–3)

Time's impotent senility treads the verge of the comic, but it is a comedy that does not alienate the reader's human sympathy, just as the comic grotesqueness of the mask does not conceal its menace.

Shelley exploits both the strengths and the weaknesses of the ballad style to create a balance between anger and comedy. Like Brecht, he uses comedy to discipline anger, to reconcile anger with the demands of ordinary communication. The technique allows him to describe Eldon without giving way to the disturbing paranoia that he reveals in other references to the Lord Chancellor. [14] But the balance the poem achieves is uneasy. The comic surface of the poem is threatened by the hatred beneath it; the comic pose as the simple-minded balladeer is only precariously maintained. Brecht achieves much the same effect in his plays; the voice of the author's angry didacticism is only just prevented from breaking through the dramatic idiom of a particular character, the play achieves a threatened poise between the dramatic and the polemic, and the audience's sense of the tightrope that is being walked gives the play much of its theatrical excitement.

The second part of the poem records a speech made by Hope to the people of England. The distinction between Shelley's voice and the balladeer's lapses, and as a consequence the poem's language loses some of its vigour. But this is compensated by a very characteristic manoeuvre. The programme of action which Hope recommends to the people is one of peaceful, even passive, resistance to oppression. They should send representatives to a great assembly which should proclaim its independence of the government. The delegates must expect attack from the army but should react passively and look for protection to the law, if that fails to the common humanity they share with the soldiers, and if that fails to the power of public scorn which will pursue the killers of unarmed citizens. Godwin himself, although he would have been alarmed by the notion of a large assembly, could not have proposed a policy of more awesome restraint. And yet Leigh Hunt refused to publish Shelley's poem in *The Examiner* in 1819. Not until 1832 when radical energy had subsided with the passing of the reform bill did he think fit to print it. Hunt explains his decision in the preface to his edition of the poem:

I did not insert it because I thought that the public at large had

not become sufficiently discerning to do justice to the
kind-heartedness of the spirit that walked in this flaming robe
of verse. His charity was avowedly more than proportionate
to his indignation; yet I thought that even the suffering part of
the people, judging, not unnaturally from their own feelings,
and from the exasperation which suffering produces before it
produces knowledge, would believe a hundred-fold in his
anger, to what they would in his good intention, and this made
me fear that the common enemy would take advantage of the
mistake to do them both a disservice. [15]

The uncharacteristic tortuousness of Hunt's prose betrays his
embarrassment in reconciling the two aspects of the poem, the
'flaming' and the 'kind-hearted'. He finally takes refuge in
paradox, explaining Shelley's 'patience' as 'checking, and in fact,
produced by 'the extreme impatience of his moral feeling'. Hunt
did not publish the poem in 1819 because he detected beneath its
avowed pacifism a dangerous countercurrent of approved violence. In the poem's second part the balance between hatred and
comedy is replaced by a balance between passivity and violence.
    The most considerable of Shelley's political essays is his
unfinished *A Philosophical View of Reform*. The essay is in three
chapters: the first describes the conflict between government and
the people from the dissolution of the Roman Empire to the
present day, and from America to India; the second concentrates
on the particular situation in England and enumerates the objects
of reform; the third discusses the means that should be used to
pursue these ends. The essay is moderate in its principles. The
people are advised that 'patience and reason and endurance' will
prove more effective weapons in the struggle than swords. The
more extreme radical demands, such as for the enfranchisement
of women, are postponed. Shelley counsels a slow but steady
progress towards a more just society rather than an immediate
revolution. But any abstraction from the essay of the principles
that it avows falsifies its meaning. The first two chapters do not
read like a summons to calm reflection but a call to action. The
execution of Charles I is admired as having given the world a
splendid example by 'bringing to public justice one of those
chiefs of a conspiracy of privileged murderers and robbers whose
impunity has been the consecration of crime'. This is not the
language of moderation. But it is not only that at some points in

the essay Shelley seems to condone violence, his prose style is in itself an incitement to revolution. Passages of analysis culminate in short epigrammatic sentences which express a nervous energy with a potential for violence. He ends a discussion of paper money by remarking: 'The rich no longer being able to rule by force, have invented this scheme that they may rule by fraud'. He notes that the real power of the land has been transferred from the king to the wealthy, from the aristocrat to the capitalist, and concludes: 'Monarchy is only the string which ties the robber's bundle'. This is superior prose, but it is the prose of the revolutionary manifesto not of a rational appeal for moderation.

A similar ambiguity is characteristic of Shelley's writings. In *Prometheus Unbound* there is an odd contradiction between Prometheus's eschewal of revenge, 'I wish no living thing to suffer pain', and the violent overthrow of Demogorgon. When Hope lies down between the army of Anarchy and the people, a Shape, associated by references to a snake and to the morning star with the archetypal rebel Satan, rises between her and the army that is about to trample over her. The Shape has a lethal effect:

And Anarchy, the ghastly birth,
Lay dead earth upon the earth;
The Horse of Death tameless as wind
Fled, and with his hoofs did grind
To dust the murderers thronged behind. (130–4)

Hope gets up and makes a speech recommending passive resistance, but she does so only after the violent rout of Anarchy's army. It is open to Shelley to claim that he has represented the destruction of vices, of Murder, Fraud etc., rather than of people, but since Murder and Fraud are personified quite literally as Castlereagh and Eldon, such a defence would be disingenuous. The suspicion remains that the Shape is a device enabling Shelley to destroy his enemies whilst saving his spokeswoman Hope from any complicity in their deaths.

The poem can, however, assimilate this inconsistency, for *The Mask of Anarchy*, as Leigh Hunt recognised, is like *A Philosophical View of Reform* in latently condoning the violence that it explicitly condemns. Hope demands that the people's delegates should passively endure the attack of the soldiery, but she adds:

On those who first should violate
Such sacred heralds in their state
Rest the blood that must ensue,
And it will not rest on you. (336–9)

The absolution that she grants the people would be redundant if she seriously expected them to react passively. The massacre of the delegates will reverberate through the country like 'a volcano heard afar'. Such rumblings portend an eruption, hardly an appropriate metaphor for a passive Godwinian campaign. Hope's metaphors are consistently at odds with her principles:

Rise like Lions after slumber
In unvanquishable number—
Shake your chains to earth like dew
Which in sleep has fallen on you—
Ye are many—they are few. (151–5 and 368–72)

This stanza, which appears twice in the poem, appears for all the world to be an incitement to violent insurrection.

Like *A Philosophical View of Reform* Shelley's ballad is addressed to the government quite as much as it is addressed to the people. Its ambiguity carries the poem's message, a warning of the bloody consequences that will follow a failure to redress the people's grievances. In its first part hatred and comedy are balanced, in its second violence and pacifism. The precariousness of the equilibrium that the poem achieves is the means by which it expresses the precariousness of the hold that the government and the moderate radical leaders maintain over the people; it is the means by which Shelley expresses his sense of his historical situation. I described the comedy of the first part of the poem as a technique which allowed Shelley to regulate his hatred. This is true, but it is in the end more important to note that it is one of the poem's threatened controls. Comedy barely maintains control of hatred in the poem's first part; pacifist principles barely maintain precedence over incitements to violence in its second part. The urbane poet patronising the ballad style and the peaceful Godwinian reformer are both presented as characters whose roles are threatened by the hating, violent revolutionary who lurks beneath the poem, and it is this precarious, threatened situation rather than anything Hope says that the poem 'means'.

Shelley has located a style designed in itself to express England in 1819.

Shelley hesitated over the spelling of the word 'Mask'; he seems finally to have chosen 'Masque'.[16] Presumably he wished to subordinate the meaning 'disguise' to the meaning 'masquerade', but he may also have wished to emphasise the relation between his poem and the formal masque of the Renaissance and the seventeenth century.[17] A masque might take the form of a procession as well as a dramatic entertainment, and it is a processional masque that Shelley dramatises in his unfinished play *Charles I*, on which he began work in 1819 just after completing *The Mask of Anarchy*. The masque is presented to the audience by two spectators, a naïve youth and a disillusioned older man. The youth is impressed by it:

How glorious! See those thronging chariots
Rolling, like painted clouds before the wind,
Behind their solemn steeds: how some are shaped
Like curved sea-shells dyed by the azure depths
Of Indian seas; some like the new-born moon;
And some like cars in which the Romans climbed
(Canopied by Victory's eagle-wings outspread)
The Capitolian—See how gloriously
The mettled horses in the torchlight stir
Their gallant riders, while they check their pride,
Like shapes of some diviner element
Than English air, and beings nobler than
The envious and admiring multitude. (Scene I, 137–49)

The youth succumbs to the effect that the masque was designed to produce. He accepts the aristocratic and courtly ethic implicit in it, acknowledging that the masquers are 'beings nobler' than the 'multitude'. But the older man is a critic after Shelley's own heart; he interprets the masque independently of the intentions of its producers in accordance with his own ethical premises, and understands it as an emblematic representation of the economic subjection of the many by the few:

These are the lilies glorious as Solomon,
Who toil not, neither do they spin,—unless
It be the webs they catch poor rogues withal.

Here is the surfeit which to them who earn
The niggard wages of the earth, scarce leaves
The tithe that will support them till they crawl
Back to her cold hard bosom. Here is health
Followed by grim disease, glory by shame,
Waste by lame famine, wealth by squalid want,
And England's sin by England's punishment.
And, as the effect pursues the cause foregone,
Lo, giving substance to my words, behold
At once the sign and the thing signified—
A troop of cripples, beggars, and lean outcasts,
Horsed upon stumbling jades, carted with dung,
Dragged for a day from cellars and low cabins
And rotten hiding-holes, to point the moral
Of this presentment, and bring up the rear
Of painted pomp with misery! (Scene I, 156–74)

The Youth imagines that his companion has misunderstood the
meaning of the anti-masque, and he points out its conventional
significance:

'Tis but
The anti-masque, and serves as discords do
In sweetest music. (Scene I, 174–6)

But his friend has not misread the masque out of ignorance, he
has rejected its intended significance on moral grounds.

The youth understands the anti-masque in relation to the
masque, but to the man the anti-masque of the downtrodden is
the point of reference from which the masque must be judged.
The conflict between their two viewpoints is fundamental: it is
the conflict between an aristocratic ethic and a democratic ethic.
The conventional dramatic masque ends with the expulsion of
the anti-masquers. Only after this can the masquers join with the
audience in a dance celebrating the social harmony of all present.
Masques erect an ideal of the good life that entails the exclusion
of those elements inconsistent with the ideal. The youth accepts
this, but to the man the exclusiveness of the ideal exposes its
inadequacy. He judges the masque not by the aesthetic quality of
the order that it achieves but by the cost to others of that
achievement.

The older man shows that it is possible to read a masque through a looking-glass. Read in this way the threat to social harmony comes not from the anti-masquers but the masquers. Their pursuit of an ideal that is necessarily exclusive is a threat to the potential unity of the whole of society. True social unity will only be made possible by the expulsion, or transformation, not of the anti-masquers but of the masquers.

The Mask of Anarchy is a looking-glass masque, a selfconscious reversal of the action characteristic of the conventional masque and of the ethic that such an action implies. Shelley suggests this by building reversal into the language of his poem. Murder wears 'a mask like Castlereagh'; instead of a man wearing an emblematic mask, an abstraction disguises himself as a real person. Similarly the masque, the celebration in pageant or in drama of the harmony and order of a king-centred society, is reversed and exposed as the expression of an ethic that is socially divisive, anarchic. In the centre of Shelley's procession, proceeded by Castlereagh, Eldon etc., and followed by the army, in the place that one would expect to be occupied by a divine or kingly figure, rides a man who proclaims himself as '*God, and King, and Law*'. He claims to represent the summation of the forces of social cohesion: his name is Anarchy.[18]

Shelley's ballad begins as a processional masque, but when the Shape intervenes between Hope and the army it becomes dramatic. Hope is a 'maniac maid', and she is accompanied by her father Time who is 'palsied' and 'idiot-like'. These two confront a crowned figure on horseback who is preceded by important dignitaries and followed by an army. Hope and her father, paupers, comic grotesques, are candidates for inclusion in just such an anti-masque as Shelley describes in *Charles I*. They confront a procession of dignitaries whose social status entitles them to appear as masquers. A divine presence, the Shape, appears, exactly the kind of celestial intervention used in the conventional masque to effect the expulsion, or transformation, or circumvention of the anti-masquers. But Shelley's Shape is satanic, an inverted deity, and he puts to flight not the anti-masquers Hope and Time, but the King, his officers and his army.[19] The Shape expels the masquers who prevented the achievement of true social harmony, and only after their expulsion is Hope free to address the people of England as 'Nurslings of one mighty Mother'. Shelley's reversal of the conventional masque action is pointed and precise.

The Shape's rout of the masquers represents on a symbolic level an action that Hope predicts will take place literally in the future. The people's assembly will be attacked by the soldiery; the agents of government order will attempt to preserve that order by crushing the people's representatives. But the government and its agents will necessarily fail, because they are outnumbered. The exclusiveness of the aristocratic ethic makes inevitable its defeat. The anti-masquers outnumber the masquers: 'Ye are many—they are few'. Shelley's poem is a generic expression of popular strength and durability. It is both a popular ballad and a masque; it plays both with an aristocratic genre and a popular genre, and the ballad is triumphant. The masque that the poem contains must be reconstructed; it is a fossil preserved by the ballad. The masque is an event in literary history, but the popular ballad existed before it, it was available for Shelley in 1819, and for Brecht in 1945. Richard Holmes says of Shelley's poem: 'The very roughness of the verse, the deliberate ruggedness of grammar and style, pushes aside the dilettante and the *littérateur*'.[20] This is true more precisely than Holmes supposes, for the poem contains the 'literature' that it pushes aside, it recreates the masque that it allows to be overpowered by the ballad. Shelley's poem is a generic expression of the inevitability of the triumph of the people over their oppressors; in it the ballad triumphs over the masque.

But here is the paradox. Holmes will not approve of my description of the poem, for to locate in it a generic game of the kind that I have described is to deny that it is a popular poem, it is to suggest that *The Mask of Anarchy* is itself the work of a *littérateur*. But this is a paradox from which we should not flinch. Shelley, as I have insisted, patronises the ballad; he makes his reader aware of a distinction between the poet and the simple balladeer. The balladeer is (for once the cliché is useful) a persona, Shelley is himself a masquer. It is part of the poem's point that it fails to express what Holmes claims for it, 'triumphant solidarity with the underprivileged, oppressed, and unrepresented against the élite class in power'. Shelley, like Byron though less stridently, was aware that such a solidarity was impossible, and to claim it dishonest. He was separated from the balladeer by the culture he was heir to, an élitist culture, his participation in which made him a masquer. Shelley predicts through Hope the victory of the people, but he also expresses through the poem his own separateness from them. Hope's pronouns are carefully chosen: 'Ye are many—they are few'. The refusal to write 'we' is an honesty. The people occupy one side of the line, the government occupies the other—Shelley sits on the dash. He writes a looking-glass masque that repudiates the ethic implicit in the conventional masque, but the masque is the product of a culture alien to the balladeer, and to recreate it even in parody is for Shelley to distinguish himself from the people whose victory he predicts and celebrates. *The Mask of Anarchy* sides wholeheartedly with the people, but it would be a lesser, a less honest poem, if it did not also express the situation of the upper-class rebel.

The Witch of Atlas

By the time Shelley died five cantos of *Don Juan* had been published, and he had come to regard it as the greatest poem of his age. There is evidence that in the last years of Shelley's life he began to find his relationship with Byron stifling,[21] but before this, in 1819 and 1820, he made a sustained attempt to cope with *Don Juan*, to assimilate its techniques for his own purposes. In these years he wrote *Peter Bell the Third* and *The Witch of Atlas* and translated the Homeric *Hymn to Mercury*. In all these poems Shelley is indebted to his reading of *Don Juan*. They are poems which result from a critical effort to understand Byron's poem, and in them more clearly than his other work Shelley's poetry is revealed as the result of a literary criticism. In order to appreciate them it helps to understand what Shelley admired in *Don Juan*.

In Canto I of *Don Juan* Shelley especially praised the letter of farewell written by Julia to Juan after the discovery of their affair.[22] He praises it as 'a masterpiece of portraiture', admiring no doubt Byron's sensitivity to a woman's predicament and his successful recreation of a feminine voice. But Shelley admired not only the letter itself, but also 'the account of its being written', and the account is very different in its manner:

This note was written upon gilt-edged paper
  With a neat little crow-quill, slight and new;
Her small white hand could hardly reach the taper

It trembled as magnetic needles do,
And yet she did not let one tear escape her;
The seal a sun-flower; '*Elle vous suit partout*,'
The motto, cut upon a white cornelian;
The wax was superfine, its hue vermilion. (Canto I, stanza
198)

Julia's fastidious concern for elegant detail in the presentation of
her letter suggests that her despair is a charming adaptation to a
conventionally required posture: her kinship is with Madame
Bovary rather than with Eloise. This stanza Shelley admired, but
he added: 'I cannot say I equally approve of the service to which
the letter was put: or that I altogether think the bitter mockery of
our common nature of which this is one of the expressions, quite
worthy of your genius'. Presumably the passage to which he
objects is Juan's farewell speech to Spain and to Julia, made as his
ship sails away from land, after rereading Julia's letter. Juan
fights a battle between his desire to give noble expression to his
grief and his increasing nausea, and nausea wins: ' "Beloved
Julia, hear me still beseeching!"/(Here he grew inarticulate with
retching.)' (Canto II, stanza 20). In a typical manoeuvre Byron
exposes the vulnerability of the highest emotions to vulgar
physiology. Romantic love encounters, and is vanquished by,
seasickness: a mouthful of fine words is interrupted by a
mouthful of vomit. Shelley was perhaps oversensitive in the face
of the rumbustious comedy of the scene. He was offended by the
use of man's animal frailties, 'our common nature', to mock all
emotion that aspires beyond the merely animal. But it might be
argued that a similar relationship exists between Julia's letter and
the account of its being written. The account ridicules the letter
by exposing it as a sophisticated convention to which Julia
conforms rather than a spontaneous overflow of powerful
feeling. Such an argument would surely be misleading. Byron's
technique in the seasickness passage was offensive to Shelley
because the reader is persuaded that nausea is a feeling 'truer' than
the noble emotions, love of Spain and love of Julia. The
technique in this passage is exclusive and levelling. Seasickness is
used to expose the lowest common denominator of the human,
and to ridicule the aspiration towards any higher factors. The
relationship between Julia's letter and the account of its being
written is rather different. The account persuades the reader of a

certain artificiality in Julia's response to her situation, but it does not ridicule the emotion that she expresses. Julia becomes a sentimentalist, but there is no indication that her sentiments are false, only that she seeks comfort in the choice of an appropriate role, and finds some satisfaction in the quality of her perform- ance. The account deepens rather than punctures the sympathy with Julia aroused by her letter: it encourages the reader not only to pity her pain, but also to admire her resilience. The technique is inclusive; it results not in a brutal reduction of man to the animal bedrock of his being, but in an amused, affectionate awareness of human complexity.

Shelley most admired *Don Juan* when Byron's stance is least like Swift's, when it directs the reader towards a tolerant, qualifying, complex attitude to experience rather than an attitude which is hostile, simplifying and exclusive. He admired *Don Juan* as a comedy, not as a satire.

Shelley wrote *Peter Bell the Third* in October 1819 after reading a review by Leigh Hunt that conducted a comic comparison between Wordsworth's *Peter Bell* and Reynolds's parody of it. Shelley, like Reynolds, parodied Wordsworth's poem before he had read it, and his Peter Bell rapidly becomes a pseudonym for Wordsworth. The poem centres on a comic description of Wordsworth's career. It is uneven; there is evidence that Shelley was not yet at ease in this style of writing. It is at its best when Shelley leans most heavily on those techniques developed by Byron in *Don Juan*:

He had also dim recollections
  Of pedlars tramping on their rounds;
Milk-pans and pails; and odd collections
Of saws, and proverbs; and reflections
  Old parsons make in burying-grounds.

But Peter's verse was clear, and came
  Announcing from the frozen hearth
Of a cold age, that none might tame
The soul of that diviner flame
  It augured to the Earth:

Like gentle rains, on the dry plains,
  Making that green which late was gray,
Or like the sudden moon, that stains

Some gloomy chamber's window-panes
With a broad light like day.

For language was in Peter's hand
Like clay while he was yet a potter . . . (428–44)

The chattering syntax of the first stanza is interrupted in the second by the grand cadences of the tribute to Wordsworth's greatness. The abrupt change in diction and in rhythm expresses the incongruity between Wordsworth's materials and the poems fashioned from them, and also, more strikingly, Wordsworth's advent into a banal literary situation, his Messianic redemption of English poetry. The tribute continues for two stanzas, but in the opening lines of the next Shelley slips by means of a simile (a characteristic Byronic device)[23] back into the comic base tone of his poem: 'For language was in Peter's hand/Like clay while he was yet a potter . . .'. A tribute to Wordsworth's mastery of words turns into a comic recollection of Peter Bell's profession, and prepares the reader for a comic description of Wordsworth's vanity and social pretensions.

The whole poem expresses what Shelley thought of as an incongruity between the man and the poet, but Wordsworth's personal failings are not used as a lever with which to demolish his poetic achievement. Both are true, both are accepted. Like those passages in *Don Juan* which Shelley most admired the effect of the poem is inclusive, not reductive; it results in an amused recognition of human variousness, not a fierce exposure of man's pettiness. The most important technique that Shelley learned from *Don Juan* was the possibility of employing an uneven or mixed style, so that the reader is prevented from finding a point of reference in any one of the poem's styles and forced to consider the relation between styles as the poem's meaning.

Don Juan is the masterpiece among a group of poems written in this period which exploit the possibility of choosing between styles, in particular of choosing between a 'realist' and a 'romantic' style. In the prologue to *Peter Bell* Wordsworth represents this act of choice in a rather stiff allegory, but there is also a number of poems, *Don Juan* is one of them, that work by moving between the two styles. Keats's *Lamia* is a representative of this group especially pertinent as an introduction to *The Witch of Atlas* because the two poems are thematically similar.

The story of Keat's poem dramatises the conflict between illusion and the reasonable gaze of the philosopher. Lycius, a young Corinthian, falls in love with a snake, Lamia, which, thanks to a spell cast by Hermes, has assumed the appearance of a woman. Lycius and Lamia set up home together in an illusory mansion. Lycius's tutor, the philosopher Apollonius, gate-crashes their wedding, and subjects Lamia to a withering rational stare that dissolves her into nothingness. Lycius dies of grief and shock. Both he and Lamia would have survived had they, as Lamia asked, lived together in their dream home isolated from all other people, but for a man like Lycius such an existence would be intolerable: 'Love in a palace is perhaps at last/More grievous torment than a hermit's fast . . .' (Part II, 3–4). He insists that they take their place in the social world, and so he arranges the wedding feast. Lycius cannot live without reality, but neither can he live without illusion; when Lamia disappears, he dies. This is the dilemma that the poem explores, a dilemma from which only the gods, for whom dream is identical with reality, are free: 'Real are the dreams of Gods, and smoothly pass/Their pleasures in a long immortal dream'. (Part I, 127–8).

The style of the poem is accommodated to this theme. Keats prepared for its composition by studying Dryden's fables and translations. Its opening lines are a close imitation of a passage from Dryden:[24]

Upon a time before the faery broods
Drove Nymph and Satyr from the prosperous woods,
Before king Oberon's bright diadem,
Sceptre, and mantle, clasp'd with dewy gem,
Frighted away the Dryads and the Fauns
From rushes green, and brakes, and cowslip'd lawns . . . (Part I, 1–6)

The poised, strongly jointed movement of the verse detaches the poet from his fairytale subject-matter. The poem is begun from a point of view firmly rooted in commonsense reality, and Keats reverts to this tone from time to time throughout the poem's course. But the poem has another style. Consider the description of the dream home's porch:

While yet he spake they had arrived before
A pillar'd porch, with lofty portal door,

> Where hung a silver lamp, whose phosphor glow
> Reflected in the slabbed steps below,
> Mild as a star in water; for so new,
> And so unsullied was the marble's hue,
> So through the crystal polish, liquid fine,
> Ran the dark veins, that none but feet divine
> Could e'er have touch'd there. (Part I, 378–86)

In the description the stone of which the palace is composed is melted. The 'pillar'd porch' and the 'lofty portal door' of the opening couplet establish an architectural frame, formal, distanced, which disappears as the description proceeds. The effect is created partly by a narrowing of focus, the eye moves from the entire facade to the dark veins in the marble; the solidity of the building is dissolved like matter viewed under a microscope. Partly it is created by Keat's metaphors: lamplight is reflected in the marble, 'Mild as a star in water'. We glimpse the image that made Venice a city central to the Romantic imagination, the reflection of buildings in water, their three-dimensional solidity transformed into the flat precariousness of a reflection. But the progression in the passage is not only a narrowing of focus, nor only a movement from architectural images to the image of stone dissolved into water, it is also stylistic. The passage moves from the conversational opening couplet to the extreme mannerism of the line: 'So through the crystal polish, liquid fine . . .'. The mannerism is pivotal, forcing the reader to decide his relation with the whole description, whether to recognise and stand detached from its oddity, or whether to accept it, and, so to speak, look with the style rather than at it. The progression of the whole passage impels the reader towards the second possibility. The passage is a movement between the two ruling styles of *Lamia*, the urbane and somewhat sceptical style that Keats learned from Dryden, and that other style which interpenetrates its content to create what Keats calls within the poem 'flitter-wingèd verse'; between a style that accepts that in this world reality and dream are incompatible, and a style that insists that poetry is divine and that 'real are the dreams of Gods'.

The poem ends with the death of Lycius:

> his friends came round—
> Supported him—no pulse, or breath they found,

And, in its marriage robe, the heavy body wound. (Part II,
                                                        309–11)

It ends with the victory of the reality principle, a victory in which
not only the 'flitter-wingèd verse' is destroyed, but also the
assured urbanity of the poem's other style. The lines concentrate
on a perfunctory notation of fact. The corpse resists any
imaginative transmutation of the kind that dissolved the palace
into water, it remains 'the heavy body', but equally it refuses to
be subsumed within the easy, gentlemanly control of the poem's
Dryden-like verse. *Lamia* ends by associating both its styles as
victims of the withering gaze of the philosopher.

   The Witch of Atlas is prefixed by a dedication to Mary that
defines both the manner and the matter of the whole poem. It has
been well discussed by Harold Bloom, who, along with Wilson
Knight and Carl Grabo, has been largely responsible for the
introduction of the *Witch* into the canon of Shelley's major
poetry.[25] But the elevation of the poem by these critics has been
accomplished at some cost. Each of them diverts the reader's
attention from the poem's tone, essentially a comic tone, in order
to direct him to those other characteristics of the poem which are
more obviously serious.

   The first three stanzas of the dedication meet an objection by
Mary that the poem lacks human interest, that the verses 'tell no
story false or true', and its final three stanzas institute a
comparison between Shelley's poem and Wordsworth's *Peter
Bell*, which Shelley takes as an example of the type of poetry that
Mary demands. In the first three stanzas Shelley's urbane
mockery both of Mary and of himself, and the poised selfconsciousness with which he handles words, provide a standard of
sophisticated detachment and verbal agility which ought to
control our reading of the whole poem. Shelley admits the
modest pretensions of his poem, and his modesty becomes the
means by which Mary's serious moral objection to it is exposed
as clumsily inappropriate, ridiculously solemn, and even rather
cruel, a sledgehammer used to stun a butterfly:

What hand would crush the silken-wingèd fly,
   The youngest of inconstant April's minions,
Because it cannot climb the purest sky,
   Where the swan sings, amid the sun's dominions?
Not thine. (9–13)

The controlling influence here is Spenser. Harold Bloom has pointed out the verbal echoes in this stanza of Spenser's description of Clarion in *Muiopotmos*.[26] Shelley presents his own poem as a version of the comic epyllion, a form in which Spenser both in *Muiopotmos* and in the translation of *Culex, Virgil's Gnat*, is the English master. In presenting his poem as a butterfly like Clarion, Mary's killing insensitivity to it is made to seem as ugly as Aragnoll's slaying of Clarion, her rejection of the gift as ungrateful as the shepherd's swatting of the gnat who has awakened him to the danger of the snake. Bloom describes *The Witch of Atlas* as 'barbed' against criticism. This is well said, but the defences that protect the poem from Mary's attack are a development of an anticritical bias characteristic of the comic epyllion:

> let this much then excuse
> This Gnats small Poeme, that th'whole history
> Is but a jest, though envie it abuse;
> But who such sports and sweet delights doth blame,
> Shall lighter seeme than this Gnats idle name.[27]

To attack such a poem for lack of seriousness is to misread its nature, to misinterpret naïvely the relationship between the poem and its author. Spenser maintains throughout both poems a sage and serious tone, adhering more closely than in *The Faerie Queene* to a standard of decorous elegance in his diction. Shelley imitates this. His epithets are conventionally elegant. April is 'inconstant', the fly is 'silver-wingèd'. In the context of this style any straining after the individual, after a phrase like 'the tiger moth's deep-damask'd wings', would appear vulgarly ostentatious. The sophistication of the poem's manner is detached from the playfulness of its content. 'Virgil', Spenser and Shelley present their poems as a harmless relaxation from the epic task, the *Aeneid, The Faerie Queene, Prometheus Unbound*. Shelley may confess himself childish, a 'kitten', but the style of the confession belies the charge. It is Mary whose relation to the poem is truly that of the earnest unsophisticated child, and she is addressed as such, cajoled. Who would kill a butterfly because it is not a swan? Not you, you know better than that:

> Thou knowest 'tis its doom to die,
> When Day shall hide within her twilight pinions

The lucent eyes, and the eternal smile,
Serene as thine, which lent it life awhile. (13–16)

In the second three stanzas of the dedication the Spenserian
mock-heroic is replaced by a broader, more Byronic comedy.
Shelley contrasts his own poem with Wordsworth's *Peter Bell*.
The comparison is slyly humorous in Shelley's most engaging
vein. The Witch is described in a fluently trochaic line: 'Light the
vest of flowing metre/She wears . . .', and Peter, 'proud as dandy
with his stays', is made to imitate this rhythm stiffly. The Witch
and Peter are juxtaposed incongruously. Incongruity is to
become the poem's central device. It may take the form of an
incongruity between style and content, as in Spenser's two
poems, or, more often, an incongruity between different verbal
registers and the areas of experience with which they are
associated, as in *Don Juan*.

The reference to *Peter Bell* is not haphazard. Harold Bloom
was the first to suggest that we should associate the Witch's boat
with the aeronautic 'canoe' which Wordsworth dismisses in his
prologue to *Peter Bell*. Wordsworth's boat is the vehicle of
immature poets who have not yet learned to grapple with the
problems of the real world; it represents an imaginative world
unconnected with reality. Wordsworth's decision to bid farewell
to the boat on the basis that it is a nobler and more adult duty to
keep one's feet on the ground prepares the way for the
unimpeachably earthbound poem that follows. In the final two
stanzas of Shelley's dedication Peter is aligned with Othello, Lear
and a comic Satan. Opposed to this formidable group stand the
Witch and, by implication, Spenser's Clarion. *The Witch of Atlas*
and *Muiopotmos*, 'visionary rhymes', are contrasted with
Shakespearean tragedy, *Paradise Lost* and *Peter Bell*, poems of
moral conflict. That *Peter Bell* is chosen as the representative of
this latter class prevents the distinction from being evaluative and
safeguards Shelley's comic tone. In the dedication Shelley
represents in literary terms what will become the basis of the
dialectic of the whole poem.

It is easy to see that a poem can only be described as a
representative of a certain sort of poetry, the visionary rhyme,
and as a comparison between the attitude to experience expressed
in that sort of poetry with the attitude expressed in a contrasting
sort of poetry, the poetry of moral conflict, if the writer practises

a Nabokovian aloofness from the conventions within which he is writing. The comic technique derived from Spenser, and also from the Italian comic romances that Shelley had been reading,[28] enables him to achieve this sophisticated detachment from his own medium. The technique developed from *Don Juan* provides the means by which Shelley conducts his investigation.

The Witch is introduced in the first stanza: 'A lady-witch there lived on Atlas' mountain/Within a cavern, by a secret fountain' (55–6). The information is delivered in a deliberately perfunctory manner, as if all witches live on mountains in caverns near fountains, or at similar addresses, and so there is no need for further elaboration. The term 'lady-witch' makes the absurd claim that a class structure flourishes even in the underworld of the imagination. Both these devices insist on Shelley's detachment from the convention within which he is writing, and most of the romance props introduced into the poem receive similiar treatment.

The dignity of the Witch is constantly kept at the mercy of Shelley's language. The description of the procession of animals and gods which arrives to pay homage to the Witch on her incarnation is similar to the passage describing the worship of Una by the 'woodborne people' in *The Faerie Queene*,[29] but stanzas 8, 9 and 11 all end in bathos. 'Universal Pan' approaches: 'And felt that wondrous lady all alone, –/And she felt him, upon her emerald throne' (119–20). Stanza 12 describes the power that has drawn all these people to the Witch: 'For she was beautiful –'. The cause seems wildly inadequate to the effect. But this stanza has a development in contrast to the preceding stanzas. It demonstrates the art of rising, not sinking, in poetry. The Beauty Queen is transformed into an embodiment of ideal beauty:

> her beauty made
> The bright world dim, and everything beside
> Seemed like the fleeting image of a shade:
> No thought of living spirit could abide,
> Which to her looks had ever been betrayed,
> On any object in the world so wide,
> On any hope within the circling skies,
> But on her form, and in her inmost eyes. (137–44)

The double-focus is epitomised in the poem's use of the word 'form'. In stanza 5 it refers to the womanly figure, but in this stanza the word is used Platonically to refer to the non-sensual essence of a thing. If anyone glimpses this form he becomes, like the hero of *Alastor*, enslaved by his vision: 'Which when the lady knew, she took her spindle . . .'. The tone changes abruptly and Shelley again sidesteps seriousness. The action is announced in a Miltonic construction, which leads us to expect that it will be impressive. But after the conjunctions syntax becomes colloquial and the subject-matter mundane.

The stanza continues:

> And twined three threads of fleecy mist, and three
> Long lines of light, such as the dawn may kindle
>   The clouds and waves and mountains with; and she
> As many star-beams, ere their lamps could dwindle
>   In the belated moon, wound skilfully;
> And with these threads a subtle veil she wove –
> A shadow for the splendour of her love. (146–52)

Wilson Knight and Harold Bloom both praise the language of this stanza for making the abstract tangible.[30] But their praise is misdirected. The introduction of a tonguetwister like 'three threads of fleecy mist' hardly suggests that Shelley is being serious. The mist from which the threads are drawn is called 'fleecy', and thread can be manufactured from fleeces, but the adjective surely does not make the notion of mist-thread seem more probable. It suggests that an obvious metaphor has been construed absurdly literally. Similarly the Witch's practical good sense demonstrated in her winding the star-beams before they vanish in the light of the moon only acts as a foil to her being able to wind star-beams at all. A discrepancy is allowed to develop between her activities and her materials.

Shelley is interested in exploring the difference between the 'real' and the 'imaginary'. The images do not fuse, they confuse the two, and this is characteristic of much of the poem's imagery. Among the stores in the Witch's cave are 'sounds of air' which are said to be 'Folded in cells of crystal silence'. The effect of the verb is to make sound and silence appear not less but more intangible than they are. The relationship expressed by the verb shocks our sense of reality. But the last four lines of stanza 14 relate these folded sounds to our feeling of loss as we grow old. They are sounds:

> Such as we hear in youth, and think the feeling
>   Will never die – yet ere we are aware,
> The feeling and the sound are fled and gone,
> And the regret they leave remains alone. (157–60)

The absence of metaphor, the colloquialism 'fled and gone', and the half rhyme, all help to convey a change of tone from fancifulness to the voice of personal experience. The stanza effects an uneasy conjunction between the surreal and the real. Stanza 16 is somewhat similar. Odours are trapped in a net 'woven from dew-beams', and beat their wings like 'bats at the wired window of a dairy'. The dairy does nothing to realise the dew-beam net. The two parts of the simile stand apart from, and laugh at, each other. The dairy laughs at the fancifulness of the dew-beam net and the net laughs at the grossness of the dairy.

In the following three stanzas the Witch is made the vehicle of Shelley's wish-fulfilling dreams. Stored in her cave are cures for all the evils of the world. The point of the poem's strange incongruities becomes apparent. The Witch is being related to the real world in which men live and suffer. The result is predicted by the fate of the imagery. Folded air and the anxieties of middle age, the odours trapped in a dew-beam net and the bats in the dairy, refused to coalesce. They insisted despite the syntax that they were inhabitants of different worlds. In the prologue to *Peter Bell* Wordsworth decides that boat-trips are incompatible with the real business of life, and the language of this poem enacts the same predicament.

The crucial event of the first part of the poem, the Witch's rejection of the nymphs' offer to serve her, is a direct statement of this position. Her speech in stanzas 23 and 24 is deeply serious, but it is important to realise that its seriousness derives directly from the humour of the first part of the poem. Humour has been created by the juxtaposition of incompatible words and ideas. Similarly the Witch recognises the incompatibility of her own immortality with the transience of the nymphs. The effect is no longer comic simply because incongruity, instead of emerging slyly from Shelley's language so that it forces on the reader an ironic awareness of the events recorded in the poem, is recognised and felt by the Witch herself.

The first part of the Witch's speech describes the transience of all natural things. The second recognises that the nymphs are a part of this process. The first stanza exhilarates:

> The boundless ocean like a drop of dew
> Will be consumed—the stubborn centre must
> Be scattered, like a cloud of summer dust. (230–2)

The stanza makes use of the human fascination with chaos. The destruction does not threaten us. We are presented with a god's-eye view of the world to which the ocean is no more than a dewdrop and the earth's core no more than a dustcloud. The close rhetorical patterning of the stanza brings the destruction, which is its subject, under verbal control. A terrifying event is verbally mastered, so that when we read the stanza we share in the mastery. But in the following stanza the pattern breaks:

> And ye with them will perish, one by one; –
>   If I must sigh to think that this shall be,
> If I must weep when the surviving Sun
>   Shall smile on your decay – oh, ask not me
> To love you till your little race is run;
>   I cannot die as ye must – over me
> Your leaves shall glance – the streams in which ye dwell
> Shall be my paths henceforth, and so – farewell! – (233–40)

The stanza is dominated by personal pronouns. The god's-eye view is replaced by a personal view, and the mood changes from exhilaration to pathos. The language, instead of expressing control over experience, expresses by its disjointed syntax, by interjections, by short clauses suggesting sobbing, a failure to master experience. The contrast between the two stanzas expresses the dilemma that is at the heart of the first part of the poem. The Witch's power is contingent on her remaining abstracted from any personal relationship with transient beings. When in the second part of the stanza she allows herself to feel sympathy for the nymphs her strength is threatened, and so like Blake's Thel the Witch retreats back into the vale of Har.

The first part of the poem ends with stanza 30 which describes the Witch's hibernation in a well of fire. Her 'open eyes, closed feet, and folded palm' suggest perfect self-completeness and self-absorption. She has arrived at that state sought by Buddhists and Hindus in which nothing external can affect the individual's inner calm. But the natural world around her of which she is unaware is also beautifully described:

> And when the windless snow descended thicker
> Than autumn leaves, she watched it as it came
> Melt on the surface of the level flame. (286–8)

The melting snow is to us an emblem of transience, but the Witch is unaffected by it. The first part of the poem ends with this image of the inevitable separation of the Witch from the condition of mortality. The main purpose of the poem thus far has been to express the incompatibility of the world of the Witch and the world of mortality, the 'real' world. The main purpose of its second part will be to explore the relative value of the two worlds.

It begins by offering two possible accounts of the manufacture of the Witch's boat. Either it was manufactured by Vulcan as a vehicle for Venus's star, but was found to be insufficiently heatproof for that function, or it was fashioned from a gourd grown by Cupid on the planet Venus from a seed he had stolen from Chaos. Again the humour of each description derives from an odd mixture of realism and fancy. Cupid steals a seed from Chaos but is careful to wrap it up in mould like a human gardener. The process of photosynthesis by which the plant grows is described with a precision worthy of Erasmus Darwin, but the plant that undergoes the process remains a fanciful invention.

To power the boat the Witch creates the Hermaphrodite. The role of this creature in the poem is simply as an alter ego of the Witch. The Hermaphrodite is fashioned from fire and snow, and in stanza 30 when the Witch lay in the well of fire watching snow melt on the flames she was related to these two substances. The Hermaphrodite lying in the bottom of the boat 'With folded wings and unawakened eyes' recalls the description of the Witch in her contemplative hibernation. The Hermaphrodite is called a 'sexless thing' and the Witch is later compared to a 'sexless bee'. The Witch created the Hermaphrodite in her own image. Its hermaphroditism is a symbol of her own existence, both in the world and out of it. It is used to express the radical ambivalence of the Witch's own character. It is an image of 'perfect purity', but it can also be called 'a sexless thing', a description that makes it seem ridiculous, and insists that it is a 'thing', an object.

Stanzas 37–47 describe the Witch's boat-trips. The language in these stanzas searches after paradox; the shade in the forest casts 'a pleasure hid/In melancholy gloom', Sunbows are said to be 'lighting [the boat] far upon its lampless way'. Descriptions stress contrast; the Hermaphrodite's wings are said to be like day and spring and also like winter and night. The concern with contrast and paradox reflects the theme of the poem, its concern to bring together contradictory sorts of experience. The world of the poem is 'the noon of interlunar night'.

The Witch journeys to Antarctica, and finds a smooth stretch of water surrounded by stormy seas. Stanza 50 contrasts the storm and the calm. The contrast expresses one version of a major theme of the poem:

> And whilst the outer lake beneath the lash
> Of the wind's scourge, foamed like a wounded thing,
> And the incessant hail with stony clash
> Ploughed up the waters, and the flagging wing
> Of the roused cormorant in the lightning flash
> Looked like the wreck of some wind-wandering
> Fragment of inky thunder-smoke—this haven
> Was as a gem to copy Heaven engraven,—... (441–8)

The cormorant struggling against the storm is a powerful emblem of man in a world of moral conflict. The calm inner lake is described as a 'haven', a 'gem', and a 'copy' of heaven. A haven suggests a negative value, a hidingplace from storm; a gem is precious, pretty, but also small and inhumanly hard; it is a copy not an original, but it copies heaven. The value of the haven is left in doubt until the following stanza. There it appears as a playground, childish and absurd when used by a grown-up person like the Witch. She plays, circling a star: 'Even as a tiger on Hydaspes' banks/Outspeeds the antelopes which speediest are...' (451–2). Again the two parts of the simile serve to criticise each other. The comparison recalls the contrast between the kitten and the predatory grown cat made in the dedication. The Witch outspeeds the star in play: the tiger outspeeds the antelope to kill it. The Witch's world still seems trivial, but whereas the cormorant made the other world appear heroic, the tiger makes it seem destructive.

Stanzas 52–4 parody Books I and II of *Paradise Lost*, the summoning of the fallen angels by Satan and the Parliament of Hell. After 1819 parody becomes one of Shelley's favourite devices. It is a device especially attractive to radical authors, Brecht for example, because it allows them to use and to reject their literary traditions at one and the same time. In these stanzas there is a tendency for Milton's metaphors to become literal in Shelley's parody. The ensign unfurled by Azriel 'Shone like a meteor':[31] the Witch's armies carry 'meteor flags'. Pandemonium 'Rose like an exhalation':[32] the Witch's tent is framed of 'woven exhalations'. The effect of this is to suggest a contrast between the solidity of Pandemonium and the flimsiness of the Witch's palace. Pandemonium is built on the shore of a lake, the Witch's palace is built on the lake itself. The Witch and Satan are related as antitheses. The Witch is compared in line 479 to the obscured moon, Milton compares Satan to the obscured sun.[33] Pandemonium is built on the shore of a burning lake, the Witch camps on a lake situated near the South Pole. Satan sat in state to preside over the mighty Parliament of Hell.[34] The Witch also sat in state:

> And on a throne o'erlaid with starlight, caught
>   Upon those wandering isles of aëry dew,
> Which highest shoals of mountain shipwreck not,
>   She sate, and heard all that had happened new
> Between the earth and moon, since they had brought
>   The last intelligence . . . (473–8)

Debate becomes gossip. The comparison ridicules the Witch.

The Witch's sports, described in the following stanzas, resemble the recreations of the fallen angels in Hell. Both sing. The fallen angels sing 'Their own heroic deeds and hapless fall'.[35] Their song is heroic poetry. But the Witch's song is non-imitative. Those who hear it understand it as a divination of something beyond life:

> Mortals found
> That on those days the sky was calm and fair,
> And mystic snatches of harmonious sound
> Wandered upon the earth where'er she passed,
> And happy thoughts of hope, too sweet to last. (492–6)

For Shelley all value is relative to man, but this stanza insists that the visionary rhyme as well as the poetry of human conflict has a human value. The visionary rhyme gives man 'happy thoughts of hope', in contrast to the song of the angels which records a 'hapless fall'. The Witch's 'choice sport', a journey down the Nile, contrasts with Satan's expedition to Eden. The ease of her progress, gliding, contrasts with the difficulty of his. Both instil dreams in mortals, but the effect of the Witch's dreams is beneficent, the effect of Satan's is malignant. Parody is used in these stanzas just as verbal incongruity is used elsewhere in the poem to bring together two worlds, the world of the Witch, and that other world represented here by *Paradise Lost*. Shelley provokes a complex comparison between the two worlds. Parody, an indirect means of investigating the relative value of the two worlds, is used, because only an indirect method could gracefully accommodate the inconsistency of the results. The Witch is alternately ridiculed and elevated by the comparison.

In stanza 61 the Witch observes sleeping mankind. A series of generalised but precise pictures together form a pageant of human life. 'Old age with snow-bright hair and folded palm' reminds us of the Witch in line 272 and of her *alter ego* the Hermaphrodite in line 362. But contemplative old age completes a cycle. The Witch's life cannot have this aesthetically satisfying shapeliness. The mortal pageant, as it is described in this stanza, expresses the beauty of man's progress through life. In the following stanza the pattern is disrupted by 'distortions foul', the repressive influences of religion and habit. We are grieved: it is our loss. The Witch's comment: '"This," said the wizard maiden, " is the strife/Which stirs the liquid surface of man's life."'. . . (543–4), is expressed in a neat couplet bound tightly together by alliteration. The neatness of her remark is chilling, the aphorism of the detached observer. The following stanza makes the same contrast between the Witch's detachment and human involvement. It is similar to the contrast made in stanza 50 between the calm inner and the stormy outer lake:

And little did the sight disturb her soul—
We, the weak mariners of that wide lake
Where'er its shores extend or billows roll,
Our course unpiloted and starless make
O'er its wild surface to an unknown goal:—
But she in the calm depths her way could take,
Where in bright bowers immortal forms abide
Beneath the weltering of the restless tide. (545–52)

The cormorant struggling against the storm becomes the weak
mariners. The gem-like haven becomes the calm submarine
world beneath the waves. Again in this stanza the human
predicament seems heroic. There is an exhilarating sense of pride
in the extent of human voyages, and there is heroism in the
rashness of the enterprise. We respond to the voyage in the dark
on the restless sea with that part of us which demands uncertainty. But the Witch walks 'in bright bowers', and the words
which describe her dwelling-place, 'where immortal forms
abide', suggest permanence and the absence of struggle.

The area of experience that the Witch embodies is becoming
increasingly clearly defined. In the following stanzas her ability
to see through superficial appearances to the spiritual reality that
lies beneath is described. In stanza 65 the body is designated in a
favourite Shelleyan figure, the veil of the soul. But the rhythm is
deliberately conversational:

all the forms in which those spirits lay
Were to her sight like the diaphanous
Veils... (561–3)

The transparency of the veils (all that the ladies are concealing is
'their scorn of all concealment') is treated as a joke. The joke
reveals the paradox inherent in the metaphor. The body's veiling
of the soul is compared to a garment's clothing of the body, so
that our pleasure in seeing ladies' bodies is converted by a sleight
of hand into a pleasure at seeing through their bodies into their
souls. But in the following stanza the same event is recorded with
complete seriousness: 'She, all those human figures breathing
there,/Beheld as living spirits...' (569–70). The verb 'Beheld'
comes between 'human figures' and 'living spirits': its position
mimics the transfiguring glance of the Witch. All events in the

poem are at the mercy of language. The Witch is an idealist, but how seriously idealism is to be taken is left in doubt.

The final stanzas of the poem parallel those that described the stores in the Witch's cave. I said then that she was being used as a vehicle for Shelley's wish-fulfilling imagination. It would be truer to to say that wish-fulfilment is one of the characteristics that she embodies. Stanza 70 describes the death of those to whom she has given her panacea:

> For on the night when they were buried, she
>> Restored the embalmers' ruining, and shook
> The light out of the funeral lamps, to be
>> A mimic day within that deathy nook;
> And she unwound the woven imagery
>> Of second childhood's swaddling bands, and took
> The coffin, its last cradle, from its niche,
> And threw it with contempt into a ditch. (601–8)

The syntax of the stanza, one action following another without causal connection, suggests in this context a ceremony. The language is highly figurative; the shroud is 'second childhood's swaddling bands', the coffin is the body's 'last cradle'. The paradoxes recall all the Christian quibbling with the ideas of life and death. The Witch is presiding over a ritualistic rebirth. But the ceremonial unwinding of the stanza is shattered in its last line, when the Witch took the coffin: 'And threw it with contempt into a ditch'. Instead of the restrained, prescribed actions of ceremony the verb suggests an energetic spontaneous action. Instead of the emotional neutrality of the officiating priest the Witch acted 'with contempt'. Instead of a ritualistic view of life in which things are important not for their real but for their symbolic value as 'woven imagery' we find a crudely material ditch. The Witch's contempt of the coffin, the emblem of death, expresses man's refusal to accept his own mortality. We react to the incongruity with a fierce joy. The Witch has become one part of our attitude to life.

The concluding stanzas of the poem revert to a comic tone. The rhymes (geese/diocese, for instance) are Byronic. Stanzas 73–7 imagine a comic overthrow of priestly, governmental and moral tyranny, but the comic tone prevents us from taking these revolutions seriously. The Witch represents the impulse towards the rejection of reality, but the impulse may be manifested in sublime vision or idle daydream. The last stanza of the poem brings it to a close in a tone of self-mocking urbane grace:

> These were the pranks she played among the cities
>   Of mortal men, and what she did to Sprites
> And Gods, entangling them in her sweet ditties
>   To do her will, and show their subtle sleights,
> I will declare another time; for it is
>   A tale more fit for the weird winter nights
> Than for these garish summer days, when we
> Scarcely believe much more than we can see. (665–72)

The Witch of Atlas is an answer to the criticism of it by Mary which Shelley reports in his dedication, an irony that may have amused him. It can be seen as a sceptical myth designed to explore the function of poetry. The Witch herself would then represent the visionary rhyme, poetry which does not take as its basis the 'real' world. In the dedication this sort of poetry is contrasted with that chosen by Wordsworth in the prologue to *Peter Bell*, the poetry of the 'real' world of moral conflict. Shelley has accepted the challenge thrown out by Wordsworth in conversation with his boat:

> Take with you some ambitious Youth
> For, restless Wanderer! I, in truth,
> Am all unfit to be your mate.[36]

The second type of poetry intrudes into Shelley's poem sometimes through literary allusion, sometimes through the poem's imagery, and sometimes through planned indecorums. Each kind of poetry criticizes the other. The relationship between the two is constantly changing for everything in the poem is at the mercy of language. The Witch herself can seem sublime or ridiculous. Shelley employs a verbal technique of extraordinary agility. Each event, attitude or character in the poem is surrounded by distorting mirrors. The image is traced now in one, now in another. To attempt to identify which reflection is true is to run counter to Shelley's manner. The purpose of the ironical shifting of tones is to preserve his sceptical detachment from the problem he is exploring. The virtuoso sophistication of the poem's tone is itself a satire on the gauche single-mindedness of Wordsworth's tone in *Peter Bell*. The relevance of the antithesis explored in the poem obviously extends beyond poetry, but any reduction of its meaning is made extremely difficult by the nature of its technique.

It is perhaps best to summarise the poem's theme by indicating its descendants, Tennyson's *The Palace of Art* and, more strikingly, *The Lady of Shalott*, and Yeats's Byzantium poems.[37] The Lady of Shalott, like the Witch, has an immunity from time that is contingent on her remaining abstracted from the real world; when she turns away from her mirror and leaves her tower, she dies. The contrast in *Sailing to Byzantium* between 'whatever is begotten born and dies' and the gold mosaics of the city recalls the central contrasts in *The Witch of Atlas*. But Tennyson refuses the rough, comic edge that is the Byronic element in Shelley's poem, and Yeats refuses Shelley's light gaiety in pursuit of a more massive statement of the dilemma. Neither follows Shelley in exploring the possibilities of mixing styles as a means of exploring a contrast and yet suspending judgement on it, as a means of achieving a comic scepticism.

I began this chapter by suggesting that *The Mask of Anarchy* and *The Witch of Atlas* represented the extreme poles of Shelley's achievement. In obvious senses this is true, and yet it is surely also true that the two poems have such in common. Both explore the possibilities of violent contrast, in *The Mask of Anarchy* a generic contrast between masque and ballad, and in *The Witch of Atlas* stylistic and semantic contrasts. But more than that, both poems are fully available only to the reader willing to understand Shelley through his techniques, not to the reader who tries to disentangle the poem from its techniques. Shelley attempts in the poems of his maturity to discover styles and genres that will, in themselves, express his themes. In *The Mask of Anarchy* the conflict within the poem between the masque and the ballad is, in itself, a way of expressing the conflict between the people and the powerful élite which is the poem's theme. The durability of the ballad as compared with the masque becomes a generic expression of the inevitability of the people's eventual victory. The poet exists within the poem through his techniques, exists as both simple balladeer and as the sophisticated poet who had recently been reading Petrarch's *Triumphs*. The generic conflict is a means of expressing a conflict within the poet, and the poem ends by predicting and applauding a victory in which the poet cannot share. Just as Shelley is both the masquer and the balladeer in *The Mask of Anarchy*, he is also both the visionary poet, and the moral poet who ridicules mere vision in *The Witch of Atlas*, and just as *The Mask of Anarchy* insists on the incompatibility of masque and ballad, so *The Witch of Atlas* expresses the incompatibility of the 'visionary' and the 'real': the Witch's beauty and power is contingent on her remaining abstracted from all things mortal, the bats in the dairy and the odours trapped in a dew-beam net remained obstinately separate from each other.

Two conclusions may be drawn from the study of these poems that are generally applicable to Shelley's best work. The poem 'means' its techniques, its language and its genre are not vehicles of the poem's meaning but expressions of it: the idea is fully integrated with the word. The poem's meaning cannot be located in any of its parts, it is a function of the interrelation of its parts: meaning is propositioned.

3 The Language of Self-love

Man, argues Hume, is a creature capable of limited generosity but extended sympathy. He feels called upon to relieve the distress only of those close to himself, but he can sympathise inactively with the plight of others at a much greater remove. Morality is a direct product of the sympathetic capacity in man, because it enables him to adjust or even to overrule those reactions which arise from his 'particular and momentary situation'. For example, it enables him to estimate justly the good qualities of an enemy, even though, in the present situation, those qualities may make him the more dangerous. 'The imagination adheres to the general view of things', and hence morality, the child of the imagination, is separable from self-interest, which is peculiar to each individual.[1]

Shelley's defence of the utility of poetry is founded on Hume's demonstration that 'sympathy', or the 'imagination', is the basis of morality:

> The great secret of morals is love, or a going out of our own nature and an identification of ourselves with the beautiful which exists in thought, action, or person, not our own. A man, to be greatly good, must imagine intensely and comprehensively; he must put himself in the place of another and of many others: the pains and pleasures of his own species must become his own. The great instrument of moral good is the imagination, and poetry administers to the effect by acting upon the cause.[2]

Hume uses his theory of sympathy as a means of explaining the almost universal coincidence of moral taste, and is doubtful of how far man's extended sympathy interacts with his limited generosity. But Shelley, a reforming moralist, is convinced that a strengthening of the power of the imagination must result in an extension of the individual's sphere of active benevolence. The poet has an effect like that which Wordsworth ascribes to the old Cumberland beggar. The beggar is useful not in spite of, but because of, his decrepitude and his dependence on charity. His helplessness 'compels' those who see him 'to acts of love'. Just as the beggar has this effect merely by being, so the poet acts as a force for moral good whether or not his poems have a moral purport. Reading poetry strengthens the imagination, which is the cause of virtuous behaviour. In the *Defence* Shelley even argues that the poet who attempts to inculcate moral sentiments directly assumes 'an inferior office'. A poet 'would do ill to embody his own conceptions of right and wrong, which are usually those of his place and time'. By concerning himself with the effects of a healthy imagination in the moral arena, the poet 'would resign the glory of a participation in the cause'.

Hume is, in many ways, a conservative moralist. His method of distinguishing virtue from vice is empirical, and claims, like much conservative thought, a basis in language:

> The very nature of language guides us almost infallibly in forming a judgement of this nature: and as every tongue possesses one set of words which are taken in a good sense, and another in the opposite, the least acquaintance with the idiom suffices without any reasoning to direct us in collecting and arranging the estimable or blameable qualities of men.[3]

The appeal to virtue becomes an appeal to common prejudice, of doubtful value to a poet who wishes to present a man like Laon, an incestuous, anti-Christian revolutionary, as a 'beautiful idealism of moral excellence'. The poem, to the reforming moralist, becomes, not a means by which he arouses a pre-existing sympathy with accepted codes of conduct, but a means by which he disrupts that prejudice by enforcing sympathy with a character or action that would otherwise have seemed indifferent or offensive to his reader.

Hume's explanation of virtue is essentially utilitarian. In moral philosophy he is a precursor of Bentham. Those qualities are virtuous which conduce to the wellbeing of society. To uphold this position he makes a sudden and illuminating leap from an empirical to a rational definition of virtue. He is well aware that there is an established moral system founded on a consideration of the individual's personal integrity, unrelated to any social benefit actual or potential which may proceed from his good qualities. This is the morality peculiar to religion. That man is most virtuous who is closest to god, whether or not his intimacy with the deity renders him socially useful:

> A gloomy, hair-brained enthusiast, after his death, may have a place in the calendar; but will scarcely ever be admitted, when alive, into intimacy and society, except by those who are as delirious and dismal as himself.[4]

Hume rejects this ideal of virtue as a monkish superstition, but to the Romantic poet it offered a means of presenting a character to the reader without activating stock responses. It offered a means of superseding moral conventions. The virtue of the saint can be appreciated only by an imaginative leap into the the holy man's consciousness; it will not necessarily be manifested in his outward dealings with the world. The difference between the two ethics becomes obvious if one compares Pope's Atticus with Byron's Lara.[5] Pope is content to describe the paradoxes of Atticus's character. He concentrates his portrait on the question: what kind of man is Atticus? Just as we describe an object in terms of its properties, he describes Atticus in terms of his social behaviour, that aspect of him which is evident to others. The rhetoric of Byron's portrait owes much to Pope, but its focus is quite different. In Lara qualities are 'inexplicably mixed'. The adverb demands that the reader devote his energies not to receiving a description, but to explaining it. Byron asks not 'what?', but 'why?'. Instead of subjecting Lara to a single commanding judgement, he surrounds him with observers who have each a partial and possibly mistaken insight into his character: 'What had he been? what was he, thus unknown,/Who walk'd their world, his lineage only known?' The central core of Lara's personality is inaccessible to them, it is 'hidden', and as the portrait proceeds the reader moves from an awareness of manners to an awareness of consciousness. Only when the verse enters Lara's 'breast', describing how he feels rather than how he appears does it lose its tentativeness. Then the rhythm of the verse overpowers the tentative auxiliaries, and achieves the forceful cadences of assured statement:

In self-inflicted penance of a breast
Which tenderness might once have wrung from rest;
In vigilance of grief that would compel
The soul to hate for having loved too well.

Implicit in Pope's portrait is the notion that the behaviour of an individual can be judged by its adherence to, or divergence from, a conventional standard. Atticus is 'placed' within a framework of values that is essentially normative. Byron, on the other hand, suggests that Lara can be judged only in terms of himself. When those around him try to place him in conventional categories they are nonplussed. He can be understood, and therefore judged, only by one able to enter his consciousness, to see the world through his eyes.

To Hume Byron's technique would seem an abnegation of all moral responsibility. Moral judgement is possible only if we succeed in placing a particular situation within a general context. The peculiarity of the moral sentiment is that it is not controlled by the individual's personal perspective. It adjusts the distortions created by his self-interest rather as the brain adjusts his notion of the size of objects by relating their apparent size to their distance from the eye:

> When a man denominates another his *enemy*, his *rival*, his *antagonist*, his *adversary*, he is understood to speak the language of self-love, and to express sentiments peculiar to himself, and arising from his particular circumstances and situation. But when he bestows on any man the epithets of *vicious* or *odious* or *depraved*, he then speaks another language, and expresses sentiments, in which he expects all his audience are to concur with him.[6]

In his portrait of Lara Byron abandons, in Hume's terms, the language of morals in favour of the language of self-love. The reader is forced towards the sentimental fallacy: *tout comprendre, c'est tout pardonner*. Unpleasantness is justified because it is the outcome of wounded feelings, and the unpleasantness itself is more admired than disapproved because it is assumed with a fierce gloom which, we are persuaded, is in itself majestic. To evade conventional morality the poet adopts the technique of the hagiographer, and achieves exactly that kind of uncritical celebration of personal eccentricity that characterises the official biographies of the more alarming saints.

The technique can be used more tactfully than Byron uses it in his verse tales. In *The Thorn*, for example, the narrator, ignorant of the facts of the case, makes no judgement of the woman on the mountain. Others, convinced that she had killed her child, 'had sworn an oath that she/Should be to public justice brought'. But their meddling, legalistic minds are exposed as inadequate to a true understanding of the woman's situation. Her grief, her loneliness, have removed her from that area to which the simple, objective morality embodied in the legal code is appropriate:

> At all times of the day and night
> This wretched woman thither goes;
> And she is known to every star,
> And every wind that blows . . . (67–70)

Wordsworth moves from the level of experience that we may judge, to the level that reduces us to awe, with an economy of means unknown to Byron.

The achievement in *The Thorn* and its companion poems is considerable, but the technique is limiting. Wordsworth suggests no possible relation between the ordinary moral categories and the imaginative leap necessary to comprehend the woman. The result is that she exists on the fringe of our experience, like a saint. Most human emotions, pity for example, seem irrelevant to her predicament. Wordsworth is not always willing to reject social values so absolutely, although he never accepts their sufficiency. His attempt to combine the language of morals with the language of self-love, to relate the individual as social animal with the individual as saint, results in curiously broken-backed poems like *The Old Cumberland Beggar*. For most of its length the poem is an attack on utilitarian ethics, and the social policies that they had generated. The beggar is useless only if we define utility in material terms. Wordsworth insists that he contributes to the spiritual welfare of the community in which he lives, and that, were he to be confined to a poorhouse, this value would be lost. Throughout this argument Wordsworth expresses 'sentiments in which he expects all his audience are to concur with him'. But to stop there would be to accept tacitly the utilitarian premise— that behaviour must be judged in terms of its social utility.

Wordsworth's final address frees the beggar from any such dependence:

> Then let him pass, a blessing on his head!
> And, long as he can wander, let him breathe
> The freshness of the valleys; let his blood
> Struggle with frosty airs and winter snows;
> And let the chartered wind that sweeps the heath
> Beat his gray locks against his withered face. (171–6)

The change of key is startling. The humanitarian concern for the beggar's happiness which had been active in the first part of the poem becomes a brutal indifference to his merely physical welfare. His life is described as a heroic odyssey 'in that vast solitude/To which the tide of things has led him'. What he learns from that experience will be private, incommunicable. His life is finally justified in and for itself, as Wordsworth progresses beyond the criterion of social utility.

Look again at the quotation from Shelley's *Defence* which began this chapter. In its insistence that morality derives from emotional responses to situations rather than rational judgements of them, it stands in direct descent from that eighteenth-century tradition of moral thought of which Hume is the greatest representative. But there are important differences. Imagination, for Hume, is the faculty which controls our 'extended sympathy' rather than our 'limited generosity': 'Sentiments must touch the heart, to make them control our passions: but they need not extend beyond the imagination, to make them influence our taste'.[7] That we can imagine the pain of starvation is enough to convince us that starvation is a bad thing, but it must 'touch the heart', we must see, or be closely attached to, a starving person, before our distaste for starvation impels us to take action to relieve it. Shelley on the other hand uses 'imagination' as a synonym for 'love'. He confounds Hume's distinction between the imagination and the heart, and his motive for doing so is obvious. Hume is doubtful of how far our extended sympathy interacts with our limited generostiy, and therefore of how far a more refined moral perception impels the individual to a more active benevolence. Such scepticism Shelley finds unacceptable.

For Hume morality is a product of our 'sympathy' with other

people; but the word is too passive for Shelley, and he substitutes for it 'identification'. This threatens another of Hume's distinctions, between the language of morals and the language of self-love. Imagination is a key concept in Hume's theory because it 'adheres to the general view of things', and so becomes the means through which morality is separable from self-interest. But imagination, when it is defined as 'identification' or 'love', no longer upholds this distinction; instead of offering the individual a general perspective, allowing him to correct his individual perspective, it offers him only the individual perspective of another person.

Hume distinguishes morality from benevolence, extended sympathy from limited generosity, the language of morals from the language of self-love. Shelley refuses these distinctions, and he does so because Hume's theory explains, and in explaining justifies, an imbalance which Shelley regarded as the greatest failing of his age:

> We have more moral, political, and historical wisdom than we know how to reduce into practice. . . . We want the creative faculty to imagine that which we know: we want the generous impulse to act that which we imagine: we want the poetry of life: our calculations have outrun our conception: we have eaten more than we can digest.[8]

In describing this dilemma, Shelley instinctively adopts an aesthetic vocabulary, for an attempt to resolve it is the central project of his poetic career. He attempts to make generosity coextensive with sympathy, to make the language of self-love serve also as the language of morals, or, in less technical terms, to reconcile the ideal with the real. The task, he is aware, is impossible. Hence Shelley is pre-eminently the poet of unrealisable aspiration. But it is also, as we have seen in discussing *Lara*, a dangerous venture. Lara, the old Cumberland beggar, even the woman in *The Thorn*, instead of being freed by the imaginative leap taken by the poet into the consciousness of his character, are in danger of being reduced into mere masks of their creators, a Germanic Byron, Wordsworth in rags or in drag. The attempt to identify oneself with another individual can collapse into a technique through which the poet contrives to celebrate only himself. Shelley, at his best, is supremely aware of this danger, and his awareness of it becomes thematic in several of his major poems. In Shelley's first major poem, *Alastor*, it is central.

Alastor

The preface to *Alastor* presents the poem as an allegory of 'one of the most interesting situations of the human mind'. It tells the story of a youthful poet gifted with 'an imagination inflamed and purified', who uses this gift, not in the manner which Shelley offers in the *Defence* as a description of the moral sense, the 'identification of ourselves with the beautiful which exists in thought, action, or person, *not our own*', but to pursue the embodiment of '*his own* imaginations'. Shelley argues that the 'speedy ruin' of this young poet exposes the danger of 'self-centred seclusion'.

The first part of the preface identifies the poet's fault, the second emphasises the nobility of his failing. He is contrasted with, and preferred to, the 'unforeseeing multitudes' who also 'attempt to live without human sympathy', but whose failing is the result of lack of imagination, of spiritual torpor, rather than of an imagination too inflamed or misdirected. The preface, as has often been remarked, assumes an attitude to the poem's hero, which, if not inconsistent, is at least troublesomely complex.

An unstable relationship with their central characters is a characteristic of a number of romantic poems, in particular those of Byron. The first two cantos of *Childe Harold* are besprinkled with hints to the reader to associate Harold with Byron himself, and yet Byron was annoyed with reviewers who made this identification, and remarked: 'I would not be such a fellow as I have made my hero for all the world'.[9] There is a strange passage in Mary Wollstonecraft's *Vindication of the Rights of Woman* which illustrates this uncertainty very clearly, and which is also very close to the theme of *Alastor*. Mary Wollstonecraft is arguing that friendship, 'the most sublime of all affections', rather than the kind of love celebrated by Rousseau, ought to be the young girl's objective in marriage. The benefits of friendship are real and stable whereas love is a passing fancy. The romantic lover is described in terms which bring him very close to the hero of *Alastor*:

The lively heated imagination . . . draws the picture of love, as it draws every other picture, with the glowing colours, which the daring hand will steal from the rainbow, that is directed by a mind, condemned in a world like this, to prove its noble origin by panting after unattainable perfection, ever pursuing what it acknowledges to be a fleeting dream.[10]

This splendidly Shelleyan sentence (note the Promethean metaphor) only just sustains its disapproval of the state which it describes, so that it is no surprise when the argument pauses to claim that the 'delusions of passion', against which women are being warned, are also 'a strong proof of the immortality of the soul'. Mary Wollstonecraft ends by 'leaving superior minds to correct themselves, and pay dearly for their experience'. Like Shelley she regards the love she has described as a 'superior' failing; as in *Alastor* an imaginative involvement with the predicament of the lover struggles against a sympathetic but detached awareness of its absurdity. The conflict expresses a hesitation between two ethical systems, the one social and normative, the other individual and empathic. The language of morals struggles against the language of self-love.

Alastor records the composition by one poet of an elegy for another. The central section of the poem is a biography of the dead poet, a man who had sought ultimate knowledge, and found it, but was left unsatisfied by his discovery, just as he was unsatisfied by the love offered him by an Arab maiden. No worldly knowledge, no human lover, could satisfy his restlessness. In a dream he saw a woman, the figment of his own imagination, and enjoyed an ecstatic union with her. He awoke and felt himself an alien in an uncongenial world, through which he wandered in search of his dream lover. He found a boat, entirely unseaworthy, and set to sea aboard it. His pursuit of the dream lady had become a pursuit of death, and in surrendering himself to death he achieved a kind of exhilaration. But magically the boat carried him safe through storms, and then drifted up a river, against the current. Near the source of the river the poet disembarked and walked to a deserted clearing where he lay down until death came to him.

The obvious classical model for *Alastor*, a poem in which one poet records the suffering through unrequited love of a fellow poet is a poem well known to Shelley, Virgil's tenth eclogue, the elegy for Gallus. *Alastor* begins and ends with an invocation. Shelley begins by invoking Mother Nature to assist him in his song; he ends by addressing the dead poet. Framed by these invocations is a biography of the poet whose death he mourns. The structure of Virgil's poem is similar. Its central section consists of a speech by Gallus which is enclosed within a pastoral framework. The poem opens with an invocation in which Virgil prays for the assistance of the pastoral muse Arethusa, and at the end Virgil returns to the pastoral setting and dedicates his poem to Gallus. The form establishes the contrast between Virgil, the pastoral poet, and Gallus, the elegiac love poet.

Virgil presents his elegy, and the speech by Gallus that it contains, as a fiction, *'pauca carmina'*, a few verses, and within his poem he imagines Gallus asking the Arcadian shepherds to sing verses commemorating his love. Virgil's poem is then the gift which, within the poem, Virgil imagines Gallus requesting. The poem is, so to speak, a response to itself. Virgil, from within a rich pastoral setting, imagines Gallus in a harsh, cold, mountain landscape, and Gallus, in his speech, imagines the pastoral landscape in which Virgil sings. In composing Gallus's speech Virgil imagines the passionately unsatisfied love of the elegiac poet, and within the same speech Gallus imagines the less demanding happier love of the pastoral world, the love that he might have felt for Amaryllis or Menalcas. Gallus and Virgil contrast with one another, but they also reflect one another's worlds, and their two worlds interpenetrate. Pastoralism as Gallus conceives it is influenced by his soldier's imagination. Instead of goatherding, he thinks of himself hunting wild boar. The pastoralism of Virgil's world is compromised by the rigours of Gallus's world, so that his song becomes a 'labor' rather than a spontaneous product of pastoral otium.

Gallus's speech expresses a farewell to poetry: his love for Lycoris can no longer be subdued by expression within the form of elegiac poetry. He ends his speech in submission to the power of love: *'Omnia vincit Amor; et nos cedamus Amori'* (69). Poetry, even love poetry, can, in a sense, only be written in defiance of the omnipotence of love. Gallus's submission is, as he realises, a vow of silence, and, because the poem which contains it is an elegy, it is also conceived as a kind of death. Virgil's poem is also a farewell. Virgil represents it as his last exercise in the pastoral mode, his *'extremum laborem'*.

But the situation is more complicated than this. Virgil's pastoral poem attempts to embrace a different kind of poetry, Gallus's elegiac lament. Similarly, when Gallus imagines the pastoral life, elegiac poetry attempts to embrace the pastoral. The poem's mirror images force together Gallus and Virgil. Gallus imagines carving Lycoris's name on the bark of trees: '*crescent illae, crescetis, amores*', as the names grow, may my love grow. In the poem's conclusion Virgil returns to his grief for Gallus: '*cuius amor tantum mihi crescit in horas/quantum vere novo viridis se subicit alnus*' (73–4). The same verb, *crescere*, and a similar botanical simile, describe both Gallus's love for Lycoris, and Virgil's love for Gallus. The two perspectives that the poem contains, the pastoral and the elegiac, become one, as Virgil realises that the fiction he has created, the speech in which Gallus expresses his unfulfillable, unconquerable love for Lycoris, is a song sung by himself, a commemoration of his own love for Gallus; that the last line of Gallus's speech might just as well have served as the first line of his own conclusion: '*Omnia vincit Amor; et nos cedamus Amori*'. The pronoun, *nos*, is no longer general; it forces Gallus and Virgil together as fellow prisoners of love.

The poem ends in the serenity of a Virgilian evening, but the evening hides menace, its darkness is noxious and threatens the crops and the singer's voice. Virgil represents himself weaving a basket: the basket is his poem, but he may also be alluding to Theocritus's first idyll, the model for the tenth eclogue. In the Greek poem a goatherd offers to the singer Thyrsis a cup on which is engraven a boy—concentrating on weaving a basket he has forgotten his duties as guard, and is oblivious to the fox which is rifling his vineyard. Engrossed in composing a poem for Gallus Virgil has unwittingly destroyed the pastoral world which has been his peculiar poetic province.

Virgil's poem reaches its climax when Virgil recognises that he has not written a pastoral poem which includes an elegiac poem, but an elegiac poem in which Gallus is to him what Lycoris is to Gallus. The complexities of the poem's structure are revealed as integral to its theme. From within a pastoral setting Virgil imagines an elegiac love poem within which Gallus imagines pastoralism. Structurally the tenth eclogue is a pastoral poem which subsumes an elegiac lament; thematically it is an elegiac love poem which subsumes its pastoral framework. In devising a fiction in which Gallus recognises, and submits to, the omnip-

otence of love, Virgil achieves a recognition of the nature of his
own love for Gallus, and in doing so destroys his pastoral world.
It is a poem which dramatises a process of learning about oneself,
not through introspection, but by devising a fiction.

Alastor is in no sense an imitation of eclogue X. The similarities
between the two poems are only general. A reading of eclogue X
is however useful in suggesting a suitable approach to *Alastor*.
Both poems are rooms of mirrors; both are concerned to
delineate a process, a movement towards a new awareness of
oneself.[11]

The early careers of the narrator and his hero exactly
correspond. Both pursue 'Nature's most secret steps'; the
narrator by sleeping in graveyards, and dabbling in witchcraft,
the hero by studying the magical monuments of ancient
civilisations. But the narrator, although he does not attain full
knowledge of nature's 'inmost sanctuary', experiences a revelation satisfying enough to leave him serenely still:

> moveless, as a long-forgotten lyre
> Suspended in the solitary dome
> Of some mysterious and deserted fane . . . (42–4)

His hero, however, studies mystic hieroglyphs:

> till meaning on his vacant mind
> Flashed like strong inspiration, and he saw
> The thrilling secrets of the birth of time. (126–8)

But his knowledge leaves him still restless, and he wanders on
until he dreams of the woman that he will pursue until his death.

The central contrast is between the satisfaction of the narrator,
expressed in his stationary situation, and the dissatisfaction of his
hero, expressed in his endless wandering. The hero, despairing
of finding his ideal lady, eventually gives himself up to death. His
corpse is described as: 'A fragile lute, on whose harmonious
strings/The breath of heaven did wander . . .' (667–8). It is
precisely the same comparison that the narrator had used to
describe his own self-satisfaction. As when Virgil claims that his
love for Gallus, *'crescit in horas/Quantum vere novo viridis se subicit
alnus'*, the dead hero and the narrator who commemorates him
merge, and that is the point to which the poem has been driving.

To Shelley poetry is the expression of 'beautiful idealisms';
writing a poem is exactly analogous to the hero's dream of an
ideal woman. The narrator's poem is then equivalent to the
hero's dream, and in the end the narrator recognises that the
story he has told is not an idle fiction, but an allegory of his own
life. The narrator's hero looks at a stream, and realises:

Thou imagest my life. Thy darksome stillness
Thy dazzling waves, thy loud and hollow gulfs,
Thy searchless fountains, and invisible course
Have each their type in me. (505–8)

Whatever the narrator's hero looks at transmits back to him a
reflection or an allegory of himself. Similarly, after his hero has
died, the narrator reviews his hero's career, and realises that he
was: 'a dream/Of youth, which night and time have quenched
forever'(669–70). The hero who dreamed of an ideal lady, and
died pursuing his dream, is himself a dream. The narrator, like
his hero, sees only reflections of himself. Just as the lady his hero
dreams is an idealised self, so the hero that the narrator imagines
is only an idealised self.

The contrast between the satisfied, stationary narrator, and the
restless, dissatisfied hero is apparent, not real, for writing a poem
is the expression of the restlessness that the narrator denies, and
his hero's physical wanderings are images of the narrator's
mental travels, a stream into which the narrator projects an
allegory of his own life. In the same way, the girl that the hero
dreams, 'herself a poet', is in the same relation to the hero that
hero, himself a poet, occupies as regards the narrator, the writer
of the poem.

Alastor is a complex series of mirror images, and Shelley
suggests as much within the poem. Its central images are images
of reflection. Awakening from his dream the hero looks on the
scene before him, 'as vacantly/As ocean's moon looks on the
moon in heaven' (201–2). Later he sees on the bank of a stream
yellow flowers, presumably narcissi, which 'For ever gaze on
their own drooping eyes,/Reflected in the crystal calm' (407–
8).Later still he looks into a well, which 'Images all the woven
boughs above' (459), and:

His eyes beheld
Their own wan light through the reflected lines

Of his thin hair, distinct in the dark depth
Of that still fountain: as the human heart
Gazing in dreams over the gloomy grave,
Sees its own treacherous likeness there. (469–74)

Related to these images of reflection are the characteristic
verbal figures of the poem, the self-reflexive simile, the simile
that compares a thing to itself, and other reflexive constructions.
The voice of the lady of the hero's dream is 'like the voice of his
own soul'. He sees her limbs 'by the warm light of their own
life'. Compare these expressions to the description of the hero's
love, which 'ever feeds on its decaying flame'. Death lures him
with a 'doubtful smile mocking its own strange charms', and at
this point he is 'Startled by his own thoughts'. The poem's
structure is itself reflexive, for the narrator's fiction reflects his
own predicament, his hero is a mirror image of himself. *Alastor* is
a poem about the nightmare of solipsism, in which everything
the mind sees becomes a reflection of itself, and this absolute
isolation of the self is, as Shelley suggests in his preface and as the
career of the poem's hero makes clear, equivalent to death.

Keats's *Endymion* is the product of an intelligent reading of
Alastor.[12] Endymion, like the hero of Shelley's poem, falls in
love with the creature of his own dream, the goddess of the
moon, and his love, like that of Shelley's hero, is necessarily
frustrated. But Endymion learns in the end not to ask for the
moon (it is typical of Keats that this homely proverb should be at
the centre of his myth); he accepts instead a human lover, and in
rejecting the impossible ideal, accepting the real, he gains what
he has rejected. The mortal lover reveals herself as the goddess of
the moon. Ideal love is fulfilled only through an acceptance of the
real, not by rejecting it. But this solution would not have
contented Shelley, for, to him, love of another originates in
self-love, and the rejection of the ideal that the self dreams leaves
the individual with no impulse to project his desires into the
world around him. Those who reject their ideal suffer a death
more dreadful than that which befalls his poem's hero:

They who, deluded by no generous error, instigated by no
sacred thirst of doubtful knowledge, duped by no illustrious
superstition, loving nothing on this earth, and cherishing no
hopes beyond, yet keep aloof from sympathies with their

kind, rejoicing neither in human joy nor mourning in human grief; these, and such as they, have their apportioned curse. They languish, because none feel with them their common nature. They are morally dead.

Shelley's preface to *Alastor* must be supplemented by his fragmentary *Essay on Love* if we are to understand his position. In the preface he says of the poem's hero that he 'seeks in vain for a prototype of his conception'. In the *Essay on Love* Shelley describes the origin of love as the perception within the self of 'the ideal prototype of everything excellent or lovely that we are capable of conceiving as belonging to the nature of man'. The prototype, the original, has, by definition, an existence purely mental. An embodiment of the prototype is a contradiction in terms, hence the frustration of the hero of *Alastor*. The word Shelley uses to signify the embodiment of the original which man ought to pursue is 'antitype'. But the antitype, the embodied ideal, is also an impossible goal, for no thing or person will entirely satisfy the lover's yearning for an exact embodiment of his ideal. The antitype is 'the invisible and unattainable point to which Love tends'.

Shelley appears to have made a distinction only to dismiss it as insignificant. Certainly the poised and beautiful opening of the essay, a passage which, until a more intelligent mode of reading Shelley has been generally accepted, will no doubt be dismissed by many as a chracteristic relapse into self-indulgent self-pity, would seem to suggest this:

> I know not the internal constitutions of other men, nor even yours whom I now address. I see that in some external attributes they resemble me, but when misled by that appearance I have thought to appeal to something in common, and unburden my inmost soul to them, I have found my language misunderstood like one in a distant and savage land.

The mind imagines its ideal, searches in vain for its embodiment, and feels within itself 'an insufficient void'. The essay appears to condemn man to a life of incurable frustration, and this is true. But then, through an elegant turn in the argument, that painful frustration is redeemed, recognised as the source of all that is benevolent in man. For it is man's frustration, the void within

him, that turns him outwards towards the world: 'it urges forth
the powers of man to arrest the faintest shadow of that without
the possession of which there is no respite to the heart over which
it rules'. What man finds are only the shadows of the antitype of
his dream: the heart is never at rest. But in the end the heart's
restlessness is celebrated, for the heart at rest, the mind unself-
conscious of 'an insufficient void', contains within itself no
dynamism to turn it outwards in a loving communion with the
world around it: 'So soon as this want or power is dead, man
becomes the living sepulchre of himself, and what yet survives is
the mere husk of what once he was'. Notice the use here, as in
Alastor, of a reflexive construction, man as the sepulchre of
himself, to express the mind turned inwards against the world, in
a state which both the poem and the essay suggest is equivalent to
death.

To Shelley the completion or perfection of Endymion's love
would also have seemed a kind of death, for exactly the same
reason that the extinction of the need to love is a death; both relax
the emotional pressure that drives man outwards to the world.

We can now return more confidently to the hero of *Alastor*.
His mistake is that the awareness of the void within his mind,
instead of directing his mind outwards, precipitates it inwards
into a self-destructive solipsism. The more interesting, the more
problematic case, is that of the poem's narrator. In the first line of
the poem he addresses, 'Earth, ocean, air'. Fire, the vital, the
dynamic element, is suspiciously absent. In the invocation to the
goddess of nature that follows he seems perfectly at one with his
environment, conscious of no void within himself. And this is
death. The narrator recognises this when he repeats a simile, the
comparison of himself to an aeolian lyre, when describing the
dead body of his hero.

In the poem's introduction the narrator recalls how he had
once engaged in researches into nature 'Like an inspired and
desperate alchymist'. His studies did not bring him ultimate
knowledge, and yet he claims to be serene. By the end of the
poem, the narrator has realised that his serenity was founded on
self-ignorance, for the story he has told, the fiction he has
created, has given ample evidence of a restlessness that has not
been satisfied. In the poem's conclusion he longs again for
'Medea's wondrous alchemy'. He longs to resuscitate his dead
hero, and to grant him the gift of eternal life:

Which but one living man has drained, who now,
Vessel of deathless wrath, a slave that feels
No proud exemption in the blighting curse
He bears, over the world wanders for ever,
Lone as incarnate death! (677–81)

The reference is to Ahasuerus, the wandering Jew, who was
granted eternal life as a curse rather than a blessing, as a
punishment for having mocked Christ on the cross. These lines
rehearse in miniature the poem's entire procedure. In the course
of telling his tale the narrator has become more and more
convinced of the identity of himself and his hero. His plea that his
hero be restored to life is both a covert plea for himself, and an
expression of the last distinction between himself and his hero. In
so far as the narrator still considers life a blessing he remains
separate from his suicidal *alter ego*. But even as the wish is
articulated, the narrator realises that he does not desire it, that
eternal life now seems to him, as it would have seemed to his
hero, a curse rather than a blessing. His identification of himself
and his hero is complete. In articulating a sentiment, the desire
for eternal life, the narrator understands his true feelings towards
it. Similarly, in telling a story about a poet, the narrator is forced
to discover himself.

For Shelley, language becomes poetry when expression
becomes discovery. Poetry, like metaphor with which it is
closely associated, is an instrument for discovering the 'before
unapprehended'. The narrator's poem, like all poetry, has
resulted in a progress towards self-knowledge; *Alastor* is a
dramatisation of this progress. The narrator develops from one
kind of death to another, from the death of those who feel no
void within themselves, to the death of his hero, whose
consciousness of this void leaves him suicidal. The narrator,
aroused from one extreme, has created a fiction which precipitates him into the other. By the end of the poem he is sunk in 'pale
despair and cold tranquillity', exactly in the situation of his hero
when he lay down to die. Shelley's preface describes only two
kinds of people; those whose 'self-centred seclusion' brings them
to speedy ruin, and the others, worse than they, the 'selfish, blind
and torpid' who feel within themselves no insufficient void. In
writing his poem the narrator has extricated himself from this
second category, he has rediscovered the void within himself,

but he has succeeded only in joining the first category, in
becoming one with his hero. He has progressed from selfishness
to solipsism, from one kind of death to another. He is unable to
take that further step which Shelley accomplishes so elegantly in
his *Essay on Love*. He becomes a prisoner of his own fiction, the
solipsistic world of mirrors in which his hero lived, from which
there is no escape but in death.

Laon and Cythna

Laon and Cythna, Shelley's longest and least admired poem,[13]
tells the story of a young man who wanders away to an isolated
cliff to indulge his despair at the failure of the French Revolution.
From the cliff he witnesses a combat between an eagle and a
snake. The defeated snake swims to shore where it is succoured
by a woman who has watched the contest from the beach. She
invites the young man to accompany her, and the snake on a
voyage during which she explains to him the significance of the
battle he has witnessed, and tells him her own story. The boat
carries this odd group to a mysterious temple, a kind of Valhalla
for dead revolutionaries. There the young man hears a recent
arrival, Laon, tell the story of his life. The rest of the poem,
despite an odd grammatical lapse, consists of Laon's account.

Laon, a young Greek, had early recognised the oppressive
tyranny over his people exercised by the Turkish emperor. He
found a sympathetic audience for his revolutionary poems and
ideas in his sister, Cythna. Their intimacy was interrupted when
their house was raided by a band of the tyrant's soldiers. Laon
was chained naked to the top of a tower, and left to die; Cythna
was forcibly enrolled in the tyrant's harem. Laon contrived to
escape with the assistance of an aged, but enlightened, hermit,
who took Laon away to his house to recuperate; he was
convalescent for some years. After recovering he heard of a
young woman who was leading a revolt against the emperor. He
hurried to join the insurgents, and after the rebels' victory,
recognised and was reunited with his sister. The success of the
rebels was shortlived, and the revolution was crushed after a
counterattack by the tyrant's allies. Laon and Cythna escaped,
took refuge in a ruined building, and enjoyed an ecstatic
marriage night. There Cythna told Laon of her own adventures

during their separation. After being raped by the tyrant she was discharged from his harem on the grounds of insanity, and confined in a submarine cave to which she was conveyed by a pearl diver in the tyrant's employ. A sea eagle acted as her gaoler. She gave birth to a baby daughter, which the pearl diver must have retrieved and taken back to the emperor. Fortunately an earthquake brought the cave to the surface of the sea, and Cythna was rescued by some passing sailors. She immediately set about organising a revolution. Although the revolt had been crushed, the tyrant and his soldiers continued their search for its two acknowledged leaders. Laon surrendered on condition that Cythna be allowed to emigrate to America, but Cythna was determined to share her lover's fate, and the tyrant's chief adviser persuaded the tyrant that a promise made to a revolutionary is not binding. So Laon and Cythna were executed together, burnt at the stake, and journeyed after their deaths to that temple where the young man hears Laon's story.

Laon is evidently conceived as a correction of the hero of *Alastor*. He fell in love with a woman created by himself in a dream. Laon's love for Cythna, like the hero of *Alastor*'s for the dream lady, is a love of his own ideal self. But whereas the hero of *Alastor* despairs when he finds no reality commensurate with his ideal, and is precipitated inwards into a solipsistic world in which he gazes endlessly at his own reflection, Laon is propelled by his love outwards to the world. He struggles to create a reality commensurate with his ideal by engaging in political action, and fails. In his political struggle he is defeated. But *Laon and Cythna* is an attempt to demonstrate that the impulse to create a better world is its own reward, and has a value independent of its success or failure.

The first step towards understanding *Laon and Cythna* is to grasp the tradition within which it belongs. This is the more important because the other poems that make up the tradition are largely forgotten. In Shelley's poem a popular revolution against an autocrat at first succeeds, and is then defeated. There are obvious and detailed parallels between the events presented in the poem and the history of the French Revolution.[14] The practice of presenting within a historical or imaginary narrative a story fraught with veiled reference to contemporary events was, by 1817, well established. The two most significant poems of this kind for Shelley are Southey's first epic, *Joan of Arc*, and

Landor's *Gebir. Joan of Arc* was published in 1796, and *Gebir* followed in 1798. Both poems were written into a contemporary historical situation, Britain's war with France, and both concern the evils of foreign invasion. In the preface to the 1803 edition of *Gebir* Landor writes: 'In the moral are exhibited the folly, the injustice, and the punishment that ever attend the superfluous colonization of a peopled country'. Southey's poem which ends with Joan's defeat of the invading English armies clearly expresses the same warning. Both poems are examples of a curiously hybrid Romantic genre that we may term epic journalism, poems of epic pretension that do not seek to embody an age so much as to engage a particular contemporary issue.

In *Laon and Cythna* Shelley revived a type of poem twenty years out of date. *Gebir* and *Joan of Arc* along with Blake's *The French Revolution* and *America* were products of the 1790s, products of the sympathy which the French Revolution initially aroused among English Whigs and radicals, a sympathy shaken by the Terror, and finally extinguished when Napoleon converted a popular uprising into a war of imperial conquest. Shelley's avowed purpose is to correct the reaction of despair which these events had occasioned in the English supporters of the revolution.

Shelley recognised that the major impediment to reform in England was the traumatic memory of the French Revolution. *Laon and Cythna* is an attempt to revive the memory in order that the trauma it produced might be healed. That is why the poem is a revival of a kind typical of the 1790s, the crucial decade in the English response to the revolution.

The problem out of which Shelley's poem arises is not why the French revolution failed; the reasons for that failure are described almost as though they are self-evident in the preface. The problem is the reaction to its failure of the English radicals who had at first applauded it. This explains what at first seems to be a glaring weakness in the poem's plot. Laon and Cythna successfully achieve a bloodless revolution. The people they free appear to be miraculously unpolluted by the moral disease which Shelley convincingly argues in his preface is inevitably contracted by a people who have lived under an unjust and despotic government. Nevertheless, the revolution is defeated, not by any moral weakness in the revolutionaries, but by the superior power of the invading armies that come to the assistance of the fallen king. Shelley's poem seems neither to offer a credible account of a revolution like that in France to explain why the French revolution failed, nor a blueprint for a successful revolution.

This difficulty is explained by Shelley in a letter to a publisher in which he remarks that the revolution his poem describes is 'the *beau ideal* as it were of the French revolution'.[15] He cannot mean that the poem describes his own revolutionary ideal, ideally he would have wished a revolution to succeed. He means rather that the revolution he describes is the revolution that the radicals of the 1790s imagined that the French Revolution would be. Laon's bloodless revolution is 'the *beau ideal*', unconnected with reality, that had existed in the minds of Southey, Coleridge, Wordsworth and company, and which prompted their initial enthusiasm for the French Revolution. Shelley uses the word 'ideal', as one might expect, in a precise sense. The revolution his poem describes is a revolution that only ever had a mental existence in the imaginations of the English enthusiasts who fixed their utopian dreams on the events taking place in France, and therefore made the ideal, like Napoleon, vulnerable to defeat by political and military circumstances.

Laon and Cythna are not conceived as corrections of either Robespierre or Napoleon, but as corrections of Southey and Wordsworth. Their steadfast hope, their resolute belief in the validity of the ideal for which they fought in the face of its temporary defeat, is to be contrasted with the abandonment of the same ideal by Southey and Wordsworth in similar circumstances. Laon's story cures the visionary's despair; the visionary is the English radical disillusioned by the course that events in France have taken, and he is cured because Laon's story rehearses and corrects his *mental* experience of the French revolution.

In his preface Shelley claims that the disillusionment of the revolution's early enthusiasts resulted from 'a sanguine eagerness for good' unschooled by a recognition that 'resolute perseverance and indefatigable hope, and long-suffering and long-believing courage, and the systematic efforts of generations of men of intellect and virtue' are necessary before that eagerness may be satisfied. Their political ideals, he argues, were maintained in ignorance of human realities, and were therefore destroyed when the subsequent history of the French revolution obtruded those realities forcibly on their attention. *Laon and*

Cythna is an attempt to demonstrate, through its hero and heroine, how despair may be avoided by building one's ideal not on ignorance but on a defiant recognition of the realities to which it is vulnerable.

The poem is best approached through its structure, an achievement on which Shelley prided himself.[16] Shelley's poem is both a history of a defeated revolt and a love story. Laon and Cythna grew up together as children. They are separated in canto II when a band of soldiers raid their house. Laon recounts his history up to his reunion with Cythna in cantos III to V; Cythna tells Laon of her own experiences in these years in cantos VII to IX. Their experiences are linked by a series of parallel and complementary episodes. Laon, after his capture is subjected to a distinctly sexual form of torture. He is chained naked, and spreadeagled on a grill at the top of a tower. He sinks into a fever during which he sees or dreams four corpses hanging from the tower. One of them he recognises as Cythna, and grasps her rotting body, sinking his teeth in her flesh in a gesture which is partly an attempt to eat and partly a grotesque embrace. Cythna, on the other hand, is drafted into the tyrant's harem, raped by him, runs mad, and is imprisoned on the tyrant's orders in an underground cave. In the cave she is fed by a tame sea-eagle, but she dreams in her madness that the eagle is bringing her gobbets of Laon's flesh for her dinner. Laon suffers a sexual form of torture; Cythna suffers a torturous form of sex. She describes her rape as having been: 'Foul as in dream's most fearful imagery/To dally with the mowing dead...' (2877–8). When Laon dreamed that he embraced Cythna's worm-eaten body, he did precisely this. Both Laon and Cythna suffer weird cannibalistic hallucinations; Laon dreams of biting Cythna's cheek, she dreams of being served Laon's flesh to eat. Laon is rescued from the tower by a benign old hermit who transports him to an island refuge. Cythna in her cave gives birth to a child, the product of the rape. Laon with his aged father-figure is complemented by Cythna with her baby. The old hermit, a widely read man, cures Laon's insanity, and then tutors him. Cythna cures herself, and grows wise by studying the interior of her cave which she identifies as an image of her own mind. Laon's discursive knowledge is complemented by Cythna's intuitive knowledge, but both undergo a period of retirement from which they emerge wiser, and strengthened in their revolutionary purposes.

Laon recognises Cythna's story when she tells it him. It seems to him 'Like broken memories of many a heart/Woven into one'. This is hardly surprising, for Cythna's story is a version of his own. But Cythna's story is like broken memories of 'many a heart'. The parallel between the lovers' experiences is not a merely formal symmetry, but an attempt to delineate an archetypal biography of the revolutionary, a biography that will be recognised by all erstwhile sympathisers with the French Revolution as 'broken memories' of their own hearts. Its main features are reflected twice more in the poem, in the history of the snake-loving lady in canto I, and in Shelley's own history as he records it in the poem's dedication, in which, as a contemporary reviewer noted, he and Mary foreshadow Laon and Cythna. All four characters fall in love with a person and with an ideal, suffer a period of madness, and emerge from it strong enough to triumph over the temporary defeat of the cause they have espoused.

Shelley attempts in *Laon and Cythna* to write a poem which will be recognised by all those who have ever sympathised with revolutionary activities as a therapeutic articulation of their own 'broken memories'. It is vulnerable to the argument that Shelley has succeeded only in expressing his own 'broken memories', memories which relate only to his own fantasies, and which are projected arbitrarily onto several characters in the poem. Shelley believed with Wordsworth (Cythna quotes the line) that 'we have all of us one human heart', but he had an intelligent awareness that such a belief might become the refuge of a solipsist. He several times suggests that the exploration of the common human heart is his poetic province, but always indicates his recognition of the risk he runs.[17] Shelley is interested not in individual psychology, but in the common or collective human personality. The most important evidence defining that personality is within himself. He is aware of the danger of presuming his own central experience to be common to all men, but to refuse trust in subjective evidence would be, in this case, to abandon any possibility of knowledge.

In *Laon and Cythna* Shelley makes attempts to protect himself against the risk involved in his procedure. The characters of his poem are created by merging characters from his own personal mythology with characters from the public life of the recent past and characters from the poems of Southey and Wordsworth, the poets who represent for Shelley the apostate class to whom his poem is addressed. Take, for example, the aged hermit who rescues Laon from the tower and nurses him through his sickness. Mary Shelley notes that this character 'is founded on that of Doctor Lind, who, when Shelley was at Eton, had often stood by to befriend and support him . . .';[18] in particular Lind had nursed Shelley, as the hermit nurses Laon, through a feverish illness. But a contemporary reviewer suggested that the old man represented Godwin,[19] and the suggestion has point. Like Godwin he is a radical theoretician; he has spread abroad 'Doctrines of human power', but he is 'cold in seeming'; he lacks the ability to inspire which he recognises in Laon. All this might be a character sketch of Godwin. The old man confesses that until he heard of Laon he had become disillusioned. In this he recalls another old man, the Solitary, who, in Wordsworth's *Excursion* has retreated into a misanthropic retirement after becoming disillusioned with the political events in America and France. In so far as the hermit is Doctor Lind he is a figure from Shelley's private mythology; in so far as he is Godwin, he is a figure out of a *public* allegory of the history of the recent past, for Godwin had tutored a whole generation of English radicals; in so far as the hermit is a therapeutic revision of Wordsworth's Solitary he is part of an attempt to rewrite the mythology established by contemporary poets to express their disillusionment with the French revolution.

The snake-loving lady in the first canto who fell in love with the morning star is a typically Shelleyan lover, but she is also any woman, Mary Wollstonecraft for example, who aspires to a revolutionary ideal, and in addition she recalls Kailyal, the heroine of Southey's poem *The Curse of Kehama*, who falls in love with a Hindu spirit, the Glendoveer. The Iberian priest who demands the execution of Laon and Cythna is only partially a product of Shelley's private anti-Christian hysteria, he also represents Castlereagh and Metternich and the other diplomats who forged the Holy Alliance as a means of stamping out revolutionary movements, and he closely resembles the Indian and Aztec priests who, in Southey's *Madoc*, plot deviously to bring the poem's hero to the sacrificial altar.

The system of correspondences that links Cythna's story with Laon's, and both their stories with those of the snake-loving lady and of Shelley and Mary, and the technique of characterisation that I have described, attempt to establish the poem as the 'broken memories of many a heart', to establish it as a typical representation of the experience of the radical Englishman in the 1790s, and a revision of his reaction to the experience.

But Shelley's poem contains not only a love story, and a collection of minor characters, but also a political narrative (in its revised form the poem was entitled 'The Revolt of Islam'), and its political theme is also carefully structured. The history of the revolt is prefigured in the conflict between the snake and eagle in the first canto. The snake at first appears to have the upper hand, but the eagle recovers, and at last drops the snake wounded but still alive into the sea, winning a victory that we are assured is only temporary. Similarly, the poem's political history describes a successful revolt which is immediately crushed by a savage counter revolution culminating in the sacrificial execution of Laon and Cythna. But the tyrant's victory, like the eagle's, is, we are told, temporary.

The two great movements of the poem's political plot, the ebb of oppressive power followed by its flow, are held together by a series of fierce contrasts. After the success of their revolution the people build an altar, a work 'of genius', which Laon and Cythna mount as priest and priestess of the new secular religion (lines 2071–2106). After the success of the counter-revolution the invading armies, afflicted by famine, build to appease the angry gods a sacrificial altar on which they plan to burn Laon and Cythna. Their altar is far from artistic; it is a heap of wood garnished with various noxious insects and reptiles (lines 4162–70). Laon joins Cythna on the triumphal pyramid; Cythna joins Laon on the sacrificial altar. The revolutionaries are a 'band of brothers' (line 2407); the holy alliance of nations which comes to the tyrant's rescue forms a 'brotherhood of ill' (line 3839). The rebels celebrate their victory with a vegetarian feast (lines 2299–2316), but, after defeating them, the conquering armies are reduced to cannibalism (line 3955–63). Laon prevents his soldiers from marring their victory by vengeful killing by quoting Christ's response to those who would stone the woman taken in adultery (lines 2017–25). When the conquering armies are afflicted with famine and disease they begin to think that their gods are punishing them for allying with heathen nations. The Iberian priest averts sectarian strife by offering them Laon and Cythna as sacrifices (lines 4099–4143). Both Laon and the priest pacify their armies. But Laon pacifies the insurgents in love, the Iberian priest pacifies his armies by offering them a common object for their hatred. 'Christian' Socialism becomes National Socialism.[20]

Laon and Cythna is both a love story and a political poem, and in this dual interest it is typical of the poems of the 1790s that Shelley imitates. In *Joan of Arc*, for example, the epic conflict is not between the English and the French, but between the claims of retirement and domestic happiness, and the claims of active involvement in a political movement. Joan, to fulfil her destiny, must abandon Theodore, a village boy who loves her and offers her a life of rural peace. Joan is not wrong to make this decision; she is 'the destined maid', and she must fulfil her destiny, but its effects are calamitous. Theodore follows Joan to the wars and is killed. Southey consistently represents war as the wrecker of domestic happiness and domestic virtue. Repeatedly he exposes the savagery of war by juxtaposing scenes of battle and descriptions of the quiet, domestic life from which the fighting soldiers have been snatched. *Gebir* is oddly similar. Gebir, the soldier king, has a brother Tamar, a shepherd. Gebir's martial virtues bring him victory in war, but result in the death of the woman he loves. Tamar, the pacific shepherd, on the other hand, is happily united with his nymph. In *The Excursion* the Solitary takes no interest in politics until his wife and children have died.

Joan of Arc, *Gebir*, and *The Excursion* each accredit the private and the public life with separate and incompatible virtues. Shelley, as he reflected on the failure of the radicals of the 1790s to maintain their revolutionary enthusiasm, must have identified this separation between private and public values as one of its causes: political commitment could be maintained only by suppressing, or lacking, other equally valuable commitments. *Laon and Cythna* is an attempt to cure this schism, to reunite private and public life. For Laon and Cythna revolutionary principles are not upheld in opposition to the claims of love, rather each is an aspect of the other; their love for each other is fulfilled through their political struggle.

Shelley's concern to assimilate the public with the private is best illustrated by those passages in the poem which describe the merging of the inner world of private dream with the outer world of public experience. When Laon is first captured by the tyrant's soldiers they burst in on his sleep. In a fine passage

Shelley describes Laon's attempt to merge the noise of their entry
with his dream:

> And I lay struggling in the impotence
> Of sleep, while outward life had burst its bound,
> Though, still deluded, strove the tortured sense
> To its dire wanderings to adapt the sound
> Which in the light of morn was poured around
> Our dwelling . . . (1153–8)

Laon, chained on the tower, sinks into a fever in which real
events and fantasies merge indistinguishably; Cythna in the
submarine cave is for a long time in a similar plight. Their
inability to distinguish the real from the imaginary is madness,
but it is a therapeutic madness from which they emerge
strengthened. Southey, Landor and Wordsworth escaped such
madness by separating the private and the public, love and war,
but the cost of such an antidote was to leave their public
principles brittle. The central images of Shelley's poem express
his concern to merge the public and the private; dungeons and
chains are now physical impediments, now mental fetters.
Cythna's cave is a real prison, but in line 3101 it becomes a
metaphor for her mind. An unstable relationship between the
literal and the metaphoric is, in the terms of Shelley's poem, a
badge of mental strength. The poem is designed to drive
together the world of public event and of private imagining, to
represent the one as the product of the other.

The divorce of love and politics was only one aspect of the
failure of the radicals in the 1790s to assimilate with their idealism
an awareness of human realities. An ideal was espoused that
could not survive the Terror, the revelation of the dark recesses
of the human personality. *Joan of Arc* might be read as the
prediction of this failure, for it ends with Joan crowning her king
at Rheims, as though her subsequent betrayal and execution
were matters which Southey's idealistic faith could not comprehend.

Cannibalism in *Laon and Cythna* is a central metaphor; when
the invading armies buy and eat human flesh their action
expresses the complex association of lust, sadism and selfishness
on which tyranny is based. Laon and Cythna can confront
unappalled such a demonstration of human depravity, because

they have experienced it and recognised it within themselves. In their madness they both experienced cannibal fantasies in which they ate each other's bodies. As a result their revolutionary principles are stronger than those of the radicals of the 1790s; they recognise that the manifestations of tyranny that they abhor are not imposed on a naïvely innocent human personality, but rise from forces active deep within the human soul. The most disgusting barbarities, Laon and Cythna learn in madness, are only the incarnations of human dreams.

In Southey's romances (*The Curse of Kehama* is the best example), evil may perplex the hero's physical life, but his moral self is invulnerable to its assaults. His virtue is revealed in the complete disjunction between his moral life and that of the evil man. In this world they exist on the same physical level but on moral planes that never intersect. Shelley recognised that such a moral system left the individual with no means of accepting the reality of the Terror without rejecting the ideal from which it had arisen.

Shelley avoids this predicament by insisting that the ideal must be pursued in full recognition of the forces that threaten it. Cythna, when she makes her revolutionary appeal to the sailors who have rescued her, demands repeatedly that they 'know themselves', that they do not 'disguise' from themselves their inner depravity. They must recognise that their violence, their cunning, their avarice and their cruelty are not peculiar perversions, but aspects of human nature: 'Disguise it not—we have one human heart—/All mortal thoughts confess a common home . . .' (3361–2). Against Southey's facile separation of good and evil Cythna counsels a Wordsworthian acceptance of the human mind's capacity to contain both heaven and hell. But in Wordsworth that recognition bred a deepseated pessimism concerning the possibility of social regeneration which Shelley denounced as 'moral ruin'. Wordsworth's self-knowledge, Shelley would argue, resulted only in self-reproach. *The Excursion* would have seemed to him an elaborate exercise in self-loathing, a mechanism through which, in the person of the Solitary, the embittered idealist, Wordsworth could punish the aspect of himself, the part of his own biography, that he had come to reject.

Cythna demands that the sailors accept what they are, but that they avoid self-contempt: 'Reproach not thine own soul, but know thyself,/Nor hate another's crime, nor loathe thine own, (3388–9). To do otherwise, to 'repent', is to fall victim to 'the dark idolatry of self'. It is a brilliant phrase. Self-knowledge which leads to self-loathing transforms the past into an idol to which the present self must minister, so that Wordsworth in 1814 is still trapped in an impossible attempt to redeem the Wordsworth of the 1790s. In hating that aspect of himself he has kept it alive; it has grown old with him, the Solitary by the pedlar's side. In *The Excursion* the pedlar, the narrator and the pastor (the father, the son and holy ghost, a trinity of orthodox voices) all do service to the Solitary, the dark idol of Wordsworth's imagination, and in the end their redemption of him is no more than an unconvincing rhetorical trick.

Cythna insists that the sailors know themselves, but only so that they can reject their own evil. Cythna and Laon accept the hallucinations they experienced in madness; they do not deny them, but neither are they precipitated by them into a horror of their own inmost natures.

The epic struggle in *Laon and Cythna* is to achieve the rejection of evil that Cythna recommends. When the eagle and the snake, the principles of evil and good, are first seen by the visionary, they are 'wreathed', tangled together in the struggle. The poem attempts to separate them. One of its best moments occurs when Laon first approaches the revolutionaries' camp. He finds it silent, all save the sentries sleeping:

> Oh, what a might
> Of human thought was cradled in that night!
> How many hearts impenetrably veiled
> Beat underneath its shade! what secret fight
> Evil, and good, in woven passions mailed
> Waged through that silent throng . . . (1732–7)

The battle between mailed warriors, the epic conflict, takes place at night, when all are asleep, within the minds of men. The physical battle that follows is only a postscript to it. In the same way, the poem's second battle is not really Laon's losing struggle against the tyrant's counterattack, it is fought in canto IX, when Cythna salvages moral victory from physical defeat by demonstrating that the ideal for which she and Laon had struggled has a vitality which can survive the defeat and death of its adherents.

Success in these, the real battles of the poem, achieves a separation between good and evil, but since evil as well as good has its origin within the mind of man, this separation results in a precarious, tense balance between the two qualities. The good, the beautiful, is always likely to precipitate, or to be transformed into, its opposite. Laon, chained on the tower, sinks into a fever in which Cythna appears to him as a rotting, wormeaten corpse. But the most powerful expression of this theme occurs at the end of canto VI. Laon leaves Cythna in the 'green ruin', their honeymoon hotel, and rides off in search of food. In the town he finds only one survivor from the depredations of the plague:

No living thing was there besides one woman,
Whom I found wandering in the streets, and she
Was withered from the likeness of aught human
Into a fiend . . . (2758–61)

She has run mad, claims that she is 'Pestilence', and weds herself to Laon with a nightmare kiss. The woman is Cythna's antitype: the ideal has projected its own antithesis.

The point of the complex parallelism that links the progress of the revolution with that of the counter-revolution, that links the 'band of brothers' with the 'brotherhood of ill', the triumphal pyramid with the sacrificial altar, and Laon with the Iberian priest, now becomes clear. The same relation exists between the two political movements of the poem that links Cythna, the spiritual healer, with the woman who calls herself 'Pestilence'. The revolution is the embodiment of an ideal, and it projects its own antithesis.

The radicals of the 1790s, in espousing an ideal, ran the risk that their bride would be transformed into Pestilence, that the beautiful woman would wither into a fiend. Shelley's poem attempts to explain how it was that the bloodletting in Paris and the military ambition of a Napoleon, phenomena which in the context of human history seem sadly humdrum, should have delivered such a profound shock to a generation of Englishmen. They responded to an ugliness that was commensurate with the beauty of the ideal that had preceded it; that was, in a sense, the product of the beauty. They had greeted the French Revolution as an embodied ideal, and when it could no longer be considered an ideal they suffered a traumatic disillusionment. Their reaction was to dismiss the ideal, to reject it as a destructive aspiration towards the unrealisable, but in this, *Laon and Cythna* suggests, they were mistaken.

Laon is kissed by the woman who calls herself Pestilence, but he does not react by abandoning Cythna, he returns to her. In canto I the woman who fell in love with the morning star sees her star as a snake, but she does not therefore repent of her passion; she accepts the snake and loves it, waits patiently for it to reassume its proper form. When their ideal revolution has been supplanted by the barbaric counter-revolution, its nightmare parody, Laon and Cythna do not become disillusioned in their ideal; they retain their faith in its eventual reincarnation. The mistake of Wordsworth and Southey was not to espouse an ideal, but that they lacked strength to withstand the shock when they glimpsed the nightmare that must ever accompany the dream, a shock that Laon and Cythna triumphantly overcome.

To dream of ideal beauty, whether it be the beauty of a woman or the beauty of a political system, is then to incur a risk. The evil that the dreamer rejects is an evil within himself. The tendency of the ideal to project its own antithesis is the natural tendency of the rejected quality to reassert itself. The proper defence against this possibility is not, as Wordsworth might have suggested, and as so many of Shelley's twentieth-century readers insist, to dismiss the dream as an ideal which contradicts human nature, but to recognise, even when rejecting evil, that one is rejecting a part of oneself. This is the burden of Cythna's advice to the sailors. The dreamer who knows himself is steeled to withstand the nightmare parody of his dream, the appearance of the morning star as a snake, of a beautiful woman as a rotting corpse, the degeneration of what had seemed an ideal revolution into an orgy of mob violence.

If the man who commits himself to good runs a risk, then so does the man who commits himself to evil. He, just as much as the dreamer of the ideal, flouts an aspect of human nature, and risks that aspect reasserting itself. The tyrant rapes Cythna; his action is totally evil, and yet Cythna gives birth to a daughter who, both in physical appearance and in moral character, is not the tyrant's child, but the child of Laon and Cythna. The child is taken from Cythna and brought up by the tyrant, and yet, when Laon and Cythna are executed, she recognises her true parents, and dies in sympathy with them. In committing himself to evil the tyrant has succeeded in bringing forth good.

In all this Shelley is invulnerable to the most repeated of the charges brought against him, the charge of sentimental optimism. But he goes farther. The true form of the spirit of good is the morning star, its appearance as a snake is only a temporary disguise, a delusion. Its defeat by the eagle is only a temporary setback in a struggle it is fated to win. Cythna's appearance as a rotting corpse is a hallucination. The tyrant's victory is necessarily temporary. When man rejects evil, he rejects a part of himself which is real but temporary, or which has the reality of a hallucination. When he rejects good, he rejects the essentially human, and will necessarily be defeated. This extension of Shelley's scheme is not rationally defensible; it is a matter of faith. But the possession of such a faith need not justify the charge of sentimental optimism. A faith, Shelley would have argued, is, by definition incapable of rational demonstration, just like every other human principle, but it can be justified pragmatically, as giving a basis for positive benevolent action. Shelley's disillusioned revolutionary is offered a faith pragmatically justified, a faith that will save him from the living death of those who attempt to live without ideals.

Julian and Maddalo

Julian and Maddalo is an account by Julian of the crucial experience in his life. The poem begins on the Venetian Lido, where Julian is riding with Maddalo, an Italian nobleman. Maddalo is a man remarkable for his genius and his pride, and these two qualities combine to make him gloomily introverted. Julian is a young English gentleman who advocates perfectibility, is a notorious free-thinker, but is said by his friends to possess some good qualities ('How far this is possible the pious reader will determine'). On their way home from the beach, they begin an argument on the problem of whether man is essentially imperfect, or whether his imperfection is a defect that he can himself remedy. Maddalo's pessimism counters Julian's optimism. The argument continues the following morning. Maddalo admits that Julian's system might be made 'refutation-tight/As far as words go', but insists that it is humanly impossible. To prove his point, he refers to a lunatic of his acquaintance who once thought as Julian did, and whose madness, he suggests, is a direct consequence of his theories. Julian retorts, pointedly, that he thinks it more likely that he was driven mad by his own pride. To resolve the dispute the two friends visit the madman, and overhear a confused outburst in which the madman recalls his personal history, and discusses his present predicament. Such is the effect of this monologue that their 'argument was quite forgot'. Julian forms a plan to stay in Venice, to improve his friendship with Maddalo, and to attempt a cure of the madman's illness, but pressure of business forces him to return home. Only many years later does he come back to Venice. Maddalo is away, travelling, but he meets and speaks with Maddalo's daughter, who on his previous visit had been a toddler, but is now a radiant young woman. She tells him the madman's subsequent history, but since Julian refuses to confide it to the reader, the poem ends.[21]

Shelley considered *Julian and Maddalo* an experiment in a new poetic manner. He explained to his publisher: 'It is an attempt in a different style, in which I am not yet sure of myself, a *sermo pedestris* way of treating human nature quite opposed to the idealism of that drama' (*Prometheus Unbound*).[22] To Leigh Hunt he wrote: 'I have employed a certain familiar style of language to express the actual way in which people talk to each other whom education and a certain refinement of sentiment have placed above the use of vulgar idioms'.[23] The phrase *'sermo pedestris'* is used by Horace to describe the proper language for tragic lament[24], but during the eighteenth century it was used with a more general Horatian reference to describe any colloquial style that seemed to derive from Horace's manner in his satires or *sermones*. Pope's *Imitations of Horace*, for example, were attacked by a contemporary for their 'affectation of the *sermo pedestris*'. Shelley's use of the phrase suggests that *Julian and Maddalo* is a poem loosely within the Horatian tradition, and the verse form Shelley uses, heroic couplets, suggests that it is a tradition that Shelley receives through the eighteenth century, in particular, perhaps, through Pope. The poem has a place within the contemporary critical debate concerning the merits or demerits of the poetry of Pope and his school. It was probably written in the year 1819, the year in which Byron began his controversy with the Reverend William Lisle Bowles in which he defended

Pope against the attack on his reputation in which Bowles, Coleridge, Keats and Hunt had all joined.[25]

In his defence of Pope Byron argues that the highest of all poetry is 'ethical poetry'. He uses the terms 'ethical poetry' and 'didactic poetry' as synonyms, but the terms leave him uneasy: 'ethical poetry, or didactic poetry, or by whatever name you term it'.[26] His unease derives, I believe, from a recognition that there is no adequate translation of the Greek word *'ethos'*. Quintilian met the same difficulty: *'ethos*, a word for which in my opinion Latin has no equivalent'.[27] The problem for Quintilian, and for Byron, is that 'ethical poetry' is both a description of the poem's content, and of the character of its writer. Byron feels called upon to defend not only Pope's themes and his handling of them, but also his personal character. Ethical poetry may be defined as that poetry in which the poet assumes a character designed to persuade his reader to admire the virtues which he himself embodies. Not to assume the appearance of a virtuous man is to fail: 'For the orator who gives the impression of being a bad man while he is speaking, is actually speaking badly, since his words seem to be insincere owing to the absence of *ethos* which would otherwise have revealed itself'.[28] When Bowles suggests that only a bad man could have written the couplet on Lady Mary Wortley Montague in *Epistle to a Lady*, he is making an aesthetic attack on the poem.

Ethical poetry, then, is both poetry that embodies the character of its author, and poetry that teaches virtue. Lord Monboddo adheres to the former definition (to him even a poem that revealed the character of its author to be bad would be ethical);[29] Byron suggests the latter. Pope, in his *Moral Essays* and especially in his *Imitations of Horace* is a supreme example of the union of the two kinds of *ethos*, for the poems both make moral judgements, and dramatise the character of the poet. Wordsworth perceptively remarks that the 'characteristic and impassioned Epistles' written by Pope might be 'considered a species of monodrama'.[30]

Quintilian follows the Greek rhetoricians in contrasting *ethos* with *pathos*. The two differ in their intensity: ethos persuades the listener to agree; pathos, by appealing directly to the listener's imagination, enforces his agreement. The ethical speaker dramatises himself, the pathetic speaker dramatises his subject; he seems 'not so much to narrate as to exhibit the actual scene', and he achieves this effect by means of *'phantasias* or *visiones'*.[31] The ethical speaker asks that his listener sympathise with him, the pathetic speaker asks that the listener join him in an empathic relationship with his subject. If we accept that for the Romantic poet the primary subject is the activity of his own consciousness, then we can describe the Romantic rejection of Pope as a rejection of the ethical in favour of the pathetic, a rejection of the imagination defined by Hume which 'adheres to the general view of things' in favour of the imagination spoken of by Shelley as a synonym for identification. The terms *ethos* and *pathos* place in a rhetorical context a distinction like that which Hume draws between the language of morals and the language of self-love.

The Popean epistle becomes Coleridge's conversation poem, a poem in which Coleridge does not seek to create himself, like Pope, as a character, but asks the reader to share a sequence of thoughts and images; the poem recreates a series of impressions, so that in reading the poem the reader seems to become the consciousness into which the impressions flow. Pope asks his reader to admire him, or to sympathise or agree with him; Coleridge asks his reader to become him.

But the relationship between the Augustan and the Romantic is more easily seen if we compare any of Pope's epistles with Shelley's *Letter to Maria Gisborne*. Shelley's letter contains a series of verse portraits, which, like Byron's portrait of Lara, use a rhetoric handed down from Dryden and Pope:

> You will see Coleridge – he who sits obscure
> In the exceeding lustre and the pure
> Intense irradiation of a mind
> Which, with its own internal lightning blind,
> Flags wearily through darkness and despair –
> A cloud-encircled meteor of the air,
> A hooded eagle among blinking owls—(202–8)

The portrait, like many of Pope's, is assembled out of a single contrast, although Shelley, characteristically, chooses to juggle with light and darknesss rather than human qualities, and it culminates in two epigrammatic lines. But the differences from Pope's characteristic technique are more interesting than the similarities. Shelley's syntax twists between the couplets, suggesting a tentative exploration of character, rather than a massively final summation. Augustan antitheses become Romantic paradoxes, evoking wonder rather than amused contempt.

In the end Shelley's letter is more like Coleridge's conversation poems than Pope's epistles. It attempts to express a stream of thought rather than to address itself to a particular theme. The primary reality it embodies is the consciousness through which the impressions pass rather than the external reality that the impressions portend.

The letter is written from the Gisborne's house in Italy, from the study in which Maria's son has experimented, made models, drawn plans, in pursuance of his project, the design and construction of a steamboat, an enterprise that Shelley financed. Shelley sits in the room surrounded by detached fragments of the machine. These fragments act within the poem as an emblem of the disconnected impressions out of which the letter is written. The boat which Shelley sees as so many disconnected and apparently insignificant fragments, exists entire within the imagination of Maria Gisborne's son. Similarly, the disconnected fragments from which Shelley assembles his letter become whole, are unified, by the writer's consciousness. Shelley's letter, like the steamboat, exists as a whole in its author's mind. Shelley suggests the parallel when he speaks of the 'self-impelling steam-wheels of the mind'. If we attend only to its subjects, its themes, it will seem as bewildering a hotchpotch as the fragments of machinery seem to Shelley.

The letter is concerned to express the mercurial nature of Shelley's consciousness (one of the articles Shelley notes in the room is a bowl of mercury); it tries to express both the disjointedness of the mind's impressions, and the procedures by which it organises its experience. Take, for example, the description of Leigh Hunt:

> And there is he with his eternal puns,
> Which beat the dullest brain for smiles, like duns
> Thundering for money at a poet's door;
> Alas! it is no use to say, 'I'm poor!' (219–22)

The debt collectors, first offered as a means of expressing the irresistibility of Hunt's jokes, step out of the simile which contains them to allude to Hunt's precarious financial situation.

The volatile relationship between figurative and literal expression, the duns as a witty comparison and as a sad reality, acts here, as elsewhere in Shelley, to blur the distinction of which Shelley was sceptical between the mental and the objective, the internal and external, but it is also the means by which he forges a connection between Hunt's jokes and his debts. He welds, as it were, two of the steamboat's fragments together, but the weld emphasises their difference, their incongruity, quite as much as their connection. The sentence expresses both the flashing inconsequentiality of Shelley's mind, and its organising power – hence the appropriateness of its subject, puns. The poem is full of examples of the same kind of dexterity, some extending over long verse paragraphs, others wittily compressed. When Maria and Shelley meet again in Italy, they will: 'ask one week, to make another week/As like his father, as I'm unlike mine . . .' (299–300).

In the first paragraph of the poem Shelley repeats and accepts the insult of the 'moralists' who accuse him of being a 'worm', but by modifying their description, and presenting himself as a silkworm, he turns the insult into a delicate compliment to his poetry, 'fine threads of rare and subtle thought', and to the butterfly-like immortality that he hopes to earn. The moralists' criticism is not discussed, and then rejected, it is simply presented as inappropriate. Similarly, later in the poem, Shelley speaks of 'the self-impelling steam-wheels of his mind:

> Which pump up oaths from clergymen, and grind
> The gentle spirit of our meek reviews
> Into a powdery foam of salt abuse . . . (109–11)

The apoplectic vicars, and the fastidious reviewers are not exposed as wrongheaded, but absurd. The poem's embodiment of the volatile, darting movements of the consciousness renders incongruous the kind of moral judgement to which Shelley had been subjected. In Pope's verse epistles, the poet dramatises himself. A moral reaction is not only justified, it is demanded. Pope is an ethical poet. *Letter to Maria Gisborne* offers the reader, not a character, but a consciousness, and it is a Romantic discovery of the first importance, though a very dangerous one, that the exhibition of consciousness can evade, supersede, or render inappropriate the conventional ethical reactions. Con-

sciousness may be deployed against morality, *pathos* against
ethos, the language of self-love against the language of morality.
In *Letter to Maria Gisborne* this is achieved with a charming
exuberance unlikely to offend. *Julian and Maddalo* is a more
complex and problematical presentation of the same theme.

The first paragraph of the poem describes Julian's ride with
Maddalo along the Lido. It may usefully be compared with
Crabbe's description of the River Yar in *Peter Grimes*:

> Thus by himself compelled to live each day,
> To wait for certain hours the tide's delay;
> At the same time the same dull views to see,
> The bounding marsh-bank and the blighted tree,
> The water only, when the tides were high,
> When low, the mud half-covered and half-dry;
> The sun-burnt tar that blisters on the planks,
> And bank-side stakes in their uneven ranks;
> Heaps of entangling weeds that slowly float,
> As the tide rolls by the impeded boat.

Crabbe uses the description to express the torpor of Peter's
mind. Phrases linked by commas take the place of a more
energetic syntax, suggesting Peter's inertia in the face of
experience, his failure to create an order from the scattered
phenomena presented to him. The passage both describes a
landscape and expresses a mind. Peter Grimes, the poem's hero,
is both a character and a consciousness. Crabbe both becomes his
protagonist, and remains detached from him, and this produces
the reader's strange response to the poem. A moral reaction to
Peter is both demanded and forbidden – demanded in so far as he
is a character to be judged, forbidden in so far as he is a
consciousness which can only be experienced.

The sentence which begins *Julian and Maddalo* is apparently
very different:

> I rode one evening with Count Maddalo
> Upon the bank of land which breaks the flow
> Of Adria towards Venice: a bare strand
> Of hillocks, heaped from ever-shifting sand,
> Matted with thistles and amphibious weeds,
> Such as from earth's embrace the salt ooze breeds,

Is this; an uninhabited sea-side,
Which the lone fisher when his nets are dried
Abandons; and no other object breaks
The waste, but one dwarf tree and some few stakes
Broken and unrepaired, and the tide makes
A narrow space of level sand thereon
Where 'twas our wont to ride while day went down. (1–13)

Julian dominates the landscape with his own organising mind. He assembles patterns of similarity and contrast, the most important being that between the sea and the land. The beach is composed of 'hillocks', which we think of as semi-permanent geographical features, but these hillocks are composed of 'ever-shifting sand'. We are carefully placed on the frontier between stable land and the flux of the sea. The reference to 'amphibious weeds' emphasises the beach as the place where land and sea interact. Throughout the passage the observer makes distinctions and modifications: 'and no other object breaks/The waste, but one dwarf tree and some few stakes . . .'. He arranges phenomena in a meaningful order. The phrases, 'but one' and 'some few', enforce an order which is both logical, first the general rule and then the exceptions, and arithmetical, from 'none' to 'one' to 'some few'. The shape of the sentence itself suggests a scene humanly dominated. It begins: 'I rode one evening with Count Maddalo', and ends: 'Where 'twas our wont to ride while day went down'. Human activity frames the inanimate landscape.

Both Crabbe and Shelley use description to define the mood or character of the observer: Peter, sunk in apathy, and the intellectually agile and emotionally buoyant Julian. Peter succumbs to his landscape. He awaits the tide's delay, conforming the rhythm of his human life to a mechanical natural process. He is deadened by the deadness of the objects around him. Julian responds actively to his surroundings, and converts the most unlikely scenery into a metaphor for his own magnanimity:

I love all waste
And solitary places, where we taste
The pleasure of believing what we see
Is boundless, as we wish our souls to be. (14–17)

The reader is aware in both passages that the poet is creating a character and inhabiting a consciousness. In so far as he creates a character, we are aware of a disparity between the landscape as it is, and the landscape as it is perceived, the discrepancy between the two defining the perceiver's character. In so far as he inhabits a consciousness a notion of the landscape 'as it is' disappears: the individual's perception becomes the sole reality. *Julian and Maddalo* begins on a frontier between two modes of comprehending reality, and therefore of understanding people. It begins on the beach, the frontier between the sea and the land, where Julian and Maddalo ride until sunset, the frontier between night and day. The description concentrates on meeting places, and, at the beginning of the poem this is understood as an emblem of the meeting between Julian and Maddalo, two disparate personalities. But as the poem develops the significance of its symbols extends.

On their way home, as darkness falls, the conversation between the two friends becomes more serious. They hold a debate:

> Concerning God, freewill and destiny:
> Of all that earth has been or yet may be,
> All that vain men imagine or believe,
> Or hope can paint or suffering may achieve . . . (42–5)

The lines alternate between a despairing recognition of human futility, and a celebration of human potential; between the point of view of Julian, who believes that we should 'make the best of ill', and that of Maddalo, who takes 'the darker side'. An exuberant Shelleyan satanism contrasts with a Byronic Calvinistic satanism.

But the contrast between the two men is defined most completely, not in the form of a discursive argument, but by two descriptions of sunset. To Julian sunset is a vision which confirms the perfection to which he aspires as a valid goal:

> And then – as if the Earth and Sea had been
> Dissolved into one lake of fire, were seen
> Those mountains towering as from waves of flame
> Around the vaporous sun, from which there came

The inmost purple spirit of light, and made
Their very peaks transparent. (80–5)

Sunset is a vision of unity, dissolving all things into 'one lake of fire'. The unity is expressed by a sustained verbal merging of the four elements; earth, air, water and fire. To Julian this vision confirms the possibility of a life in which reality is commensurate with the human imagination, in which we are, as he claims we might be, 'all/We dream of'. He addresses Italy as a 'Paradise of exiles', and sunset suggests to him the possibility that this expression might not be an impossible paradox. The 'waves of flame' ensure the possibility that Eden and exile might also be harmonised.

But Maddalo promises to show Julian a 'better station' from which to view the sunset. They row over the lagoon, and come to a point at which an ugly building rears itself between them and the sun. The building is:

A windowless, deformed and dreary pile;
And on the top an open tower where hung
A bell, which in the radiance swayed and swung;
We could just hear its hoarse and iron tongue . . . (101–4)

Maddalo's world is at odds with itself. Julian's sunset reconciled the city with the mountains and sea that surround it. But for Maddalo no reconciliation between the natural sun, and the human artefact, the building, is possible. They stand against each other 'In strong and black relief'. To Julian man is an exile who can find his way back to paradise; to Maddalo Eden is inaccessible, man is an outcast in an alien world. The building he shows Julian is a madhouse. Its description is the most powerful moment in the poem thus far; a point at which consciousness begins to threaten character, the intensity with which the reader is persuaded to experience Maddalo's vision obstructing his ability to form a detached judgement of its quality. It predicts the function in the poem of the madman. The triplet, intruding on an unbroken succession of couplets, expresses the jarring effect of the bell, its disquieting, monotonous tolling. The rhyme sound is exactly chosen, '-ung'. Notice the delicacy with which the verb is positioned in the phrase 'where hung/A bell': it is left hanging at the end of the line. In the light of the sun the bell

'swayed and swung'. Sound enforces sense to emphasise once
more the disquieting regularity of the to-and-froing of the bell. It
has a 'hoarse and iron tongue'. Two adjectives, one human, one
inanimate, are applied to the ambiguous noun 'tongue', and the
sudden taste of metal in the mouth that the phrase provokes
clinches Maddalo's vision of a discordant world.

The bell, to Julian's contempt, rings to summon the lunatics to
evening service. Maddalo mocks his friend's anti-Christian
fervour, but then grows serious:

> And this must be the emblem and the sign
> Of what should be eternal and divine! –
> And like that black and dreary bell, the soul,
> Hung in a heaven-illumined tower, must toll
> Our thoughts and our desires to meet below
> Round the rent heart and pray – as madmen do
> For what? they know not – till the night of death
> As sunset that strange vision, severeth
> Our memory from itself, and us from all
> We sought and yet were baffled. (121–30)

The madhouse becomes Maddalo's central metaphor for the
human condition. In the poem's preface he is criticised for his
introversion. Struck by the meanness of all around him, he has
retreated into himself. To him the individual is a tower in which
are grouped thoughts and desires which turn inwards towards
'the rent heart'. The tower acts as a protective carapace that man
builds around himself as a defence against a hostile environment.
The bell, or soul, is hung in a 'heaven-illumined' tower, but it
speaks only to the tower's inhabitants, not to the outside world.
Man is a creature isolated from his fellows, and in conflict with
himself. Maddalo's metaphor is religious, because his sense of
human futility is the same that leads weaker men to postulate a
god in whose sight all is clear and significant. His emblem is in
sharp contrast with Julian's:

> I love all waste
> And solitary places, where we taste
> The pleasure of believing what we see
> Is boundless, as we wish our souls to be.

Julian would like his soul to be unenclosed, embracing everything within his experience. The simplicity of the landscape
suggests to him the potential simplicity of the human personality, its freedom from the self-destructive conflict which, to
Maddalo, is the defining characteristic of the human.

Maddalo's assertion of human futility, and Julian's assertion of
human potential, are both, quite literally, aesthetic beliefs,
beliefs sanctioned by an aesthetic reaction to landscape. *Julian and
Maddalo* is a poem not about the rights and wrongs of a particular
belief, but about the aesthetics of belief, and the point to which
the first part of the poem drives is that the beliefs of Julian and
Maddalo, apparently antithetical, are identical in the inadequacy
of their aesthetic basis. Shelley is far from dismissing the validity
of aesthetic belief as such. He accepted with Hume that, on most
important matters, feeling is the only basis for believing one
thing rather than another. The beliefs of Julian and Maddalo are
inadequate because the feelings on which they are based are
limited, they do not comprehend their complete experience of
life. Their theories are therefore at odds with their practice.
Maddalo's representation of the human situation would prohibit
the easy conversation with a friend in which he is, at that
moment, engaged. Julian's desire for a soul extending to the
horizon of the world is, he admits, best indulged in 'waste and
solitary places', suggesting that the love of humanity he profes-
ses is an emotion he finds easiest to cultivate in solitude. Theory
is disjoined from practice, and there is a further disjunction
between the aesthetic and the theoretical statement of the belief,
between Julian's glowing description of sunset, and the unnerv-
ing glibness of a couplet like this: 'for ever still/Is it not wise to
make the best of ill?' (46–7).

The following morning Julian visits Maddalo, and, while
waiting for him to dress, plays with his daughter:

A serious, subtle, wild, yet gentle being,
Graceful without design and unforeseeing,
With eyes – Oh speak not of her eyes! – which seem
Twin mirrors of Italian Heaven, yet gleam
With such deep meaning, as we never see
But in the human countenance . . . (145–50)

The description is not entirely successful, but it is an attempt to express the mystery of childhood, and the Wordsworthian cadence in its final two lines is appropriate. When Maddalo enters, Julian resumes their conversation of the preceding evening. Maddalo's mistake, he claims, is to think of man as a passive rather than an active creature, unable to make his own happiness. This time he does not point to a sunset to illustrate his belief, but to a human being, Maddalo's daughter:

> See
> This lovely child, blithe, innocent and free;
> She spends a happy time with little care,
> While we to such sick thoughts subjected are,
> As came on you last night . . . (167–70)

In being used as an illustration the child degenerates from a human being to a stereotype. Her seriousness, her subtlety, her depth are dissolved into a confection of adult sentiment. The inconsistency exposes the absurdity of Julian's claim. The goal he proposes for man's energetic activity appears to be a relapse into childhood.

The issue at stake becomes clearer when Maddalo refers Julian to the maniac, a man, he claims, who once held views like those asserted by Julian, but who was driven mad by a revelation of the distance between his aspirations and reality. Maddalo suggests to Julian that they visit him, and listen to his 'wild talk', an exercise which, according to Maddalo, will expose to Julian the futility of his 'aspiring theories'. Julian retorts, 'I hope to prove the induction otherwise'. His response is a startling confirmation of the reader's doubts about his character. The coldly logical expression applied to a painful human predicament impresses the reader as callous. Shelley could not but have been aware of the response that he was provoking. In Book I of *The Excursion*, a poem that Shelley read with careful attention, the pedlar and his young disciple are troubled by exactly this problem, the morality of using painful human experience as a dumbbell with which to exercise the moral imagination.

Julian hopes to prove that the madman was driven mad by his inability to sustain the search for 'a "soul of goodness" in things ill', that his madness resulted from his inability to accept that his love might not be reciprocated, and that these failures result from his being, like Maddalo, 'by nature proud'. Maddalo suggests that the maniac's madness is the result of a temperament like Julian's; Julian retorts that he is probably more like Maddalo. They agree to accept the madman as the arbitrator between their positions, and set out to visit him. Shelley's poem is written from within a tradition originating with Horace that he receives through the eighteenth century. The flexible couplets of the poem's first part are developed from the colloquial ease of Pope in poems like his *Imitations of Horace*, unlike, say, Hunt's couplets, which are written in conscious difiance of Pope's tradition. Thus far the poem has apparently been concerned to establish an opposition between two general points of view, Julian's optimistic voluntarism and Maddalo's pessimistic fatalism, particularised by the personalities of their adherents. To resolve such disputes the Augustan poet seeks a middle path between the two extremes. So, in the *Epistle to Bathurst*, after contrasting the frugality of the elder Cotta with the extravagance of his son, Pope turns to Bathurst to be taught: 'That secret rare, between th'extremes to move/Of mad good-nature and of mean self-love'. Shelley's poem with its concentration on positions of poise between two states; the beach between the sea and the land, sunset between night and day, has prepared the reader for a similar manoeuvre. But the central section of the poem does not present a normative viewpoint reconciling Maddalo's recognition of the reality of human weakness with Julian's insistence that man is capable of bettering his situation; it consists of the rambling monologue of a lunatic.

The Augustan technique establishes the point of virtue by bisecting a line drawn between two antithetical vices. But Shelley's concern is not to demonstrate rationally the correctness of a particular ethical theory – such a demonstration he would probably have regarded as theoretically impossible – but to force moral theory to implicate itself with the whole man. For all its elegant symmetry Pope's manoeuvre is only pseudo-rational. The contrasting vices themselves define the point of virtue, which in turn establishes the vices as deviations from the virtuous norm. The implicit argument is circular. The technique is conservative and rhetorical rather than exploratory. The validity of Bathurst's ethic is not tested, its gracefulness is celebrated by the elegance of Pope's exposition of it. But the madman's monologue forces both Julian and Maddalo to realise the human implications of their theories by testing them against

an extreme situation. 'We want,' Shelley argues, 'the creative
faculty to imagine that which we know . . . we want the poetry
of life . . .'.[32] The madman forces the two friends to imagine
what they know: his speech is, as they recognise after overhearing it, 'the poetry of life'. The disjunction within the poem that
separates the madman's monologue from its frame is thematic; it
embodies the disjunction within Julian and Maddalo of moral
theory and living experience, of ethos and pathos, of the
language of morals and the language of self-love.

The two friends stand outside the madman's room to overhear
his words. He has been driven mad by a disappointment in love,
a conventional enough predicament, except that his outburst is
frightening in its intensity and directness. He imagines himself
talking to his lady, and remembers how she had wished:

> That you had never seen me – never heard
> My voice, and more than all had ne'er endured
> The deep pollution of my loathed embrace –
> That your eyes ne'er had lied love in my face –
> That, like some maniac monk, I had torn out
> The nerves of manhood by their bleeding root
> With mine own quivering fingers . . . (420–6)

Not until Browning, who knew this poem well, wrote *The Ring
and the Book* do we find again an expression of sexual disgust as
direct as this in narrative poetry. His rebuff obsesses the maniac:

> Thou wilt tell
> With the grimace of hate, how horrible
> It was to meet my love when thine grew less . . . (460–2)

The first part of the poem dramatises a social or public
argument, to resolve which Julian and Maddalo listen to a
madman's monologue concerning his own ultimately private
predicament. The terms of the two parts of the poem do not
appear to overlap. And that is the point. There is no way in
which the friends can assimilate such an outburst with their
comfortably serious debate. After overhearing it, Julian recalls,
'our argument was quite forgot'. It reveals the theoretical debate
as insignificant, valueless, because neither theorist can assimilate
the madman's extreme, though undeniably human, situation

within his theory. Shelley confronts his two theorists with an extreme human situation, but their theories crumple under the impact.

The maniac's sexual insecurity could not be contained: it has forced itself outwards until it has effected the destruction of his social personality. It has made it impossible for him to secure that distinction between private emotion and public behaviour on which almost all forms of normal activity depend. The maniac denies this. He claims that 'what may tame/My heart, must leave the understanding free'. But his speech shows otherwise. His confusion is dramatised by his hallucinations. When he speaks to his lady, is he using a rhetorical device, or does he imagine her present? The question has lost significance for him. Sometimes he imagines that he is writing his speech: 'from my pen the words flow as I write'. But he adds that the sheet of paper burns into his brain, 'blotting all things fair/And wise which time had written there'. Paper, ink and pen swing wildly between a literal and a metaphorical reference. The maniac is no longer capable of distinguishing the real from the hallucinatory, the literal from the metaphorical, the public from the private. In this he contrasts with Julian and Maddalo. They distinguish clearly between the tenor and the vehicle of their metaphors. Julian's comparison between 'waste and desolate places' and 'the boundless soul' to which he aspires is lucidly articulated. Maddalo announces his intention to use the madhouse as a metaphor by referring to it as an 'emblem' and a 'sign'. The clarity of their figures demonstrates, in comparison with the madman, their sanity, but it also embodies the separation each maintains between theory and practice. Maddalo's theory is nihilistic, and yet he is a pleasant friend, and a benevolent man, who has done all that was in his power to ameliorate the madman's situation. Julian has a rare gift for responding to places and to people, and yet, in pursuit of a theory, he can reduce the madman to so much data from which he hopes to prove an induction. One remembers that Laon and Cythna whose theory and practice are perfectly one, both suffered illnesses in which they, like the madman, lost their sanity, and were unable to distinguish reality from hallucination.

Maddalo thought of man as a tower which turns a blank face to the world, and houses in secret its conflicting emotions. His expression of this predicament was complacent. Manifest in it was a Byronic enjoyment of its fiercely assumed gloominess.

But the madman, unlike Maddalo, is enclosed in an actual tower. He is the real victim of the psychic plight which Maddalo, as it were, entertains. The need to hide his pain from others, to enclose it in a fortified tower, is to the madman not an aesthetically pleasing conceit, but a torture:

> O, not to dare
> To give a human voice to my despair,
> But live and move, and wretched thing! smile on
> As if I never went aside to groan . . . (304–7)

Maddalo maintained his complacency by characterising the life of the psyche innocuously as 'thoughts and desires'. But the madman's thoughts and desires are specific, and of an intolerable intensity. The maniac exposes Maddalo's melancholia as an aesthetic pose. Listening to the madman forces Maddalo to understand his theory as living experience, to comprehend it in the full rather than the limiting sense of the word aesthetically.

Julian wished his soul to be 'boundless'. He wished that it extended over the whole of the perceived universe. The madman has achieved this state. He sympathises with the pain of others 'even as a man with his peculiar wrong'. But this is not, for him, a condition to be celebrated naïvely: 'Me – who am as a nerve o'er which do creep/The else unfelt oppressions of the earth . . .' (449–50). His extraordinary sensitivity leaves him a prey to other people's distresses; they crawl over him like lice. Julian's confidence is supreme:

> We are assured
> Much may be conquered, much may be endured
> Of what degrades and crushes us. (182–4)

But the madman, who, unlike Julian, speaks from experience, makes the same claim 'far more sadly': 'I live to show/How much men bear and die not' (459–60). Suffering has incapacitated him from any normal activity. That death is withheld is more a curse than a blessing. The last words that he speaks are a wish to die.

In listening to the madman, Julian and Maddalo both experience the emotional consequences of the theories they have espoused, and the intensity of the experience obliterates the theories: 'our argument was quite fotgot'. They are struck instead by the quality of the madman's speech. Julian remarks that: 'the wild language of his grief was high/Such as in measure were called poetry' (541–2). Maddalo crystallises the same observation in a sardonic epigram:

> Most wretched men
> Are cradled into poetry by wrong,
> They learn in suffering what they teach in song. (544–6)

They both agree that the madman is a type of the poet, and their recognition of this exposes the aesthetic daring of Shelley's poem. In effect, the polished, civilised excellence of the verse in the poem's first part is rejected in favour of the rambling, chaotic verse, barely contained within the couplet form, of the madman. The verse of the first part of the poem is appropriate to Julian and Maddalo: it is sane, but it is also the verse of a divided personality, in which thought and feeling exist separately, unrelated one to another. In the madman's speech thought and feeling have collapsed into one another. In him this has resulted in, or rather, is a product of, insanity, and yet his language is the chaos of a poem, whereas the language of Julian and Maddalo is an obstruction to poetry. The madman speaks such language as 'in measure were called poetry'. The word 'measure' is important to Shelley; it does not refer only to poetic metre. Language, Asia tells us, created thought, and thought is 'the measure of the universe'.[33] The madman's insanity prevents him from 'measuring' his language, from creating from words the order and unity which, for Shelley, is the supreme characteristic of art. But the poem's first section, it is suggested, is poetry only if measured language is merely a synonym for metrical language.

Julian and Maddalo begins from within a tradition which is Horatian and Popean only to become, in the madman's speech, a fierce attack upon itself. No one nowadays is likely to accept the validity of the attack, but it is a stage in an important tradition of British criticism, a tradition summed up by Arnold when he judged that Dryden and Pope produced poetry 'conceived and composed in their wits', rather than 'genuine poetry', which is 'conceived and composed in the soul'.[34] It is not necessary to agree with the criticism in order to concede its point. Agreement with Shelley is, in any case, less important that an understanding of his technique, and its difference from other verse attacks on the English Augustans, such as that contained in Keats's *Sleep and Poetry*. In Shelley's poem the Popean tradition is assimilated before it is rejected, and the accomplishment of the assimilation prevents an immediate dismissal of the rejection. Keats attacks Popean verse; Shelley, like Coleridge, understands that verse as the expression of a particular mode of thought. His attack has a breadth which Keats's lacks. The first section of *Julian and Maddalo* is splendidly written, betraying an admiration for the tradition within which the poem begins. In most of Shelley's major poems, traditions of poetry are examined and rejected, but the rejection is consistent with a genuine affection for those traditions.

After the madman's soliloquy, Maddalo disappears from the poem. In its first section he was used to oppose Julian, but the madman's soliloquy results in Julian and Maddalo coming together, their argument forgotten. The contrast between them was specious, but, in the end irrelevant; rather like the contrast between the miserly Cotta and his extravagant son. The real opposition is between the two of them, and the madman, and when the poem reaches this realisation Maddalo becomes extraneous.

After leaving the asylum Julian toys with the idea of staying in Venice, to enjoy Maddalo's conversation, the 'subtle talk' which would help him towards self-knowledge, but primarily that he might try to cure the madman by seeking 'An entrance to the caverns of his mind'. But, the following morning, business concerns force him to leave Venice. The passage in which Julian describes his dilemma, whether to stay in Venice or to leave it (lines 547–83), is the climax of the poem. Julian hesitates between the claims of 'business', and his desire to understand and to order the forces locked within the caverns of the madman's mind. The madman's monologue has struck at his self-assurance. He feels within himself a lack of self-knowledge, which he hopes to remedy by talking with Maddalo, and a strange pain, which he hopes to remedy by curing the madman: 'I sought relief/From the deep tenderness that maniac wrought/Within me...' (565–7). His desire to cure the madman is, as he realises, also the expression of a desire to cure himself. But his plans are abandoned, and now, years afterwards, they seem to him to have been fanciful:

such dreams of baseless good
Oft come and go in crowds or solitude
And leave no trace . . . (578–80)

The meaning of this failure to pursue his 'dreams' is established in the poem's final paragraph. Julian returns to Venice as an old man with 'aged eyes' and 'wrinkled cheeks':

After many years
And many changes I returned; the name
Of Venice, and its aspect, was the same;
But Maddalo was travelling far away
Among the mountains of Armenia.
His dog was dead. His child had now become
A woman . . . (583–9)

A comparison between this passage and the description of the Lido which begins the poem is revealing. Then Julian, full of youthful enthusiasm, dominated and directed his situation. His mind flowed out to its environment. Now events are recorded guardedly, as if he is afraid to implicate himself with them. Note the suspicious caution in his reference to Venice. The short, clipped sentences express a defensiveness in the face of experience. He has undergone that gradual hardening of the personality against life that is the ordinary lot of the unheroic. He has become one of those who, in the quotation from *The Excursion* prefixed to *Alastor*, are said to have hearts as 'dry as summer dust', and whose lives 'Burn to the socket'. But this condition is presented with a new sympathy.

Julian is still able to recognise the beauty of Maddalo's daughter, who seems to him 'a wonder of this earth'. But as a young man her beauty had seemed to him essentially human; now he accepts it as extraordinary. And in his tribute to her there is a new emphasis on outward manners: 'kindly she,/And with a manner beyond courtesy/Received her father's friend . . .' (592–4). He compares her to 'one of Shakespeare's women'. The compliment is splendid, but detached, as if he has withdrawn finally into a narrowly aesthetic appreciation of humanity. It is very different from the compliment that the young Julian bestowed on Maddalo's daughter many years ago. Then her eyes gleamed: 'With such deep meaning as we never see/But in the human countenance' (149-50). The young Julian confidently sought the inner recesses of the human personality, for he believed that those recesses concealed only the loveliness of humanity. He asked Maddalo: 'Where is the love, beauty and truth we seek/But in our mind?' (174-5). But when the madman disclosed the contents of his 'pent mind', he revealed love, beauty and truth tangled with their opposites, hatred, ugliness and falsehood. Julian lacked the heroism to sustain his belief in the goodness of the centrally human, when forced to recognise that this required him also to encounter the grim spectres of the consciousness. He lacked exactly that heroism which Laon and Cythna pre-eminently display.

Julian's appearance at the end of the poem reveals the nature of his failure; frightened by a revelation of the potentially destructive power of the inner forces of the human mind, he has retreated into an appreciation of the outward. The beach and sunset acted initially as emblems of the meeting between Julian and Maddalo, two contrasting personalities. They are now best understood as representations of the point at which the heroic individual takes his stand, the point where the social and the inner personalities interact. The poet, the maker or creator, and the hero, are for Shelley equivalent terms. Venice, the city salvaged from the sea, becomes an embodiment of poetry, like Coleridge's 'stately pleasure dome', and for the same reason: the city is created out of opposing principles, sea and land. When Julian thought to stay in Venice, and to pass his time learning from Maddalo's 'subtle talk', and studying 'all the beatings of [the madman's] heart', he imagined to himself a heroic, poetic role. He proposed to take his stand between the outer and the inner, between character and consciousness, to become himself a point at which opposing forces might interact. But in the end he lacked the heroism to carry through the project; he retreated inland, into reassuring daylight.

He questions Maddalo's daughter about the madman's fate, and finally succeeds in extracting from her his history. He was reunited with his lady and recovered, but she left him again, and the madman died. Julian demands that Maddalo's daughter explain these events to him. She is at first unwilling to do so, thinking it too painful, but Julian insists. She sees no need to disinter the madman's story, for she has understood it. She has accepted and comprehended his pain, and her knowledge has left her serene. Julian refused such knowledge, and as a consequence the maniac still dominates his mind, is in something of the same relation to him as the Solitary in *The Excursion* was to Wordsworth. His confrontation with the madman failed to educate him, and became instead an unresolved trauma which stifled his future development, so that his once boundless faith in humanity has become a guarded distrust of all but select individuals: 'she told me how/All happened – but the cold world shall not know' (616–17).

The final justification for Shelley beginning his poem within a Horatian and eighteenth-century tradition is that *Julian and Maddalo* expresses the same fear of, and fascination with, the potentially destructive forces of irrationality within the human personality, that dominates a poem like *The Dunciad*, and which led Swift to praise, only half ironically, the philosopher who can 'content his ideas with the films and images that fly off upon the senses from the superficies of things . . .'. But whereas Pope and Swift can assert the heroism of the holding operation conducted by reason and by commonsense against the inner forces which threaten them, Shelley represents any such defence as a weak-minded retreat from the central springs of the human personality. The true hero would not attempt to resist, or to turn away from these inner forces, but to understand and harness them. Laon and Cythna accepted their time of madness, their nightmare visions, and were left strengthened in their revolutionary purpose. But the impact of the madman on Julian had an effect precisely similar to that made by the failure of the French revolution on its feeble supporters. He succumbs.

Donald Davie dislikes Shelley's 'abstractions', but in *Julian and Maddalo* he finds them less than disastrous:

In 'Julian and Maddalo', by inventing the figure and the predicament of the maniac, Shelley excuses this incoherency and presents it (plausibly enough) as a verbatim report of the lunatic's ravings: and in this way he preserves the decorum of the conversation piece (the poem is sub-titled 'A Conversation'). As a result, the whole of this passage, tiresome and unpoetic as it is, impairs but does not ruin the whole.[35]

Davie supposes that the poem's urbane frame offers a standard

which allows the reader to identify the madman's speech as
'ravings' while saving the poem from a similar charge. The
poem's frame for him provides a standard of the 'poetic' against
which the lunatic's monologue should be judged. But Davie
defies the poem's text; Julian and Maddalo agree that the
madman's monologue is peculiarly 'poetic', and far from
judging it, they are shamed by it: their argument is 'quite forgot'.
Shelley is not interested in 'preserving the decorum of the
conversation piece', but in disrupting it. The poem's epigraph is
from eclogue X, a quotation from Gallus's speech. In eclogue X
Virgil's pastoral frames Gallus's elegy, but the decorum of
pastoral is not preserved, it is shattered; eclogue X is Virgil's
last pastoral. Similarly, *Julian and Maddalo* is not a poem
which urbanely defends itself against the lunacy it contains: it
is a poem in which urbanity crumples under the impact of lunacy.

The poem is one of Shelley's successes not because Shelley
continues within it an eighteenth-century tradition of poetry, but
because the poem's meaning is expressed through the contrast
between its two styles, not simply within them. The language of
Julian and Maddalo and the language of the madman both
express modes of thought and feeling, so that the theme of the
poem becomes the contrast between its styles. This is why *Julian
and Maddalo* is so evidently a better poem than either *Alastor* or
Laon and Cythna. In *Julian and Maddalo* language is thought, in the
other two poems it merely contains thought.

The three poems I have discussed in this chapter are variations on
a single theme, the theme that dominates all of Shelley's major
poems. I have described the theme variously, even at the risk of
confusion, for it is protean, and to express it in a single form
would be misleading. I have spoken of it as a conflict between the
language of morals and the language of self-love, between the
real and the ideal, between ethos and pathos, and between
character and consciousness. Two conclusions have emerged.
There is no such division within Shelley's work as critics have
postulated. *Alastor, Laon and Cythna*, and *Julian and Maddalo*,
the Shelleyan 'platonic', the Shelleyan 'revolutionary', and the
Shelleyan 'urbane', are recognisably products of one rather
narrow range of preoccupations. Secondly, the comparative
success of Shelley's poems cannot be established by reference to

the relative intelligence of the ideas they contain. *Alastor* and *Laon and Cythna* are intelligent explorations of Shelley's central theme; that they are both, by and large, unsatisfying cannot therefore be attributed to intellectual immaturity. It is to the relationship between the poem's theme and its form that we must look to establish why it is that *Alastor* and *Laon and Cythna* are interesting failures, whereas *Julian and Maddalo* is a thoroughly satisfying poem.

Reading *Alastor* and *Laon and Cythna* one is conscious throughout of a certain laxity, of insufficient pressure being exerted on the poem's language and its shape. The same laxity results in both the superficial gloss of *Alastor*, a stylistic assurance borrowed rather than earned, and in the frequently ludicrous clumsiness of *Laon and Cythna*. *Alastor* exists passively within its Virgilian tradition, as does *Laon and Cythna* within the tradition of the Southeyan epic. Shelley's correction of Southey is an intellectual rather than an aesthetic challenge to the tradition, just as his rescue of the snake as a symbol of the good, in the poem's first canto, is a conceptual exercise, rather than a challenge to the conventions inherent in the English language. *Julian and Maddalo* is different in that Shelley's exploration of the poem's theme becomes also an exploration of a particular kind of poetry. Aesthetic and intellectual values coalesce. Take the disjunction between the madman's soliloquy, and the two passages that frame it, the poem's central structural characteristic. The structural disjunction embodies the different levels of the personality inhabited by Julian and Maddalo on the one hand, and the madman on the other. But it also signifies the point at which Shelley rejects the tradition within which the poem begins. The poem contains an aesthetic argument, an argument about the nature of poetry, which parallels its narrative argument. In the recognition that the madman is the type of the poet, these arguments fuse. Intelligence is evident in *Alastor* and *Laon and Cythna*, but only in *Julian and Maddalo* is the intelligence displayed essentially aesthetic, revealing itself through the poem rather than simply within the poem. In *Julian and Maddalo* the contrast between the two friends and the madman is also a contrast between two literary traditions. The poem is pivotal (Pope, as Shelley remarked to Byron, was, for the Romantics a 'pivot of a dispute in taste').[36] It becomes a means by which Shelley tests the ethical base of the tradition of poetry that culminated in the eighteenth century, and establishes the point at which he rejects it. So his poem both points backwards towards the eighteenth century, and forwards towards Browning's development of the dramatic monologue and the dramatised debate. In this it is characteristic of all Shelley's major poems.

4   *Prometheus Unbound*

Prometheus Unbound has provoked a bewildering variety of conflicting interpretations. 'Of such truths each to himself must be the oracle', says Asia in Demogorgon's cave, and a student of the poem's critics might be forgiven for concluding that the meaning of Shelley's drama is just such a truth. Newman White protested against this situation in 1925 in an article entitled '*Prometheus Unbound*, or Every Man His Own Allegorist',[1] but his protest has done nothing to deter the poem's interpreters.

If yet another reading of *Prometheus Unbound* is not to add more silt to already muddy waters, it must then perform two tasks. It must delimit the area defined by the poem within which valid interpretations have their place – 'All high poetry is infinite: it is the first acorn which contained all oaks potentially'.[2] But to accept that the meaning of a poem may be infinite is not to deny the possibility of misreading. Some trees are not oaks, and it is possible to define the qualities common to oaks as opposed to, say, beeches or poplars. Secondly, a reading of *Prometheus Unbound* ought to suggest why it is that the poem has provoked such richly but confusingly varied readings. The first task is best accomplished by examining the poem's structure, its shape, for any valid interpretation must conform to that shape. The second requires attention to the poem's theme. *Prometheus Unbound* is a drama centrally concerned with perception: it is a play about various modes of seeing the world. It offers its reader not so much an object to look at as a lens to look with. That a lens can be focused on all manner of objects, and that it is only performing its proper function when it is focused on an object, seems to me the proper explanation both for the variety of interpretations that *Prometheus Unbound* has yielded and for the determination of critics to fly in the face of Newman White by continuing to offer interpretations of it. These will be the two concerns of the discussion that follows.

The structure of *Prometheus Unbound* has been described most

133

entertainingly by those critics who disapprove of it. Olwen Campbell writes:

> A drama must end to some extent in the key in which it began. What an offence against the inner logic of the three unities is a play which begins with Prometheus and the Furies in Time and Caucasus, and ends with the Sun and Moon in Elysium and Eternity! When Shelley unbinds his Prometheus, his drama falls all to bits, and his stage becomes a chaos. The real actors are crowded out of it, while portions of the scenery, the full orchestra and the flashing lights make glorious havoc of the whole.[3]

It is possible to be in broad agreement with this description without accepting the adverse judgement that it supports. Campbell believes that 'a drama must end to some extent in the key in which it began'. She has a notion of the well-made play that exists independently of the action that the play dramatises. But Shelley's play is an embodiment of the dramatic action that it represents; it is not a container for that action but a means through which the action is expressed. *Prometheus Unbound* has often been criticised on the grounds that it contains only one dramatic action, Prometheus's revocation of his curse. Though an overstatement, this approaches the truth. But Shelley wrote a play almost without action, because the central dramatic activity that the play represents is the evolving shape of the play itself.

In his preface Shelley compares his drama with Aeschylus's *Prometheus Bound* and with *Paradise Lost*. For both his models he expresses a high but qualified admiration. He has chosen not to attempt to restore the lost plays of Aeschylus partly because he feared the result of 'the high comparison such an event would challenge', but principally because he was 'averse from a catastrophe so feeble as that of reconciling the Champion with the Oppressor of mankind'. He compares Prometheus with Milton's Satan, but insists that Milton's 'magnificent fiction' is flawed by his representation of Satan as a character combining 'courage, and majesty, and firm and patient opposition to omnipotent force' with other vicious traits, 'envy, revenge, and a desire for personal aggrandisement'. Shelley takes as his models two masterpieces of which he disapproves. But only admiration is apparent in the play's first speech. Prometheus chained on Caucasus addresses Jupiter:

Monarch of Gods and Daemons, and all Spirits
But One, who throng those bright and rolling worlds...

The syntax and the diction are borrowed from Books I and II of *Paradise Lost*, the substance of the speech closely follows Aeschylus.[4] *Prometheus Unbound* begins as an imitation of Greek drama written in a blank verse imitated from Milton.

For Shelley the defining quality of poetry is its achieved unity of form and content. As he puts it in his preface: 'nothing can be equally well expressed in prose that is not tedious and supererogatory in verse'. Therefore the action in the play must be unified with the action of the play. Prometheus's first action is to seek a confrontation with his own past self, to ask to hear again the curse with which he had instituted his 3000-year struggle against Jupiter, and similarly the play itself begins in a confrontation with its models. The raising of the ghosts of Aeschylus and Milton in the form of the play is analogous to the raising of the ghost of Jupiter who repeats Prometheus's curse in its action. The ghosts are raised in order to be laid. In *Prometheus Unbound* the past is invoked only that the future might be freed from its grasp. In this it is quite different from Shelley's later lyrical drama *Hellas*.

Hellas is a dismal celebration of the Greek struggle for independence from Turkish rule, dismal because although Shelley prophesies a Turkish defeat, he nowhere predicts that the Greeks will achieve their end. The play makes best sense if one understands it as a representation of a conflict that both sides are destined to lose, and to lose for precisely the same reason. The Sultan Mahmud, wishing to learn the future of his dynasty, takes counsel of the magus Ahasuerus. He hears his ruin prophesied by the ghost of his great ancestor Mahomet the Second. The Sultan is condemned to look back at past greatness and this makes inevitable his defeat. But the Greeks, represented in the play by a chorus of Greek women, are in exactly the same predicament. They yearn for the golden age of Greek democracy to be restored; they too are committed to an ideal embodied in the past, and in the play's final chorus they realise the futility of their aspiration. The chorus begins confidently and conventionally:

'The world's great age begins anew,/The golden years return...'. The heroic exploits of legendary Greece will be repeated. The chorus becomes anxious as it recalls some of the more disturbing events of Greek history. The return of the past entails the return of the Trojan wars, of the miseries of Oedipus. For a moment they discount the logic of this disquieting perception, but in the final stanza of the chorus, the last lines of the poem, they realise it crushingly: 'O, cease! must hate and death return?/Cease! must men kill and die?' The women began by celebrating the return of the golden age, of the past: they end by wishing the past destroyed: 'The world is weary of the past,/Oh, might it die or rest at last!'

Hellas is a play about people who have abandoned the possibility of a future by committing themselves to nostalgia for a lost past. In *Hellas* retrospection is a psychic block, but in *Prometheus Unbound* it is therapeutic. The past is confronted only in order to remove the obstacles erected in the past against change.

In his first speech, Prometheus, chained to a frozen mountain summit, addresses Jupiter. The world is asleep, only Jupiter and Prometheus keep watch, 'Thou and I'. Prometheus begins the play isolated in a lonely confrontation with Jupiter. The form of Aeschylean drama and the style of *Paradise Lost* were not, for Shelley, independent of the thought that they contained. They were vehicles embodying a particular perception of the world, and they had something in common. *Prometheus Bound* and *Paradise Lost* were the two most powerful expressions available to Shelley of a particular form of dualism. Aeschylus depicts Prometheus, champion of mankind, fixed in an attitude of defiant opposition to Zeus. *Paradise Lost* begins similarly with Satan defeated, but unbowed in his opposition to god. Aeschylus represents a world with two centres, one human, one divine. The tragic hero is confronted with an impossible choice, whether to conform to a divine or a human standard of conduct. To follow the divine standard is to lose all claims to human sympathy, but to follow, like Prometheus, the human standard is to incur the wrath of the gods. Shelley makes clear in his preface that for him the situations of both Aeschylus's Prometheus and Milton's Satan were similar. Shelley's drama too begins with Prometheus fixed in defiant opposition to Jupiter; hence the stylistic indebtedness to Milton, and the substantial indebtedness to Aeschylus in Prometheus's first speech are appropriate.

Shelley's play begins from within a situation familiar to readers of Blake. The mind is divided. It has rejected a part of its own substance, accrediting to that part an independent reality. As consequence the mind is frozen (the first act is set in a 'ravine of icy rocks'); it has become a mirror image of its rejected self, unable to act by its own will any more than a reflection can move itself, unable to move that part of the self that it reflects for it has denied its identity with that part. The best-known passage in Act I creates an image of this situation:

> Ere Babylon was dust,
> The Magus Zoroaster, my dead child,
> Met his own image walking in the garden.
> That apparition, sole of men, he saw.
> For know there are two worlds of life and death:
> One that which thou beholdest; but the other
> Is underneath the grave... (I, 191–7)

There are two worlds, existing in a perfect, symmetrical relationship. Symmetry, static pattern, is described as the law of existence, and it makes any action impossible. In Act I this symmetry must be disrupted before any change is possible.

Prometheus's first speech is proud; he glories in his untamed opposition to Jupiter. He defines himself in opposition to the god that he hates. But Shelley works to deny the reality of such an opposition even as Prometheus asserts it. Prometheus begins his speech by recognising that he and Jupiter 'alone of living things' keep watch. The two are bound together by their mutual opposition, isolated not from each other, but from the world they inhabit. They are 'alone', and the word suggests not only their isolation, but also that they are in some sense one. Prometheus is determined to deny this perception, but his language repeatedly betrays him. Jupiter reigns:

> Whilst me, who am thy foe, eyeless in hate,
> Hast thou made reign and triumph, to thy scorn,
> O'er mine own misery and thy vain revenge. (I, 9–11)

Grammar insists that it is Jupiter who has made Prometheus

reign over his own misery, but word order suggests that it is
Prometheus who has allowed Jupiter to reign. Reigning and
triumphing are activities ascribed to Prometheus only by a
Satanic paradox; they are natural to Jupiter. The phrase 'eyeless
in hate' attaches itself either to Prometheus or to Jupiter
depending on the reader's intonation. The phrase 'to thy scorn'
may contain either an objective or a subjective genitive; either
Jupiter scorns Prometheus for his physical degradation, or
Prometheus scorns Jupiter for his moral baseness. The syntactic
ambiguities begin the play's opening theme, the representation
of Jupiter and Prometheus as interchangeable.

Prometheus and Jupiter are bound together by mutual hatred
and mutual scorn. Hatred and scorn are emotions that fix their
subject and object in a static relationship. The only change that
they allow is a simple reversal, and Prometheus looks forward to
such a change. He welcomes the passing hours:

> And yet to me welcome is day and night,
> Whether one breaks the hoar frost of the morn,
> Or starry, dim, and slow, the other climbs
> The leaden-coloured east; for then they lead
> The wingless, crawling hours, one among whom
> – As some dark Priest hales the reluctant victim
> Shall drag thee, cruel King, to kiss the blood
> From these pale feet, which then might trample thee
> If they disdained not such a prostrate slave. (I, 44–52)

Prometheus would then be forced from his cross, but only that
Jupiter might suffer a similar fate and become himself a sacrificial
victim. The relationship between the two would remain
unchanged. Prometheus and Jupiter are interchangeable, like
Napoleon and Louis. Such an attitude is a perversion of
Prometheus's true nature, and the verse reveals this. Prometheus
welcomes the evening when 'starry, dim, and slow it climbs/The
leaden-coloured east'. He welcomes it, he tells us, because it
brings nearer the hour of his revenge. But the description belies
the motive, or rather the motive is a betrayal of the description,
substituting for the beautiful ritual of the daily cycle the obscene
ritual enacted by the priest and his victim. The description gives
evidence of an unperverted Prometheus who has better reason
for welcoming night than that it brings closer his revenge.

In his opening soliloquy Prometheus struggles against his hatred and scorn of Jupiter. 'Disdain! Ah no! I pity thee,' he claims, and adds, 'I hate no more/As then ere misery made me wise.' But his rejections of hatred and scorn alternate with longing anticipations of revenge. In the opening soliloquy there is a contest between an old desire for revenge and a new pity, and this represents the struggle in which Prometheus has been engaged for 3000 years, since he was first bound to the mountain. It is to end this struggle that he asks to hear again the curse that had initiated his struggle with Jupiter. Both the form of the drama and its action insist that to exorcise a ghost one must first raise it. The ghost chosen to repeat Prometheus's curse is the phantasm of Jupiter.

Panthea's description of the ghost is similar to several descriptions of Prometheus in Act I[5]: 'Cruel he looks, but calm and strong,/Like one who does, not suffers wrong'. Panthea tries to distinguish the agent from the victim of suffering, but she does so ineptly. She seems to isolate calmness and strength as the distinctive characteristics of the tyrant, and these are qualities that Prometheus shares with Jupiter: 'Fiend, I defy thee with a calm, fixed mind . . .'. That the ghost of Jupiter repeats the curse first spoken by Prometheus is Shelley's succinct conclusion to the opening theme of his drama, the presentation of Jupiter and the unregenerate Prometheus as interchangeable. But Prometheus's decision not to allow his own ghost to repeat the curse is the first indication that he has it in him to break the deadlock.

As a part of his curse on Jupiter Prometheus had prayed that the hour might come 'when thou must appear to be/That which thou art internally'. That hour has now come. Jupiter appears as he is internally, and internally he is a ghost, lacking any real substance, that appears only when summoned by Prometheus. Prometheus has allowed independent reality to what in truth is only a ghost of his own imagination. But the curse is now spoken to Prometheus; it rebounds onto its original author. As the phantasm speaks it mimics Prometheus's own 'gestures' and 'looks', demonstrating that when the curse was first spoken Prometheus was 'internally' identical with Jupiter. He was Jupiter pretending to be Prometheus. The Jupiter in him spoke, although he pretended that his words were Promethean.

Curses are double-edged – they strike at their object and their subject. Prometheus discovers what Jupiter is internally, but only by discovering what he is, or was, himself. The form of the whole curse insists on this truth, for it occupies four stanzas, in the third and fourth of which Prometheus curses Jupiter, but only after having in the first two stanzas cursed himself. The curse was fulfilled at the moment it was spoken. Prometheus suffered, as he had asked, the hatred of Jupiter, and Jupiter suffered the tyrant's lot, and reigned, as Prometheus demanded that he should, in 'self-torturing solitude', condemned to fall only after 'many a false and fruitless crime'. One of the reasons that Shelley does not follow Aeschylus in dramatising the binding of Prometheus is that in his play the chains are forged and hammered home not by Hephaestus but by Prometheus himself.

The curse is symmetrical. It devotes two stanzas to Prometheus and two to Jupiter. This kind of symmetry, the symmetry of confrontation, is the presiding aesthetic pattern of Act I. The curse fixed Prometheus and Jupiter in a symmetrical relationship in which 'I' exactly reflected 'Thou', and only one development, interchange, was possible. Jupiter might become Prometheus's sacrificial victim, he might repeat Prometheus's curse.

Having heard his curse repeated, Prometheus rejects it: 'It doth repent me: words are quick and vain . . .'. The Earth reacts with despair. She understands Prometheus's change of heart as a signal of his final submission to Jupiter. But she is mistaken. Immediately after the revocation of the curse Mercury, Jove's messenger, descends to demand that Prometheus submit to Jupiter. Prometheus refuses. The contrast between him and Mercury fixes the distinction between a proper refusal to hate and an improper submission to power recognised as evil.

Prometheus began the play regarding a universe in which good was poised against evil, 'I' against 'Thou', himself against Jupiter. His manichaeanism was protective: it enabled him to dissociate himself from evil. But it was also stultifying because he imagined evil to be independent of his will. In rejecting the curse Prometheus rejects the primacy of the confrontation between Jupiter and himself. When he repents having cursed Jupiter, recognising that his words were 'quick and vain', he accepts evil or Jupiter as a part of his own nature. The sign of this is that the kind of pain to which he is subjected changes. At the beginning of the play his pain was physical, externally imposed. He was tortured by cold, earthquake, and by 'Heaven's wingèd hound'. Now that he has accepted within himself a potential for evil he becomes subject to mental pain.

The Furies unleashed against Prometheus by Mercury are, as they explain, mental realities: 'we will be dread thought beneath thy brain,/And foul desire round thine astonished heart...' (I, 488–9). They present to Prometheus a vision of a world in which good and evil are hopelessly entangled. He is shown Christ on the cross, and then the barbarities perpetrated in Christ's name. He is shown a people united in peace and love striving for freedom, who then, like the French revolutionaries, divide into murderous factions and are defeated. He is subjected to what Shelley considered the greatest temptation of the age, despair; tempted to react as Wordsworth did to the perversion of the French Revolution:

> I lost
> All feeling of conviction, and, in fine,
> Sick, wearied out with contrarieties,
> Yielded up moral questions in despair...

These 'contrarieties' are the theme of the last and most impressive vision vouchsafed by the Furies to Prometheus. The loftiest:

> dare not devise good for man's estate,
> And yet they know not that they do not dare.
> The good want power, but to weep barren tears.
> The powerful goodness want: worse need for them.
> The wise want love; and those who love want wisdom;
> And all best things are thus confused to ill.
> Many are strong and rich, and would be just,
> But live among their suffering fellow men
> As if none felt: they know not what they do. (I, 623–31)

Prometheus replies by accepting the truth of the Fury's words: 'I pity those they torture not'. This is the true resolution of the conflict represented in Act I. Prometheus has substituted pity for his initial scorn, but more than that, he has accepted pain as the badge of his own humanity. He is no longer subjected to pain, he has assumed it.

A chorus of comforting spirits arrives, the balance to the Furies that preserves the symmetrical structure of the act. Like the Furies their existence is mental, their homes are 'the dim caves of human thought'. The Furies had shown Prometheus evil hatched from good, the spirits concentrate on illustrations of how good may arise from evil. After their songs two more spirits arrive, one from the East, the other from the West. They come from opposite quarters of the globe, but Ione addresses them as 'Twin nurslings'. They sing of 'love' and 'ruin' connected by a necessary law. The 'best and gentlest':

> Dream visions of aëreal joy, and call the monster, Love,
> And wake, and find the shadow Pain, as he whom now we
> greet. (I, 778–9)

The last two spirits deal with exactly the same 'contrarieties' that had been the theme of the last Fury. The comforting spirits and the Furies merge just as the two spirits from the east and west descend as 'two doves to one belovèd nest'.

Prometheus began Act I in a universe radically divided between evil and himself, or injured merit. In remembering his curse Prometheus recognises the evil in himself. Good and evil, instead of standing against one another in static opposition, enter his mind successively as the Furies and the comforting spirits. Finally Fury and spirit merge in a single, coherent vision of a world in which good and evil mingle, and interchange. Good may result from evil, evil from good. To Prometheus this development seems a defeat. He began the act glorying in his crucifixion, proud in his opposition to Jupiter. He ends it in a mood of quiet, passive emptiness. Nevertheless, during the act he has won a limited victory. He began it in a sterile confrontation with Jupiter. By accepting both good and evil in himself he has transformed uncreative physical strife into mental strife. Progression is now possible, but it must be undertaken by someone other than himself:

> Most vain all hope but love; and thou art far,
> Asia! who, when my being overflowed,
> Wert like a golden chalice to bright wine
> Which else had sunk into the thirsty dust. (I, 808–11)

Without Asia, without love, Prometheus can find only an uncreative, onanistic relief.

Act I is concerned with the past. All its major events, from Prometheus's recalling of his curse to the vision of Christ's crucifixion and of the French Revolution are recreations of the past. Similarly the act begins in a formal imitation of Aeschylean drama and a stylistic imitation of Miltonic blank verse. But just as Prometheus remembers the past only in order to revoke it, recalls it (brings it to mind) only in order to recall it (take it back), so Shelley recalls Aeschylus and Milton in the first act only to free himself from their control. By the end of the act the character of the blank verse has changed:

> Deeply in truth; but the eastern star looks white,
> And Asia waits in that far Indian vale,
> The scene of her sad exile... (I, 825–7)

It has become authentically Shelleyan.

The first achievement of Act I is the decision to confront the ghosts of the past, the second is the refusal of the polarised world described by Aeschylus and Milton. Early in the act the Earth speaks of Zoroaster as 'my dead child'. The prophet is dead, but his teachings must also be laid to rest.[6] To describe the universe as a confrontation between mutually opposed principles is to confer on the individual only one duty. Like Prometheus at the beginning of the play he must embrace good as his 'I', and cast aside evil as a rejected 'thou'. But to reject anything is to guarantee its continued existence, for in rejecting evil, in denying that evil is a part of himself, the individual abandons his control over it; he enthrones it as Prometheus enthroned Jupiter. Prometheus emerges from this deadlock by accepting evil as a part of his own nature, while still refusing, as his reply to Mercury makes clear, to bow to its authority.

Act I is a passion, Act II is a quest. Act I is a single scene, Act II is made up of five scenes. Throughout Act I Prometheus is chained to a rock. All events and characters of the act centre on the single, static figure. Throughout Act II Asia is moving. In Act I Prometheus succeeds in diverting his mind from hatred and scorn to pity. But pity is not an emotion that can create. At its best it is an emotion that redresses the wrongs of the past. It is the emotion appropriate to Act I, for Act I is concerned with the past, with recalling. But Act II is a narrative, a movement towards the future. The emotion that controls it is not pity but

love, because, for Shelley, love is essentially active, 'a going out
of our own nature'. Pity may dominate a static scene, but the
dramatic action appropriate to love is a journey, a movement. In
Act II Asia journeys to the cave of Demogorgon.

   In Act II scene i Panthea arrives in the Indian vale where Asia
has lived since her separation from Prometheus. She bears a
message for Asia in the form of a dream, dreamt as she slept at the
feet of Prometheus. Her dream is of Prometheus transfigured;
her experience of the dream was overpoweringly sexual:

> I saw not, heard not, moved not, only felt
> His presence flow and mingle through my blood
> Till it became his life, and his grew mine . . . (II, i, 79–81)

But Asia dismisses Panthea's account of the dream:

>   Thou speakest, but thy words
> Are as the air: I feel them not: Oh, lift
> Thine eyes, that I may read his written soul! (II, i, 108–10)

In Act I Prometheus failed to understand the language of his
mother, the Earth. He heard her only as an 'inorganic voice'. The
speeches of Prometheus and the Earth form a coherent dialogue,
but this is chance, or perhaps an indication that Prometheus still
intuitively understands a language that he has consciously forgotten. Isolated in his combat with Jupiter he has lost contact
with his natural mother, and forgotten her language. Asia's
failure to understand her sister is significantly different. She
rejects all secondhand accounts of experience in favour of the
experience itself. She looks into Panthea's eyes and recreates the
dream.

   Panthea had two dreams but can remember only one. The
other dream eludes her, but it cannot elude Asia's intuitive gaze.
She sees a shape interposed between herself and Panthea:

> What shape is that between us? Its rude hair
> Roughens the wind that lifts it, its regard
> Is wild and quick, yet 'tis a thing of air,
> For through its gray robe gleams the golden dew
> Whose stars the noon has quenched not. (II, i, 127–31)

Like the bard of *Kubla Khan* the shape has 'flashing eyes' and 'floating hair'. He is the poet in his bardic, prophetic role, and he frees the poem. He initiates Asia's journey, calls on her to 'follow', and so breaks the static pattern of the play. He prompts Asia to a journey which results formally in a release from the constrictions of the Greek dramatic model and culminates dramatically in the release of Prometheus from his chains. His appearance is pivotal, because it marks Shelley's assumption of a new role. Act I began in imitation of Aeschylus and Milton: the poem began in homage to its models. But the appearance of the prophetic bard at the beginning of Act II indicates the the poem now owes its duty not to the past but to the future. The forgotten dream that Asia reveals parallels the forgotten curse that Prometheus recalls. But remembering the curse frees Prometheus from a negative emotion, hatred; it frees him from a past, but does not create a future. The recreation of the dream releases Asia into action, prompts her to engage in a quest.

Prometheus as he appeared in Act I is not the Prometheus of Panthea's dream. Panthea describes a Prometheus equipped with 'soft and flowing limbs', 'passion–parted lips' and 'keen, faint eyes', hardly an appropriate representation of the embattled Titan of Act I. That Prometheus was a Christ of the cold countries, a Germanic Christ, his heroism manifest in the greatness of his sufferings. The Prometheus described by Panthea is a Christ by Correggio,[7] experiencing his crucifixion erotically rather than tragically. The protagonist of Act I is Prometheus, but the protagonist of Act II is Asia. Her's is the controlling perspective, and the Prometheus she sees is arrayed 'In the soft light of his own smiles'. The play jumps from one mode of perception to another.

A passage from *A Defence of Poetry* is helpful in defining the distinction between the two kinds of perception:

> We want the creative faculty to imagine that which we know; we want the generous impulse to act that which we imagine; we want the poetry of life; our calculations have outrun our conception; we have eaten more than we can digest. The cultivation of those sciences which have enlarged the limits of the empire of man over the external world has for want of the poetical faculty circumscribed those of the internal world; and man, having enslaved the elements, remains himself a slave.[8]

Prometheus is the enslaver of the elements, the stealer of fire, and his inventiveness has resulted in a circumscription of the limits of the internal world; Prometheus is enchained. Man has remained himself a slave; Prometheus protests to Jupiter that the Earth is 'Made multitudinous with thy slaves'. Even at the end of Act I Prometheus is impotent. He 'would fain/Be what it is [his] destiny to be', but he is sunk in passive resignation: 'Earth can console, Heaven can torment no more'. He lacks the 'creative faculty to imagine that which he knows, and he identifies what he lacks as love: 'Most vain all hope but love, and thou art far,/Asia'. The separation between Prometheus and Asia is, then, analogous to the separation between the intellectual and the imaginative faculties that Shelly diagnosed in the world around him. The movement from Act I to Act II is a movement from one mode of perception to another.

Act II scene i begins in an atmosphere of sensual languor. Panthea's wings as she flies to Asia are 'faint with the delight of a remembered dream', and the dream she remembers is erotic. Shelley saw a relation between the decline of Greek literature and the decline of the Greek democracies. The poet writing in a society ruled by a tyrant addresses himself to 'those faculties which are the last to be destroyed' by the debilitating effects on the human personality of unjust government. He is thinking of the Greek pastoral poets, in particular of Theocritus, and the faculties most resistant to tyranny are the sensual, especially the erotic.[9] Asia has reacted to the tyranny of Jupiter just as Theocritus reacted to his Sicilian tyrant. She has created a pastoral landscape into which she has retreated. But her retreat has been at a cost. The poetry of Theocritus and his school lacks the 'harmony of the union of all faculties' that characterises the work of the greatest poets, in which the senses and the intellect are fused. Nevertheless, the poetical faculty, even when it has retreated into a pastoral vale, 'contains within itself the seeds at once of its own and social renovation'. Asia, unlike Prometheus, can act. She sees the prophetic bard and she obeys his summons to follow. She leaves her vale and goes on a journey to the top of a mountain, and then down into its crater. At the beginning of the act she is a pastoral princess, but she abandons her flowered valley for a more demanding landscape. When she descends into the mountain crater, she is an epic hero descending into the underworld. In Act II scene ii two fauns talk together somewhat coyly. The scene is modelled on Virgil's sixth eclogue,[10] but the descent to Demogorgon's cave has as its analogue the sixth aeneid. In Act II poetry breaks out of a pastoral mode towards epic, for Asia goes in search of Prometheus, in search of the 'harmony of the union of all faculties' that characterises the greatest poetry.

In scene iii Panthea and Asia have reached a rocky pinnacle where they pause before being invited by a troop of spirits to descend into the abyss. Panthea and Asia both pay tribute to the glory of the scenery around them. Asia's tribute is particularly interesting:

> How glorious art thou, Earth! And if thou be
> The shadow of some spirit lovelier still,
> Though evil stain its work, and it should be
> Like its creation, weak yet beautiful,
> I could fall down and worship that and thee. (II, iii, 12–16)

This seems a classic expression of Platonic pathos, of the refusal to admire beauty, however glorious, unless it shadows Beauty; of the refusal to admire the actual unless it figures the ideal. But it is more interesting than that. Asia attempts to hold apart two notions, the actual earth, and the ideal earth that the actual earth may only imperfectly shadow. But try as she might, and her syntax is very emphatic, the two earths collapse into one another, for Asia realises that if evil is present in the actual earth then this must betoken a flaw in the ideal earth of which it is a shadow; evil in the creation can derive only from evil in the creator. If the actual earth is 'weak yet beautiful', then so too must be any imagined original. Instead of a contrast between the imperfect world witnessed by the senses, and a perfect imagined world of ideas, Asia is left with two worlds, replicas of each other, differing only in their substantiality. It is a situation we have met with before. In Act I the Earth herself insisted that there were 'two worlds of life and death', one that which we see around us, the other inhabited by ghostly replicas of everything that is. In Act I, the Earth's scheme was a dominant emblem, figuring the static, symmetrical dualism, preventing any change against which Prometheus had to struggle. He did so by rejecting hatred and scorn, and embracing pity. Now Asia must make a similar effort. But, as her description of the Earth suggests, the terms in which the problem must be addressed have changed.

The struggle against dualism had been for Prometheus a moral struggle, but for Asia it is a problem of perception. The spirit song bidding Asia and Panthea descend into the mountain makes this clear. The spirits describe the descent as a penetration through the variegated world of appearances to a world of undifferentiated unity, 'Where there is One pervading, One alone'. It is a journey through the opposites of everyday reality, 'Through the cloudy strife/Of Death and of Life'. Prometheus struggled against a simplistic opposition of good and evil, but the contrarieties through which Asia passes are perceptual.

Act II scene iv takes place in Demogorgon's cave. Asia questions Demogorgon who ends the discussion by drawing her attention to two chariots. One of them is driven by a spirit with a 'dreadful countenance'. In this chariot Demogorgon mounts to overthrow Jupiter. The other is the chariot that will institute the new society. It is constructed from a shell, the emblem of Venus. In this chariot Panthea and Asia ascend.

The scene is focused on a long speech by Asia which is closely modelled on speeches by Prometheus in *Prometheus Bound*.[11] It is packed with allusions that drive the reader back to the Bible and to *Paradise Lost*. Shelley reverts to the techniques that he had used in the first speech of the play. In Act I Prometheus defined his regenerate self in opposition to his former self. Shelley defined his play in opposition to its models. In Act II scene iv Asia progresses to a new position by a wider ranging confrontation with the past than had been achieved in Act I.

Demogorgon introduces himself to Asia as an oracle. He promises to answer any question that she cares to put to him. Her first three questions ask who is responsible for the good in the world. To each of these Demogorgon replies, 'God'. Asia goes on to question Demogorgon about the origin of evil. Again she asks three questions, to each of which Demogorgon replies, 'He reigns'. As she asks her first three questions Asia grows in confidence; her speeches increase in length. But as she questions Demogorgon on the origin of evil, her speeches are progressively shortened, so that the last of them is a disjointed, strangulated cry: 'I feel, I know it: who?' Demogorgon simply repeats his enigmatic answer: 'He reigns'.

Asia herself directs Demogorgon's answers. She realises as much before the end of the scene. Her first efforts to understand the nature of the world's constitution are stifled, just as

Prometheus is stifled at the beginning of Act I. She attempts to understand the world in terms of a simple opposition between good and evil. Such a procedure, as Prometheus learned, is hostile to any real change, for if good is independent of evil, then evil is eternal. Asia realises the need to change her scheme, and she does so by attempting to construct a myth of the world's history in which evil is recognised as entangled with good. Just as Prometheus came to recognise the association of good and evil within the psyche, Asia realises their association in the external world. Act II, scene iv reverts to the techniques of Act I, because in this scene Asia repeats the progression to self-knowledge made by Prometheus in the first act. But before discussing her version of universal history, we must return to the beginning of the scene.

Demogorgon is first seen veiled, but then the veil falls, and Panthea describes his appearance:

> I see a mighty darkness
> Filling the seat of power, and rays of gloom
> Dart round, as light from the meridian sun.
> – Ungazed upon and shapeless; neither limb,
> Nor form, nor outline; yet we feel it is
> A living Spirit. (II, iv, 2–7)

The shapelessness of Demogorgon, as has often been remarked, is the shapelessness of Milton's Death 'that shape had none/ Distinguishable in member, joint or limb'. But his bright darkness is just as clearly an allusion to Milton's God 'Dark with excessive bright'.[12] Demogorgon is described as a compendium of God and Death, of the 'Author of all being', and the destroyer of life. As the scene develops Asia progresses towards self-knowledge by recognising Demogorgon, and Panthea's description suggests how this must be accomplished – by discarding Milton's dualism, or rather by working out an alternative to dualism in active opposition to Milton's theogony and the theogony of the Bible.

Asia begins by denying that there ever was a beginning: 'There was the Heaven and Earth at first,/And Light and Love ...' (II, iv, 32–3). She begins by challenging the first verse of Genesis: 'In the beginning God created the heaven and the earth'. The biblical account is rejected, because, in supposing a creation, it at once asserts the primacy of a creator. Any creation myth is pernicious because it implies the contingency of man, his dependence on the fiat of a divine overlord. The denial of a creation is therefore a necessary first step in the construction of a man-centred mythology. But Asia's words carry another suggestion: in the beginning the universe was divided between Heaven and Earth. It is this notion that Asia will attempt to supplant.

Asia divides history into a Saturnian age and the age of Jupiter. Life under Saturn was as intolerable as life in Eden, and for the same reason. Saturn refused men 'The birthright of their being, knowledge, power... For thirst of which they fainted'. To remedy this situation Prometheus empowered Jupiter to overthrow Saturn:

> Then Prometheus
> Gave wisdom, which is strength, to Jupiter,
> And with this law alone, 'Let man be free,'
> Clothed him with the dominion of wide Heaven. (II, iv, 43–6)

In Genesis God grants dominion to man, but here Prometheus, man's champion, grants it to Jupiter. Both Prometheus and the Christian God attached a condition to their gift, but God's condition was repressive – it denied men 'the birthright of their being' –, Prometheus's condition was moral and beneficent.

Nevertheless Prometheus had made a crucial error, as Asia goes on to explain: 'To know nor faith, nor love, nor law; to be/Omnipotent but friendless is to reign...' (II, iv, 47–8). That Jupiter's government is evil ought not to be explained as a moral lapse on the governor's part, but as a necessary consequence of the position assigned to him by Prometheus. To be faithless, loveless and lawless are consequences of the role Jupiter has been given. In giving absolute sovereignty to one faculty, in creating a God or a King (Asia's speech may be translated into psychological, theological or political terms), Prometheus has condemned both himself and mankind to misery. In Act I Prometheus was shown to have spoken the curse from which he suffers. Now, that event is explained.

Prometheus's reaction to his mistake is described in two very compressed lines: 'Prometheus saw, and waked the legioned hopes/Which sleep within folded Elysian flowers...'. Aeschylus's Prometheus helped men in the same way: 'I caused blind

hopes to dwell within their breasts'. Douglas Bush contrasts the
strength of Aeschylus's line with Shelley's flowery elaboration of
it.[13] But in Asia's speech Aeschylus is used primarily as a base
from which Shelley can conduct subversive operations against
Milton and the Bible. God looked on his creation, and saw that it
was good. Prometheus looked on his creation of Jupiter, and saw
that it was disastrous. He 'waked the legioned hopes' just as
Satan 'stood and called his legions'. But Prometheus called his
hopes not from a trance in the lake of Hell, but from their sleep in
Elysian flowers, and one of these flowers is amaranth, the flower
of Milton's Heaven. Milton's division between God and Satan,
between Heaven and Hell, is brought under a concentrated ironic
fire. Bush's simple comparison with Aeschylus in terms of
dramatic vigour misses the point.

As 'alleviations' to man's misery Prometheus institutes the
study of science and the practice of the arts. Civilisation is
explained as a response to an otherwise intolerable environment.
In a sense, Prometheus's enthronement of Jupiter was right after
all. It was a necessary stage in man's development because it
forced him to claim the birthright of his being, knowledge.
Prometheus accepted in Act I the necessity of pain in order for the
individual to develop, recognised that 'misery made [him] wise':
Asia here recognises the necessity of misery for social development.

But this era of history, the age governed by dualisms, by
Heaven and Earth, gods opposed to men, kings opposed to
people, by a divided psyche, enabled man to develop only into a
startling paradox, into that creature that reached its final
development in the eighteenth century, and was given its
ultimate expression in Pope's *Essay on Man*, the 'glory, jest and
riddle of the world'. Asia returns to her original question, asks
once more who is responsible for evil:

> which, while,
> Man looks on his creation like a God
> And sees that it is glorious, drives him on,
> The wreck of his own will, the scorn of earth,
> The outcast, the abandoned, the alone? (II, iv, 101–5)

Man as the scorn of earth is identified with Satan outcast from
Heaven, with Adam and Eve outcast from Eden, and with their

types Cain and Ahasuerus outcast even from fallen society. But man who looks on his own creation like a god, and sees that it is glorious, is the vindictive God of the Bible. Jupiter, Asia admits, is not responsible for this situation. She suspects that he too is a slave, and Demogorgon confirms her suspicions. Asia has, in fact, answered her own question in posing it. She has described man as a creature suffering from divine retribution, but also as the God who exacts that retribution. Man suffers under his own displeasure. Just as Prometheus enthroned Jupiter, the god from whose power he suffers, so man is oppressed by gods of his own creation. The mystery of evil is lightened as Asia reaches beyond the antithesis between God and man, between heaven and earth.

Asia has encountered the past in much the same way that Prometheus encountered his own past in Act I. Like him she has moved from a facile dualism, a belief in independent principles of good and evil, to the recognition that man is responsible for both, for both are contained within him.

She asks Demogorgon to identify the ultimate power of the universe, but he is unable to reply:

> If the abysm
> Could vomit forth its secrets . . . But a voice
> Is wanting, the deep truth is imageless;
> For what would it avail to bid thee gaze
> On the revolving world? What to bid speak
> Fate, Time, Occasion, Chance and Change? To these
> All things are subject but eternal Love. (II, iv, 114–20)

Asia realises that Demogorgon has only repeated her own belief:

> So much I asked before, and my heart gave
> The response thou hast given; and of such truths
> Each to itself must be the oracle. (II, iv, 121–3)

She has realised that Demogorgon is not an oracle but an echo. Just as the Furies are shapeless, and can be organised only by forces within Prometheus, so Demogorgon is in himself shapeless, and can only articulate the thoughts of those who address him. The distinction between the ignorant suppliant and the all-knowing oracle, between Aeneas and Anchises or between

Adam and Raphael, is exposed as yet another factitious dualism. The oracle sees no more than its interrogator. And that is why oracles tell the truth. To see something is to make it true, for everything exists as it is perceived.

Asia, like Prometheus, has recognised that love has power over Jupiter. But Prometheus failed to see love in himself: he saw it only in Asia, and so was condemned to await his deliverance passively: 'Most vain all hope but love; and thou art far,/Asia'. Asia feels love in herself. Her final question to Demogorgon is demanding, not supplicatory:

> One more demand; and do thou answer me
> As mine own soul would answer, did it know
> That which I ask. Prometheus shall arise
> Henceforth the sun of this rejoicing world:
> When shall the destined hour arrive? (II, iv, 124–8)

Asia has achieved a confident belief: 'Prometheus shall arise'. Her ringing indicative tense contrasts with Prometheus's feeble optative at the end of Act I: 'I would fain be what it is my destiny to be...'. The chains that bind Prometheus are mind-forged manacles. For them to disappear it is enough that his resurrection be willed. Asia demands that Demogorgon answer 'As mine own soul would answer'. He replies, 'Behold!', and the two chariots that will accomplish the revolution appear. Asia's soul, that she supposes ignorant, has enforced the answer that she desires.

Asia and Panthea mount the shell chariot. In the last scene of Act II they pause on their journey. Asia is transfigured, so that the act begins with the transfiguration of Prometheus, and ends with the transfiguration of Asia, his female counterpart.

The relationship between the first two acts of Shelley's drama may be variously described. Prometheus, in revoking the curse, in accepting within himself a capacity for both good and evil, has removed a psychic block. He has freed the healing, creative forces of the mind which had retreated to a nook deep within the psyche, and in Act II these forces go about their restorative work. But Act II might also be understood as parallel to Act I. Prometheus begins Act I as one of the participants in a cosmic conflict. He escapes from this static position by accepting an inner impulse, by revoking his curse. The action then moves progressively into Prometheus's own mind. Asia begins Act II in her Indian vale. The first scene describes a dream world: Asia has retreated from external reality to dream, from reason to intuition. When, at the end of the act, she confronts Demogorgon, she is forced to supplement dream with history, intuition with discursive reason. Act I begins with Prometheus exposed on an icy mountain, Act II with Asia nestling in a warm valley. But during the act Asia makes a journey that brings her to the summit of a mountain. In the first two acts Asia and Prometheus approach each other. Prometheus moves towards an acceptance of the inner workings of his own mind; Asia moves outwards to a confrontation with external reality. This *rapprochement* is completed in Act III in their wedding, the emblem of a new psychological and social wholeness.

In Act III, scene i, Jupiter is overthrown by Demogorgon. In scene ii Apollo and Ocean discuss the fall of the government. In scene iii Prometheus is unbound by Hercules, and invites Asia to retire with him to a cave. He gives to the Spirit of the Hour a shell, and directs him to circumnavigate the globe, blowing this conch, the emblem of Venus, Shelley's version of the last trump. In scene iv Asia and Prometheus, before retiring to their cave, hear reports on the changed situation, first from the Spirit of the Earth, and then from the Spirit of the Hour.

Once again the play has changed its form. Act I represented a single, continuous series of actions centred on one character, Prometheus. In Act II the drama was discontinuous, divided into scenes, but still represented a single series of actions, the journey of Asia and Panthea. In Act III a narrative or sequential structure is replaced by a parallel structure. Jupiter falls, Prometheus is unbound. The rest of the act consists of a series of reports on the change in world conditions expressed in a variety of manners. Douglas Bush is surely right when he argues that in *Prometheus Unbound* a dramatic structure is supplanted by a musical structure.[14] The various parts of Act III are held together not by narrative connection, but because they represent variations on a single theme, the contrast between 'then', life under Jupiter, and 'now', life after his fall.

The two events of the act, Jupiter's fall and Prometheus's release, are both problematic. Jupiter is violently overthrown; and odd conclusion to an action that began with Prometheus revoking his curse on Jupiter, his decision that he now wishes 'no living thing to suffer pain'. Instead of sliding over this inconsistency, Shelley allows Jupiter to point it out:

That thou wouldst make mine enemy my judge,
Even where he hangs, seared by my long revenge,
On Caucasus! he would not doom me thus.
Gentle, and just, and dreadless, is he not
The monarch of the world? (III, i, 65–9)

The other problem of the act is that Prometheus's decision to retire with Asia to a cave, where he plans to make daisy-chains and enjoy the rumours that reach him of mankind's progress, hardly seems an adequate resolution of his struggles.

Jupiter's downfall is represented in a grimly ironic scene. Jupiter holds a feast in heaven to celebrate the imminent incarnation of his son, the product of his rape of Thetis. The secret possessed by Aeschylus's Prometheus is that Zeus will be overthrown by the product of his rape of Thetis, but Shelley cunningly revises the Greek myth. The expected guest proves not to be Jupiter's son but Demogorgon. When it suits him Shelley reads myth as metaphor. Demogorgon, in his role as revolutionary destroyer, is in a metaphorical sense the son of Jupiter's tyranny; the one is the natural and predictable consequence of the other. But the scene is also a fiercely ironic parody of *Paradise Lost*. Jupiter looks forward to the arrival of his son because he expects the son to subdue once and for all 'the soul of man', which, despite Jupiter's reprisals, persists in 'hurling up insurrection'. The son will quell man's satanic rebelliousness. In Book VI of *Paradise Lost* God looks to His Son to end the resistance of the rebel angels. Both Demogorgon and the Messiah mount chariots, but Demogorgon, instead of casting down the rebels, casts down Jupiter. Shelley's Messiah defects to the rebels and casts God into Hell. Shelley seems to have stumbled into the parodist's cul-de-sac. Demogorgon becomes vulnerable to exactly the same charge that Shelley brought against Milton's God when he described him as 'one who in the cold security of undoubted triumph inflicts the most horrible revenge upon his enemy'.[15] In parodying Milton Shelley seems to have produced only a Miltonic parody of himself. Prometheus's revocation of his curse seems no more than a washing of the hands, a denial of moral responsibility for the violent revolution from which Prometheus benefits and the result of which he celebrates.

Jupiter is cast by Demogorgon into the 'abyss' into which Asia and Panthea had descended. The entrance to this cave is described by Panthea in Act II scene iii as a fount from which 'the oracular vapour is hurled up/Which lonely men drink wandering in their youth', become drunk, and assume the inspiring voice of the prophet, the 'voice which is contagion to the world'. The Earth describes the cave to which Asia and Prometheus plan to retire, and it is oddly similar. This cave too is a fount of vapour, that men inhaled: 'And spoke, and were oracular, and lured/The erring nations round to mutual war' (III, iii, 128–9). Both caves are outlets of a gas that has inspired prophets to go about their business of inciting people to violence.[16] This is the clue that in effect the two caves are the same. Prometheus, Asia and Jupiter all retire to the same place. To Jupiter it seems that he is cast into Hell, to Prometheus and Asia it seems a retreat to a pastoral haven. But the apparent difference in their fates is only a difference in perception.

The damnation that Jupiter suffers is simply a distorted perception of the event that occurs. Jupiter appeals to Prometheus as 'the monarch of the world', but Prometheus is not, nor will he become, a monarch. Jupiter perceives the world, as Prometheus had perceived it at the beginning of the play, as a struggle for power between himself and Prometheus, as a confrontation between 'Thou' and 'I'. When he is forced to recognise change, he understands it in the only way in which he can imagine; he understands that his role and that of Prometheus have been reversed. Like Prometheus in the play's first speech he begins to echo Milton's devils: 'No pity, no release, no respite!' He sinks 'Dizzily down, ever, for ever, down', echoing Prometheus's initial cry of pain: 'Ah me! alas, pain, pain ever, for ever!' He is violently overthrown not by Demogorgon, but because violent overthrow is all that he can imagine. Jupiter, Asia and Prometheus all retire from the play, but the nature of the retirement is determined by the individual's perception of it. To Jupiter it is Hell, to Prometheus and Asia it is a welcome release.[17]

When Jupiter asks who Demogorgon is, the latter replies, 'Eternity. Demand no direr name.' Critics have, as critics will, refused to believe him. But he tells the truth. He is the eternity of which Mary Wollstonecraft speaks (interestingly, she, like Panthea describing Demogorgon, alludes to Milton's description of Death) when she refers to 'particular men, who filled a niche in the temple of fame, and dropped into the black rolling stream of time, that silently sweeps all before it, into the shapeless void called eternity – For shape can it be called that shape hath none?'[18] Demogorgon is eternity defined as the sum total of time. So he presides over temporal change, erupting from his cave to bear down with him what has become outmoded, but he is perceived as a destroyer only by those who, like Jupiter, attempt to withstand the process of temporal change.

During Act III the focus of the play moves from the mythological characters who have dominated the first two acts to mankind. In the first two acts men have been subsidiary, adjuncts to Prometheus's conflict with Jupiter. In Act III they gradually become the focus of the play's concern. As a consequence the active supernatural characters, Jupiter, Prometheus and Asia, disappear. As independent entities they retreat into Demogorgon's cave; as partial qualities they reoccupy their proper home within the human breast, The gods of mythology are only the splinters of divided man; they disappear when man regains his original wholeness.

When Asia embarked on her journey in Act II her movement makes a break with the constraints of Greek drama, but Act III ends with the disappearance of the play's major characters, and this indicates a break not simply with Aeschylean modes of thought but with the major premise on which all drama depends, the belief in individual character. In his *Essay on Life* Shelley writes: 'The words *I* and *you* and *they* are grammatical devices, invented merely for arrangement, and totally devoid of the intense and exclusive sense usually allotted to them'.[19] Individual character is ultimately only an abstraction. The Spirit of the Hour recognises that Jupiter was all the habits, things, roles, etc. that divided one man from another. All these 'under many a name and many a form' 'Were Jupiter, the tyrant of the world'. When Hercules unbinds Prometheus, Prometheus is revealed as not a character but an allegorical personification:

> thus doth strength
> To wisdom, courage, and long-suffering love,

And thee, who art the form they animate,
Minister like a slave. (III, iii, 1–4)

Prometheus and Asia are beneficent forces, but only divisiveness or Jupiter made them appear as independent characters. The martyr and the redeemer are roles that have meaning only in a divided society. When division has been destroyed they will cease to be apparent as separate entities. They will retreat, as Jupiter retreats, into the cave of eternity, only to reappear if man fails to preserve his regained wholeness.

The central movement of Act III is a progressive celebration of the changed situation. The revolution is celebrated first by Ocean and Apollo, and later by the Spirit of the Earth and the Spirit of the Hour. The substantial changes in the world are far less significant than those that result from the changed manner in which man sees his world. The Spirit of the Earth reports that 'toads, and snakes, and efts' are now beautiful, but this transformation has been accomplished 'with little change of shape or hue'. The Spirit of the Hour:

first was disappointed not to see
Such mighty change as I had felt within
Expressed in outward things... (III, iv, 128–30)

He had expected a physical transformation of the world, but he realises that the revolution has been a mental event; everyone is changed 'within'. The world is utterly transformed because man sees both himself and his world quite differently.

Shelley dramatises this perceptual revolution when he replaces the Earth, who makes her last appearance in the play in Act-III scene iii, with the Spirit of the Earth. The Earth was Prometheus's mother: the Spirit of the Earth is a child of unknown parentage who has adopted Asia for its mother. In Act I Prometheus had to struggle against the Earth. On a physical level he had to struggle against the pain of ice, earthquake, etc.; on a mental level he had to struggle against the unregenerate craving for revenge that the Earth incited him to sustain. He was the Earth's child, but he had to grow up. In revoking his curse, in disappointing his mother by giving up his violent opposition to Jupiter, Prometheus breaks the umbilical cord that had tied him to his mother; he recognises that the Promethean must not be confined to the earthly. In Act III the old Earth is replaced by the Spirit of the Earth who recognises the parental control of Asia. Nature understands its subservience to the creative faculty, the Earth that it is properly the creature not the creator of the imagination. Man ceases to be the product of his world when he understands that he creates the world he lives in by perceiving it, and that the quality of the world is dependent on the quality of his perception.

The conversation between Ocean and Apollo and the reports of the Spirits of Earth and Hour all celebrate the revolution that has occurred in man's manner of perceiving his world. And yet the arrangement of the celebration is odd, anticlimactic. Ocean and Apollo speak in the most serenely beautiful blank verse that Shelley ever wrote, a verse that wonderfully captures the achieved harmony of the new world. But the Spirit of the Hour ends the act by reporting rather than expressing this harmony, and reporting it in a manner that evokes the old world that has been destroyed far more vividly that it suggests the new. The speech is dominated by negative constructions. It is written in Miltonic blank verse, in a periodic syntax, but the expected climax is repeatedly avoided. The relics of the monarchy and the church 'Stand, not o'erthrown, but unregarded now'. The strong verb is denied in favour of a weak one. The power of the speech is entirely in its description of the evils of the old world and its unholy images which are now 'But an astonishment', which stand 'not o'erthrown, but unregarded', that are 'mouldering fast o'er their abandoned shrines'. The evils have simply ceased to be, and the effect is oddly anticlimactic. The speech contains an explanation of the extraordinarily negative character of its celebration:

> The painted veil, by those who were, called life,
> Which mimicked as with colours idly spread,
> All men believed or hoped, is torn aside ... (III, iv, 190–2)

'All' men believed or hoped has been destroyed, for 'all' the beliefs of the old world were false, not only the belief in Jupiter, but also the belief in Prometheus and Asia. The play turns on itself, on all that has gone before, and dismisses it as a fiction, a story that had point within the old world, but must now be dismissed as an empty mockery. The Spirit of the Hour begins his speech by describing a temple in the sun at which the worshippers are 'Phidian forms' of Prometheus, Asia, the Earth and himself. The play's characters freeze into statues; its mythology recognises itself as artifice, but the artifice is at least magnificent. By the end of the speech the veil of life on which men's beliefs are painted is 'idly spread' with colours, dismissed as a childish daub. The play rejects itself.

The reappearance of Miltonic blank verse in the final speech of Act III and the concentration in that speech on the destruction of the fictions of the past remind the reader of the central activity of the first three acts. The past is confronted, and as a consequence destroyed. In Act I Prometheus confronted the ghost of his former self, in Act II Asia confronted the world's past, its history. Prometheus confronted his former self only in order to reject it; Asia confronted the world's history only to demand that history be superseded, that the destined hour arrive. Miltonic blank verse is one of the vehicles of Shelley's metaphor, a style embedded in the past that must itself be confronted and overcome.

In Act I Prometheus recalled and revoked his curse, so that at the end of the act he was empty, he had 'no agony and no solace left'. Act II ended with Asia's lyric, 'My soul is an enchanted boat', which describes a journey back through life in which all the experiences of life are negated. Act III ends with the veil of life torn aside. Man remains but shorn of most of his distinguishing characteristics except his subjection to death and change. Finally he is presented with the ambition to 'oversoar' these 'clogs', and to find his home in the vacuum of space, 'Pinnacled dim in the intense inane'. The third act ends in emptiness.

In the *Essay on Life* Shelley declares his allegiance to Sir William Drummond's 'intellectual philosophy', and then adds,

> What follows from this admission? It establishes no new truth, it gives us no additional insight into our hidden nature, neither its action nor itself. Philosophy, impatient as it may be to build, has much work yet remaining as pioneer for the overgrowth of ages. It makes one step towards this object: it destroys error and the roots of error. It leaves, what it is too often the duty of the reformer in political and ethical questions to leave, a vacancy.[20]

In their own way the first three acts of *Prometheus Unbound* have been concerned to tear away the overgrowth of ages, and in the end they leave the reader with a vacancy, leave him 'Pinnacled dim in the intense inane'.

Shelley finished Act III of the play in April 1819. He then seems to have regarded it as complete, and it was not until late in the year that he thought of adding Act IV. The history of the play's genesis has been used by critics in support of their argument that its final act is an afterthought to be appreciated independently of the play that it completes.

Without Act IV the shape of the play would parallel the shape of the diverted Miltonic sentences in the last speech of Act III. The play's resolution would be inadequate to its action; the vision of the redeemed world would fail to match the energy with which the old world had been described and destroyed. This imbalance seems for some time to have satisfied Shelley. It is certainly a principle of construction in some of his other poems, most obviously in the fine sonnet *England in 1819*. The first twelve lines of the sonnet are composed of a series of noun phrases, each driving home Shelley's charge of moral bankruptcy in the government of the country. The verb is withheld until the poem's thirteenth line, when we learn that all these instruments of corruption: 'Are graves, from which a glorious Phantom may/Burst, to illumine our tempestuous day'. The rhyme stresses the tentative auxiliary 'may'. The violent energy of the sonnet is dissipated in a prophecy which is relegated to the status of a wish. Shelley has accepted it as his duty as a political reformer to leave the reader as far as possible with a vacancy. But this structure, effective enough in a sonnet, is surely unsatisfactory in a major poem.

In Act III the theme of *Prometheus Unbound* becomes man and man's transformed perception of the universe. But the quality of that perception is reported rather than expressed. The redeemed perception of the universe is the subject rather than the object of Act IV, and therefore its actors are the fundamental categories of perception, space and time. None of the play's major characters appears in Act IV. In Act III Shelley dismissed his characters from the play for exactly the same reason as he dismisses personal pronouns in the *Essay on Life*. Dramatic characters, like personal pronouns, are products of a habit of mind that asserts distinctions between individuals. When that habit is broken, when 'men' become 'man', a 'chain of linkèd thought', they must be discarded.[21] At the end of the play this conclusion is expressed with that literal simplicity so characteristic of *Prometheus Unbound*. Demogorgon rises to deliver his summing-up of the play's action. He appeals for attention to the earth, the moon, the stars, the dead, the elements and the creatures of the earth. Finally he addresses man, and the response is spoken by 'All'. The play has represented the pursuit by man of his own identity. That pursuit is ended here in the recognition that he is 'all'. He is everything that exists, because nothing exists outside his perception of it. Nothing exists but in his thoughts, and everything in his thoughts exists. Therefore the dead exist, not supernaturally, but because they are objects of human thought, and so exist with neither more nor less certainty than the sun and the moon.

Panthea and Ione are the only survivors from the first three acts of the play to appear on stage in Act IV, but they are compères of the act rather than participants in it. The third act ended with a celebration of the individual's deliverance from all restrictive institutions, his coronation as 'king over himself'. But the liberated individual man makes no appearance in Act IV. Shelley forces the play's reader to engage the paradox that to liberate the individual is to annihilate him. Individual consciousness is apparent only when the individual is aware of a disjunction between himself and his world, and between himself and other selves. When the habits of mind and the institutions that upheld these distinctions are destroyed, the individual will be both freed and annihilated. Once unbound Prometheus has nothing to do but disappear, and the disappearance from the play of Prometheus, Asia and Jupiter foreshadows the final jettisoning of man himself. Act IV represents the new man by representing how he sees, because he exists only as a way of seeing. It is interesting that the personal pronouns that Shelley dismisses in *An Essay on Life* as delusions are all nominatives. They are functional only when the knower is distinguished from the known. Act IV is a sentence from which the subject, man, has been jettisoned because it has become redundant.

The subject of the act is the redeemed perception of the universe; its actors are space and time. At its beginning the 'dead Hours', the time of which man was a victim, make their exit from the stage, and are replaced by a new chorus of hours who dance with 'the Spirits of the human mind'. Time still passes, but man now recognises that since the awareness of duration is subjective, it is within his control, so that lovers may now catch the hours by their 'loose tresses', may lengthen the apparent duration of their moments of happiness. Ione and Panthea then watch the chariot of the moon and the sphere of the earth pass over the stage in procession. Finally the Earth and the Moon, which in themselves constitute human space, and whose dancing movements mark out the times by which men live, share a duet.

Some characteristics of the mode of perception that the act expresses may be briefly indicated by comparing its form with Act I. Prometheus begins the play demanding that all the heavenly bodies look down on the earth, look down on himself, and Prometheus looks inwards, engrossed in his own mental struggles. Only at the end of the act does he remember Asia, and that memory brings the act to an end. In Act II on the other hand Asia is impelled on her quest by a vision of Prometheus, and the crucial question she asks Demogorgon concerns not herself, but her lover. In Act III the focus of the play's attention becomes mankind. In the final act this expansive movement is completed when Panthea and Ione stand gazing outwards delighted by the dance of the universe, a perfect contrast to Prometheus who began the play demanding that the universe look inwards at him. This is the appropriate movement of the play because for Shelley 'the great secret of morals is love', and love is defined as a 'going out of our own nature'. The shape of the play is an expression of a progressive going out of our own nature.

Act I is centripetally organised. All the events and the characters are arranged around the static figure of Prometheus. That is the appropriate dramatic shape for an action set in a world governed by Jupiter, in which Prometheus the rebel is only a parody of the god he opposes. It is the dramatic shape of *Prometheus Bound*. Coleridge makes the appropriate political analogy when discussing Sophocles: 'the constitution of tragedy is monarchical . . . all the parts submitting themselves to the majesty of the heroic sceptre'. Act IV is composed largely of lyrics, each of which achieves a degree of autonomy. This is the structure appropriate to the new world, which is achieved only after all governmental institutions have been destroyed, when each man is 'king over himself'. Again Coleridge suggests a useful analogy: 'It is a fundamental principle with comedy, rather to risk all the confusion of anarchy, than to destroy the

independence and privileges of its individual constituents'.[22] Act
I is a tragedy dominated by Prometheus's cry of pain: 'Ah me!
alas, pain, pain ever, for ever!' Act IV is a comedy; in it the Earth
shouts, 'Ha! Ha! the animation of delight'. The order of Act I is
imposed; the order of Act IV is achieved by the abandonment of
each to his own joy.

I have earlier suggested that the separation of Prometheus and
Asia is best understood as a separation of the cognitive from the
creative or imaginative faculty. What is most apparent in the
lyric language of Act IV is the resolution of these two modes of
apprehension. The act has yielded to scientific commentary,[23]
but science is not its theme. Consider the Moon's celebration of
her love for the earth:

> I, thy crystal paramour
> Borne beside thee by a power
> Like the polar Paradise,
> Magnet-like of lovers' eyes;
> I, a most enamoured maiden
> Whose weak brain is overladen
> With the pleasure of her love,
> Maniac-like around thee move... (IV, 463–70)

This is a careful account of the gravitational pull of the earth on
the moon. That the moon's orbit is 'Maniac-like', for example, is
probably a reference to its libration. But the passage is equally
an expression of love. The scientific apprehension of the world in
terms of calculable forces like gravitation is united with the
mythopoeic apprehension of the world in terms of human
emotions like love. Throughout the passage gravity and love
function as metaphors for one another.

This technique is most powerfully operative in Panthea's
description of the sphere of the earth:

> And from the other opening in the wood
> Rushes, with loud and whirlwind harmony,
> A sphere, which is as many thousand spheres,
> Solid as crystal, yet through all its mass
> Flow, as through empty space, music and light:
> Ten thousand orbs involving and involved,
> Purple and azure, white, and green, and golden,
> Sphere within sphere; and every shape between

Peopled with unimaginable shapes,
Such as ghosts dream dwell in the lampless deep,
Yet each inter-transpicuous, and they whirl
Over each other with a thousand motions,
Upon a thousand sightless axles spinning,
And with the force of self-destroying swiftness,
Intensely, slowly, solemnly roll on,
Kindling with mingled sounds, and many tones,
Intelligible words and music wild. (IV, 236–52)

Harold Bloom compares this sphere with its visionary predecessors, the divine chariots of Ezekiel and Milton, whereas Carl Grabo and Desmond King-Hele explain it as a versification of an atomic theory of matter.[24] The point is that it will yield to both readings. It is best understood not so much as a description but as an expression of a mode of perception. The passage is dominated by paradox. It is 'A sphere, which is as many thousand spheres'. It is 'Solid as crystal', and yet music and light flow through it 'as through empty space'. It moves with 'self-destroying swiftness' and yet 'slowly'. The noise of its progress is like 'intelligible words' and also like 'music wild'. Paradox is a device that both tempts and frustrates logical reading, and Shelley's diction plays with this situation. His vocabulary includes words like 'inter-transpicuous' that seem to demand the scientific, logical understanding that Grabo and King-Hele bring to the passage alongside phrases that mock all such modes of thought: 'Such as ghosts dream dwell in the lampless deep'. No sooner has the reader understood that he is asked to imagine ghosts than he is faced with the impossible demand that he imagine what might be the nature of their dreams. The sphere is brought within the area of rational understanding, and then jerked light years away from it. By the end of the passage it exists in the reader's mind as an embodied paradox; as diagrammatic, like an orrery, but also as unimaginably mysterious.

Within the sphere the Spirit of the Earth lies asleep like a human child. Smiles play about its lips. Ione interrupts her sister and remarks, ''Tis only mocking the orb's harmony'. The child is amused by the mighty sphere: its mechanical precision and its unimaginable strangeness are alike mocked. The paradoxes that the sphere embodies are reconciled in the smile of a child who views each of its aspects with amused detachment. Man may see his world rationally, diagrammatically; he may perceive the world as an orrery, delightful in the complexity of its order, or he may people his world with spirits, with 'unimaginable shapes'. But the scientific and the visionary modes of apprehension cannot be irreconcilably opposed for both have the same origin, both have their home in the mind of man. That is why the child can smile as he lies at the centre of the sphere surrounded by its bewildering paradoxes. Because both terms of the paradox derive from him, he becomes himself their resolution.

The play ends when Demogorgon rises, calls for attention, and delivers a speech in which he summarises the achievement that the play has dramatised, and considers what may happen in the future. He lays claim to no special prophetic power. Man must secure his present happiness by the exercise of 'Gentleness, Wisdom, Virtue, and Endurance', and should he fail he must look to these same qualities to restore him to his present condition. Demogorgon postulates that man may lose the wholeness of vision that is celebrated in Act IV, and therefore, in the final stanzas of his speech, Prometheus is reinstated as the play's hero, a role he had ceased to occupy after Act I. Given the loss that Demogorgon fears, Prometheus, Asia and Jupiter will again become necessary configurations of the mind. Man will again be forced to rely on his Promethean qualities; he will have again to experience Prometheus's pain, and to practise once again the Titan's intransigent defiance. The play ends by returning the reader to his present, the world all before him.

Prometheus Unbound is, and will remain, vulnerable to hostile criticism. It is uneven; in fact, some of the writing is distinctly shoddy. Many of the lyrics in Act IV seem written expressly to support T. S. Eliot's charge that 'in poetry so fluent as Shelley's there is a good deal which is just bad jingling'.[25] But the poem is more than the fine passages interspersed throughout it. It is able to survive its own deficiencies because it is masterfully constructed. It moves from the rigid, frozen symmetries of Act I to the dancing symmetries of Act IV. Each act of the play develops its own dramatic technique; each act imposes on the material of which it is constructed its own peculiar form. The successive acts embody successive modes of perceiving the world, so that, as he proceeds through the play, the reader progressively redefines his awareness of what has gone before. Prometheus in Act I is the central embattled hero. In Act III he has become peripheral, the inspiration and the object of a quest. In Act II he is unbound, and, liberated; he ceases to be. The Titan becomes a personification of various moral qualities that have independent significance only when they are set in defiant opposition to their contraries. So it is that in Act IV Prometheus is forgotten, remembered only when Demogorgon suggests that at some future time his qualities may again be necessary for the redemption of man.

The play's acts are successive, provisional attempts to impose a satisfactory form on experience. In this the play resembles, as well as dramatises, the history of civilisation, for the significant moments of history, like those of Shelley's drama, are the successive attempts made by man to construct a model in terms of which he may order his world. In *A Defence of Poetry* Shelley identifies one such attempt when he pays tribute to the 'poets among the authors of the Christian and chivalric stystems of manners and religion, who created forms of opinion and action never before conceived; which, copied into the imagination of men, became as generals to the bewildered armies of their thoughts'.[26] Those who create these models Shelley describes as poets.

Each act in *Prometheus Unbound* is a fresh configuration of the mind, another gathering of the rays of thoughts. In Act I Shelley establishes, examines, and at last rejects the static, symmetrical order imposed on the universe by Aeschylus in *Prometheus Bound*. In Act II static pattern is replaced by moving, linear pattern. The bound Prometheus is replaced at the centre of the play by the journeying Asia. Act III appears to be, and in some sense is, not a fresh structure, but a structural breakdown. Act III does, after all, dramatise the final destruction of the order that Jupiter imposes on the world, or rather that man imposes on his world through the creation of Jupiter. In it a narrative pattern of successive events vies uneasily with a musical pattern in which the same theme is repeated and varied. The act ends only when the Spirit of the Hour dismisses the past as bad art:

> The painted veil, by those who were, called life,
> Which mimicked as with colours idly spread,
> All men believed or hoped, is torn aside . . . (III, iv, 190–2)

The history of mankind, which is also the first three acts of Shelley's play is summarily dismissed. Its orderings, its patternings are rejected as unsatisfactory. It was a clumsy picture, a bad poem. From the perspective that has been attained at the end of

Shelley's Poetic Thoughts

Act III Shelley can turn contemptuously on the past history of mankind and on the first three acts of his play, and reject them both. Here the play was to have ended, as an example of that kind of Romantic poem that I described in Chapter I as driving towards a recognition of its own irrelevance; the poem that eats its own tail, and ends only when it has accomplished its own disappearance. But Shelley went on to write Act IV. Act III had successfully accomplished an annihilation, had ended with the 'inane'; in Act IV a new creation takes place, like the original creation, out of nothingness. The achievement of the act is described briefly by the Spirits of the Human Mind:

> And our singing shall build
> In the void's loose field
> A world for the Spirit of Wisdom to wield . . . (IV, 153–5)

The act is designed to express a new notion of order, not an order imposed on recalcitrant materials, but an order which arises from the speakers' self-indulgence of their joy. The static pattern of Act I and the moving linear pattern of Act II are reconciled in an act which celebrates free, circular movement. The moon circles the earth so that she may rapturously admire him from every side, and in doing so she sustains the order of the universe, just as Shelley constructs his lyric stanzas, not as a means of controlling, but to express his 'animation of delight'. The imposed order of Jupiter's world, represented in Act I by the frozen symmetries of the Aeschylean dramatic pattern is balanced by the order of Act IV, an order that results not from self-discipline, but, and the pun is crucial to Shelley's thought, from self-abandon.

I began this discussion of *Prometheus Unbound* by setting myself two tasks, to examine the play's structure and to demonstrate that it is a play about modes of perception. The two arguments have persistently merged into one, for the different modes of perception that are the play's theme are embodied in the different organisations of its successive acts, and these organisations are themselves explicable only in terms of the different modes of perception that they embody. One is forced to explain content in terms of form, and form in terms of content. This makes criticism a slippery exercise, but it is the exercise demanded by all Shelley's major poems.

5   Elegy and Dream

Adonais

Adonais is an elaborate exercise in a conventional genre, pastoral elegy. Shelley's decision to write his memorial to Keats within the tradition of pastoral elegy is a choice so far from obvious as to be eccentric. A. S. P. Woodhouse and Douglas Bush, summarising the place of Milton's *Lycidas* within this tradition, conclude by remarking that at the time when 'if not moribund' the tradition 'had almost ceased to develop, it was crowned by the greatest exemplar in any language'.[1] The genre within which Shelley writes *Adonais* died with *Lycidas*; it retained thereafter only a spectral life in the imitations of *Lycidas* written in the eighteenth century. Another elegiac tradition, that deriving from Gray's *Elegy in a Country Churchyard*, was still vital in 1821. Shelley had written his early lyric, 'A Summer Evening Churchyard', within that tradition, but when he came to write his poem on Keats he chose to ignore it. *Lycidas* is the single most important model for *Adonais*, and yet Shelley echoes and imitates Milton's predecessors rather than Milton himself. In a sense, he chose to write *Adonais* as Milton's contemporary. His poem is an anachronism.

This is not altogether surprising. *Laon and Cythna*, I have argued, is a revival of a genre twenty years out of date. *Julian and Maddalo* looks back to Horatian verse of the eighteenth century. *Prometheus Unbound* begins as an imitation of Aeschylus. But two decades are less than two centuries; Augustan verse survived throughout the Romantic period in the work of Crabbe, Campbell, Rogers and Byron; and Greek tragedy was a model continuously available since the seventeenth century, and sometimes chosen by dramatists who wished to escape from the Elizabethan dramatic tradition. Shelley's revival of pastoral elegy in *Adonais* is a good deal more remarkable.

To understand *Adonais* it is necessary to know something of the tradition of pastoral elegy as Shelley received it. The tradition has two roots: one classical, one Christian. On the classical side the important models are Theocritus's first idyll, Bion's *Lament for Adonis*, the *Lament for Bion* traditionally ascribed to Moschus, and two of Virgil's eclogues, eclogue V, the elegy for Daphnis, and eclogue X, the lament for Gallus.[2] The Christian tradition met the classical through Virgil's fifth eclogue. The structure of Virgil's poem, a lament followed by a celebration was imitated by all Renaissance poets interested in Christianising the pastoral elegy. The poem yielded easily to the evangelical spirit of Renaissance imitators of the classics. But the historians of the pastoral elegy T. P. Harrison and H. J. Leon go too far when they assert that 'for later pastoralists it remained only to substitute the joys of a Christian heaven' for the astral immortality awarded to Daphnis by Menalcas.[3] Those Christian poets of the Renaissance who simply imitated Virgil's structure (the collection of elegies of Sidney edited by Spenser contains several examples) produced absurd results. 'A Pastorall Aeglogue upon the death of Sir Philip Sidney, Knight, etc.' is a particularly crass example. Two griefstricken shepherds vie with each other in expressing their sense of bereavement, until one of them repeats the refrain of the poem, 'Phillisides is dead', and instead of continuing with some expression of misery, adds, 'O happie sprite/That now in heav'n with blessed soules doest bide . . .'. The lack of inner logic in the poem's development becomes laughably apparent. The first part of the poem, the lament, is an Aunt Sally set up only to be knocked down. The point at which the poet chooses to remember his Christian doctrine is arbitrary.

In eclogue V the elegy and the apotheosis are sung by different singers. This was not a practicable procedure for a Christian poet, who could hardly dramatise a singing contest between a Christian and an unbeliever. What is more Virgil's poem suggests that Mopsus's unconsoled grief is a respectable reaction to death, a reaction superseded but not rendered absurd by Menalcas's celebration of Daphnis's immortality. Virgil's poem derives from a culture in which naturalistic notions of the finality of death, and religious notions of immortality coexisted. It is not a model appropriate for a Christian poet.

The difficulty for those Renaissance poets who attempted to Christianise the classical pastoral elegy was to find some way of progressing from lament to celebration, instead of hopping arbitrarily from one to the other. In order to understand the solutions to the problem developed by Spenser and Milton, it is necessary to know something of Christian elegy. Take, as an example, Dunbar's *Lament for the Makaris*, an exercise in Christian meditation. Death demonstrates the transience of all things earthly. It demonstrates that, 'No stait in erd heir standis sickir'. Dunbar concentrates on the death of poets as a means of bringing this truth home to himself. The poem ends when the truth has become so urgent that the poet feels impelled to act upon it, to turn his thoughts away from the life of this world which will necessarily be terminated by death to the eternal life promised by Christ:

> Sen for the deid remeid is none,
> Best is that we for dede dispone
> Eftir our deid that lif may we:
>   Timor mortis conturbat me.

The distinctive characteristic of Christian elegy is its egotism. Chaucer proudly occupies the central line of Dunbar's poem, but he does so because his demise is the most powerful example of the undiscriminating nature of death: death has killed even Chaucer who was 'of makaris flour'. If death has killed Chaucer, Dunbar can expect no reprieve. This is the point. Every stanza ends with 'me', with Dunbar himself.

The classical elegy focuses directly on the death of an individual, but distances the expression of grief for his death through the pastoral conventions in which grief is expressed. Christian elegy generalises a death into Death and works to stamp the reality of death forcibly onto the mind of the poet and his reader. In Christian elegy a particular death is a means of drawing the poet's and his reader's attention to the inevitability of their own deaths, and the consequent need to prepare for judgement. The notion of an afterlife is accidental in classical elegy, whereas it is essential to Christian elegy. In Dunbar's poem the movement from a meditation on death to a consideration of the afterlife appears not arbitrary, but necessary, because his poem is focused not on the people who have died, but on the fate of its speaker. A consideration of mortal frailty leads the speaker inevitably to a consideration of the life that follows death. Classical elegy (with the exception of eclogue X in which

Gallus is represented not as dead, but as dying) subdued the character of the poem's speaker. The poem focused on the person mourned, not the effect of his death on the elegist. When Christian poets came to write pastoral elegy, they found that the displacement of the poet's consciousness, of 'me', from the centre of the poem's concern left within the poem no dynamic capable of propelling it from a lament for the death of an individual to a celebration of his reception in heaven. The movement was in danger of becoming as in 'A Pastoral Aeglogue...' entirely arbitrary.

Spenser's solution of this difficulty is revealing. In *November* Spenser prepares for the poem's turn through a passage in which Dido's death becomes for Colin what the deaths of the poets had been for Dunbar, an example of the frailty of the merely mortal: 'O trustlesse state of earthly things, and sliper hope/Of mortal men'. The value of Dido's death becomes admonitory; it is a lesson that Colin must learn: 'Now have I learned (a lesson derely brought)/That nys on earth assurance to be sought...' (165–6). Colin, the singer, displaces Dido at the centre of the poem, so that the celebration of Dido's immortality that follows expresses a development in the state of mind of the poem's speaker. Spenser accomplishes the turn from lament to celebration by moving at the crisis away from the conventions of pastoral elegy into the conventions of Christian elegy. The focus of the poem moves from Dido to Colin as a means of propelling the poem from sadness to jubilation.

In *Lycidas* we find a very much more complex mingling of the classical and Christian, of the commemorative elegy and the admonitory elegy, of the subdued classical speaker and the egotistical Christian speaker, of the distancing conventions of classical elegy, and the urgent conventions of Christian elegy. Critics have praised in *Lycidas* the perfect fusion of its Christian and classical elements. David Daiches, for example, commends Milton's success in having written a poem which is 'both impersonal and personal, elegiac and exultant, derivative and original, topical and universal', and argues that these informing paradoxes are 'subdued and woven completely into the texture'.[4] But this hardly suggests the abrupt transitions within *Lycidas*, nor the sense the poem gives of excitingly conflicting energies. J. C. Ransom, a more subversive critic, suggests that within *Lycidas* the personality of the poem's speaker disrupts the ideal anonymity of the poem's pastoral mode,[5] and his description seems truer to one's reading experience. In *Lycidas* the discrepancy between the formal requirements of pastoral elegy, the facts of the particular death of Edward King, and the personality of the poem's speaker, create the conflicts which force the poem into its abrupt transitions.

Nowhere is this more apparent than in Milton's turn from lament to celebration. In a beautifully traditional passage Milton lists the flowers that must be brought to decorate Lycidas's bier, 'To strew the laureate hearse where Lycid lies'. The decking of the corpse with flowers is a conventional pastoral device which offers an aesthetic consolation for the fact of death. But no sooner has Milton completed the conventionl movement than he dismisses it as a 'false surmise'. King's body has not been recovered; it is still buffeted by the indifferent seas. There is no corpse available to honour. The facts of the situation have reduced the convention to the status of an idle fiction. A discrepancy is allowed to develop between the demands of convention and the demands of truth. And the discrepancy, when realised by the poem's speaker, forces him on to imagine Lycidas received in Heaven as a means of resolving it. The poem is propelled forward by an emotional pressure felt by its speaker. The decking of the corpse with flowers, the conventional reassertion of pastoral harmony in the face of death, is dismissed as fiction, as a 'false surmise'. The poet is forced to look for a harmony consistent with truth, and he finds it in Heaven. To reassert pastoral harmony Milton is forced to break with the pastoral mode, to imagine a Heaven inconsistent with the mechanism of classical pastoral. The reception of Lycidas in Heaven both completes the pastoral convention by re-establishing a harmonious relationship between the mourner, the mourned and the world, and disrupts it by the introduction of a Christian Heaven outside the frame of reference of the classical pastoral.

Lycidas is an ironic completion of the tradition of pastoral elegy, for it is also a testing and a rejection of that tradition. In this it is similar to Virgil's tenth eclogue. Both *Lycidas* and eclogue X are poems in which the convention within which the poem is written is destoryed leaving the poet at the beginning of a new stage in his career: 'Tomorrow to fresh fields and pastures new'. I have argued that the poems of Shelley's maturity, *Julian* and Maddalo, Prometheus Unbound, The Mask of Anarchy and The Witch of Atlas, are poems of exactly this kind, poems which test, and often overturn the conventions within which they are written. In Adonais Shelley accomplishes, for the first time, a successful poem that does not exist in convert antagonism to its tradition. Shelley enters the final phase of his work, in which he writes in harmony with, rather than in reaction against, the conventions within which his poem exists.

This may seem remarkable. Adonais is written within the tradition of Christianised pastoral elegy. Shelley was not a Christian; Adonais is not a Christian poem. Adonais works towards a consolation for the fact of death without reliance on any received dogma. It is a Christian pastoral elegy from which all Christian theology has disappeared. And yet Shelley found in Lycidas, fully developed, a method of progressing from one position to another by exposing the emotional demands of the poem's speaker as the driving force behind the poem's development. He found a poetic method consistent with his own kind of scepticism. He found a model which allowed him to work in harmony with his inherited tradition.

Adonais is an extremely artificial poem. Shelley himself described it as a 'highly wrought piece of art, and perhaps better in point of composition than anything I have written'.[6] It exhibits its artifice by adhering to the tradition of pastoral elegy, by its use of one of the more artificial stanza forms, by including translations of the Greek elegists, by introducing contemporary characters in pastoral disguise, and by its use of a language which is often, by present-day standards, too public. It is easy to imagine how Adonais, like Lycidas, would have disgusted Dr Johnson. It is a representative of that style of neoclassicism which he detested, and can profitably be compared with a contemporary neoclassical epitaph, Canova's monument to Maria Christina.

Canova's monument depicts a pyramid which almost encloses a procession of mourners following the Duchess's ashes into the tomb through a door set in the pyramid's centre. The relationship between the human figures and the building is defined with a harsh clarity. The bodies are curved, dressed in flowing robes, hunched forward towards the ground; the building is straight-lined, sharp-edged, and two airborne figures over the door help to give the impression that it is without weight. The heavenward-pointing pyramid, for Canova as for Shelley, is a symbol of immortality,[7] and exists in sharp, cruel contrast to the group of human mourners moving slowly towards the door of the tomb. Canova's monument is like Shelley's poem in its selfconscious adherence to a classical tradition, in its display of artistic virtuosity, and in its insistence that all emotion must be disciplined by a severe formal patterning. Only the back of an old man interrupts the triangle of the pyramid which otherwise would frame all the human activity of the sculpture.

That I have compared Shelley's poem to a sculpture is appropriate in that *Adonais*, unlike other of his longer poems, lays claim to a spatial existence. It does so by means of an elaborate patterning which can be illustrated from its first stanzas. The poem's first two lines are an imitation of Theocritus:— 'I weep for Adonais – he is dead!/O, weep for Adonais! though our tears . . .' (1–2). But whereas Theocritus uses repetition simply as a means of intensifying the emotional atmosphere, Shelley introduces a new syntactic precision:

I weep . . . he is
O, weep . . . our tears . . .

The verbs change from the first, to the third, to the second persons, and the possessive pronoun that follows is in the first person plural. This succession helps to express the effect ascribed to Adonais's death of uniting humankind in a community of grief. A similar device is used in the final three lines of the stanza:

      with me
Died Adonais; till the Future dares
Forget the Past, his fate and fame shall be
An echo and a light unto eternity! (6–9)

The verb tenses move from past, 'died', to present, 'dares forget', to future, 'shall be'. The strong positions of the verbs at the beginning or end of the line emphasise the pattern. The sense of the lines is also concerned with tense: The 'Future', the 'Past', and 'eternity', (the ever-present). The first stanza suggests that Adonais's death is a concern of all people and of all time.

But there is another pattern in the stanza. The first line ends, 'is dead', and the last ends, 'unto eternity'. The construction 'is dead' suggests that death is considered a final state. This is modified in the course of the stanza when we read: 'with me/Died Adonais'. Death is no longer represented as a state, but an event in time. The final word of the stanza replaces the idea of death as a final state with 'eternity'. The action of the stanza presents in miniature what will become the action of the poem as a whole.

The stanza's final clause, 'his fate and fame shall be/An echo and a light unto eternity', is most easily paraphrased as 'his death and poetic reputation will never be forgotten'. But this is to understand 'unto eternity' as 'until eternity', and that Adonais's fame is a light 'unto eternity', pointing the way to eternity, is the thought on which the poem ends:

> Whilst burning through the inmost veil of Heaven,
> The soul of Adonais, like a star,
> Beacons from the abode where the Eternal are. (493–5)

The intricate formal patterning works to counteract the temporal existence of the poem. The stanza demands to be recognised as a spatial pattern in itself, and also predicts the pattern that will be accomplished within the whole poem.

The second stanza also announces the poem's intentions:

> Where wert thou, mighty Mother, when he lay,
> When thy Son lay, pierced by the shaft which flies
> In darkness? where was lorn Urania
> When Adonais died? (10–13)

Again the stanza begins with a translation from the Greek,[9] and again Shelley gives a precise function to repetition. He elaborates a single sentence:

> Where + was/wert + (person a) + when + (person b) + (verb).

His purpose in doing so is apparently only ornamentation. Each of the variables in the sentence is supplied in three different ways. The persons are first referred to as unidentified pronouns, then by a noun signifying a family relationship, and finally by name. The verb first appears as the colourless 'lay', then as an ornamental circumlocution, and then starkly as 'died'. Repetition is used to make an indirect approach on the bare truth,

'Adonais died'. Similarly the first twenty-one stanzas of the poem move indirectly towards an unflinching recognition of the fact of death.

In the second part of the stanza Keats's poems are compared with flowers hiding a corpse; they are ornaments devised to hide something ugly:

> With veilèd eyes,
> 'Mid listening Echoes, in her Paradise
> She sat, while one, with soft enamoured breath,
> Rekindled all the fading melodies,
> With which, like flowers that mock the corpse beneath
> He had adorned and hid the coming bulk of death. (13–18)

The comparison recalls a motif conventional in pastoral elegy, the decking of the bier with flowers. Milton had exposed in *Lycidas* the metaphorical significance of the convention. In the first part of his poem Shelley will use language, just as the mourners spread flowers, in an attempt to hide the ugly reality of Keats's death. His poem will begin in dalliance with false surmises.

In the third stanza Urania is told not to cry, but the stanza ends in 'despair'. In the fourth she is told to 'weep again', but the stanza ends in 'light'. The stanzas move between opposite poles, suggesting a very formalised oscillation between grief and exultation. The final words of each of the first four stanzas form a large chiasmic pattern:

(a) eternity (b) death (b) despair (a) light.

The pattern again suggests how the poem will find compensation for death in the recognition of immortality, how the light of eternity will enclose the despair of human grief.

Adonais is in many ways as formalised in its presentation of the progress from death to immortality as Canova's monument. But after all the one is very different from the other. Canova's sculpture is a work of supreme self-assurance, whereas Shelley's poem, despite its technical virtuosity, is written in a language which is frequently under strain. The cancelled passages from Shelley's preface to the poem in which indignation at the critical abuse directed at Keats collapses into indignation at the wrongs suffered by himself,[10] hardly suggests the self-effacement of the formal craftsman. There is the same conflict in *Adonais* between ideal anonymity and the personality of the speaker that Ransom detected in *Lycidas*.

The third stanza presents a single argument: Weep. But why? Stop grieving over Adonais for he has gone the way of all good people. The complication comes in the seventh line:

> oh, dream not that the amorous Deep
>   Will yet restore him to the vital air;
> Death feeds on his mute voice, and laughs at our despair.
>
>   (25–7)

In contrast to the logical consecutiveness that has controlled the first part of the stanza, the syntax presents these lines as a spontaneous exclamation drawn from the heart of the elegist. He tells Urania, by implication himself, not to dream that Adonais might be resuscitated. The phrase, 'the amorous Deep', prepares the reader for a conventional consolation: Adonais is so lovable that Death will not part with him. But the last line distorts this expected development: 'Death feeds on his mute voice, and laughs at our despair'. The verb 'feeds' might be a metaphor suggesting only that Death is engrossed by Keats's poetry, but when we read on and find Death laughing cruelly at Keats's mourners, the word offers itself literally as an expression of 'the eternal Hunger' of Death; one thinks of maggots. My first description of the poem's style suggested that it worked to create patterns: the attempt was to give the poem's shape an inevitability like that of a formalised liturgy. Here the reverse occurs. The elegist's attempt to console Urania collapses as his horror of death breaks through into the poem's language. Meaning emerges independent of the apparent intention of the speaker. The stanza imitates not the prescribed movements of a ritual, or of an exercise in a convention-tied poetic genre, but the darting, unpredictable movements of the human mind, unable to direct the paths along which it will be carried. But Death's laughter is also a part of the poem's formal pattern. It is paralleled in stanza XLI by the smiling stars:

> and thou Air
> Which like a mourning veil thy scarf hadst thrown

O'er the abandoned Earth, now leave it bare
Even to the joyous stars which smile on its despair. (366–9)

Such laughter the poem realises is not really cruel, but, like the laugh of Troilus at the end of Chaucer's poem, a kindly laughter at the unnecessariness of mortal grief. The third stanza, like most of the poem, is both personal and impersonal, formal and spontaneous, but we react to its formality and its spontaneity on quite different levels.

Stanza IV is similar. It begins: 'Most musical of mourners, weep again!/Lament anew, Urania! – He died . . .' (28–9). As one reads the second line, 'he' is naturally identified as Adonais or Keats, but the references that follow identify him as Milton. The confusion created by the pronoun is active in the poem. The saddening circumstances of Milton's last years are described vigorously, but time has made apparent a startling incongruity between the defeated, dead man, who lived his last years 'Blind, old, and lonely', and the triumphant, living poet, who: 'Yet reigns o'er earth; the third among the sons of light'. The mistake encouraged by the pronoun encourages the reader to compare the earthly fates of Keats and Milton, and suggests that time will reveal a similar compensation for Keats's miserable personal biography in the posthumous fame of his poetry. In stanza III a consolation collapses into an expression of the physical horror of death; in stanza IV an expression of grief surprisingly yields a consolation. In both stanzas the poem imitates the unpredictable play of the human mind confronting experience, so that the personality of the speaker becomes central to the meaning of the poem, and the poem approximates to a soliloquy. And yet stanza IV, like stanza III, also plays a part in the poem's formal patterning. Milton, after Homer and Dante, is 'the third among the sons of light'. This trinity of poets who have achieved renown is balanced in stanza XLV by Chatterton, Sidney, and Lucan (notice how the chronological reversal perfects the symmetry), the 'inheritors of unfulfilled renown', with whom Keats takes his place. And as in stanza III the reader must react to the stanza's place within a formal pattern, and to its imitation of an undirected mental process, on different levels.

I suggested in discussing the tradition of pastoral elegy that in Spenser's *November*, and more consistently in *Lycidas*, there is a conflict between the formality of classical elegy in which the role of the elegist is subdued, and his poem focuses on the person commemorated and the conventional demands of the genre, and Christian elegy, in which the poem is focused on the conscious-ness of its speaker and death is primarily important for its admonitory effect on the elegist, warning him to discriminate sensibly between the claims of this world and the claims of the next. In *Adonais*, Shelley intensifies this conflict, but his poem remains firmly within the tradition established by Spenser and Milton. Shelley's modern admirers have tended to stress the formality of *Adonais*, but they have done so in conscious opposition to the claims of his Victorian admirers and his modern detractors that in *Adonais* Shelley's overt concern for Keats is a mask inadequately disguising his real concern for himself. Shelley's modern admirers have responded to one of the poem's elements, his detractors to the other. A critical defence of *Adonais* must therefore concentrate on its personality, and the first stage of that defence must be to indicate that the intrusion of the poem's speaker into the poem is not peculiar to *Adonais*. Egotism, as I remarked, is a distinctive feature of Christian elegy.

Stanzas V, VI and VII each attempt an approach to the fact of death through metaphor. The fifth stanza continues the theme of the fourth, translating several poetic fates into metaphors relating to light:

> And happier they their happiness who knew,
> Whose tapers yet burn through that night of time
> In which suns perish; others more sublime,
> Struck by the envious wrath of man or God,
> Have sunk, extinct in their refulgent prime... (39–43)

The metaphors are a lubricant helping the reader to glide smoothly over the difficulty evaded by the stanza. Implicit in it is a problem ineffectively disguised by Shelley's use of similar metaphors for physical death and for the death of one's reputation. The 'perished suns' are presumably those poets of antiquity whose work has not survived. The 'extinct' suns, on the other hand, seem to be those poets who died before their genius fulfilled itself. But an extinct and a perished sun are surely identical. The confusing metaphors distract the attention from a question that the stanza begs: how can one rely on mortal fame as a compensation for one's sufferings when the world has forgotten some suns, and yet retains the memory of some tapers? The following two stanzas also try to find in metaphor a protection against the nasty reality of the poet's death. The sixth compares Adonais to a flower. On the poem's personal level this is a retreat into sentimentality: on its formal level it is a retreat into an evasive myth which attempts to subsume the death of an individual, Keats, within the ritual death of the season god Adonis. The seventh attempts to view Adonais's death as a heroic act, a willing sacrifice made to ensure 'A grave among the eternal'. But the paradox contained in the phrase subversively suggests the absurdity of finding consolation for death in earthly fame.

Metaphor fails to provide Shelley with a stable, bearable attitude to death. His lack of assurance is evident in the last lines of the seventh stanza:

> Haste, while the vault of blue Italian day
> Is yet his fitting charnel-roof! while still
> He lies, as if in dewy sleep he lay;
> Awake him not! surely he takes his fill
> Of deep and liquid rest, forgetful of all ill. (59–63)

Are we told to hurry away before night falls, when the darkening sky will become unfit to act as a roof for Adonais's tomb, or before the body starts to rot, and becomes unfit to be roofed by the pure sky? 'Still' could be understood as 'not moving' or 'silent', an attempt to strengthen the fiction that Adonais is asleep, or it might mean 'yet', while the body can still be mistaken for a man asleep. 'Surely' might express the joyful certainty of the psalmist, or betray the doubt of a man anxious to convince himself of what he would like to believe. The ambiguities are an escape, suggesting that the poet is unable to convince himself of what he would like to believe, and yet unable directly to face the alternative.

In stanza VII the reader is warned either of the imminence of nightfall, or of the imminence of the body's putrefaction. In stanza VIII the one is the symbol of the other. The escape door of the preceding stanza, ambiguity, is barred. But even here an attempt is made to evade the issue:

He will awake no more,'oh, never more!
Within the twilight chamber spreads apace,
The shadow of white Death, and at the door
Invisible Corruption waits to trace
His extreme way to her dim dwelling-place;
The eternal Hunger sits, but pity and awe
Soothe her pale rage, nor dares she to deface
So fair a prey, till darkness, and the law
Of change, shall o'er his sleep the mortal curtain draw. (64–72)

Throughout the stanza the approach of corruption becomes less urgent. The shadow of white Death 'spread apace', but invisible Corruption 'waits to trace/His extreme way', and the eternal Hunger only 'sits'. As the subject comes closer to the literal fact of putrefaction the verb becomes less active. In the last lines of the stanza Shelley's desire to evade the fact triumphs. A recognition of reality, 'The eternal Hunger sits', is immediately denied, 'but pity and awe etc.'. The final clause beginning 'till' accepts the inevitability of decay, but in its expression the fact is transformed. The physical repulsion expressed in the previous references to decay is absent from the phrase, 'the law/Of change', which is comforting because it expresses stability, and because it requires only an intellectual assent. The verb, the action of corruption, is disguised in a metaphor which compares it with the drawing of curtains around a sleeping man. Stanza VIII ends the introductory movement of the poem; the final lines give the reader a comforting sense that the fact of death has been recognised and accepted. But it is a false conslusion. The final clause is inconsistent. To escape the physical horror of putrefaction the personifications of the first part of the stanza are replaced by the impersonal, asensual 'law/Of change'. But to make man the passive object of an impersonal force is to deprive him of special significance, and so the impersonal noun is attached to a complement which implies personal care. The metaphor allows Shelley to have it both ways. It is a metaphor of evasion.

The first movement ends in an impasse. Shelley has made repeated attempts to look unflinchingly at the fact of Adonais's death, and has at last succeeded only in hiding an ugly reality in a sympathetic metaphor. The following section represents a sustained attempt to 'adorn and hide the bulk of death' by the use of poetic artifice. In stanzas IX to XIII the 'quick Dreams', the materials out of which Adonais made his poems, lament him. Stanza XI may serve as an example of the style of this passage. The substance of the stanza is imitated from Bion's elegy,[11] but Shelley's manner is very different. One of the Dreams: 'Washed his light limbs as if embalming them...'. The inversion is selfconsciously ornate and witty. She washed his legs refusing to believe that he was dead, but she washed them as if embalming them. The emotions and actions of the Dreams are consistently twisted into witty patterns:

> Another clipped her profuse locks, and threw
> The wreath upon him, like an anadem,
> Which frozen tears instead of pearls begem... (93–5)

Not only is the wreath of hair like a tiara but the pearls on the tiara have their counterparts in the frozen teardrops on the hair. The poem has moved into the manner of conceited, Petrarchan verse for which Shelley's models may have been English, Italian or Spanish (Calderon). A third Dream snaps her bow; 'as if to stem/A greater loss with one which was more weak'. She breaks her bow, as people tear their hair, to relieve one pain with another. But on Adonais's face is 'barbed fire'. Death also has a dart. The Dream mimes the destruction of the power of Death, who is wittily conflated with Cupid. In either of its aspects, her action, like those of the other Dreams, is gracefully futile.

In the first eight stanzas Shelley failed in an attempt to look unflinchingly at death. His metaphors attempted to reconcile an acceptance of fact with his demand for consolation for the fact. They succeeded only through inconsistency. In the following section he attempts to achieve a stable attitude to death through artistic control, by subjugating the need to speak the truth to the need to express experience in wittily decorative patterns. Truth is made the servant of art, because art, unlike truth, is within the artist's control. As we by now expect of the mature Shelley, he looks for a style which will, in itself, express this development, and he locates it in the mannerisms of the extravagantly conceited followers of Petrarch. So the Dreams mime grief in witty patterns. They depart the scene, but Morning, Echo and Spring appear, and their grief is also mimed. In stanza XVI Spring is upset by Adonais's death, which, in a pastoral elegy, is perfectly natural, but that she behaves like Autumn and treats the

new buds as if they were dead leaves is a witty paradox.
This section ends with stanza XVII. Shelley freely translates
Moschus, arguing that the nightingale does not mourn her mate,
nor the eagle her lost offspring so much as Albion mourns
Adonais.[12] Moschus's birds are conventional emblems of grief:
Shelley chooses wittily. The nightingale is Adonais's 'spirit's
sister': Keats wrote an ode to her. The eagle 'like thee could scale
Heaven', like Keats because he wrote poems about the moon
(*Endymion*), and the sun (*Hyperion*). The eagle, alone among
birds, could look directly at the sun; 'could nourish in the sun's
domain/Her mighty youth with mourning . . .'. So could Keats,
who wrote a poem about the sun-god. But there is irony here.
The eagle rejuvenates itself by flying into the sun; Keats writes
his fragment on the sun-god and dies. The wit begins to collide
with reality. Adonais is mourned by 'Albion', a conventional
poetical name for England, but also a suitable pseudonym for
Shelley, because he writes as the representative of all English
poets, and because the word contains the name Bion, It is a witty
choice, but the disjunction between the poem's artifice, and the
reality it purports to express, has become painfully apparent.
England, far from mourning Keats, had subjected him to the
abuse and neglect which Shelley imagined had caused his death,
and Shelley could not seriously claim to be his country's
representative. The elaborate fictions of the preceding stanzas
shatter as they contact an intransigent reality. The painful
realisation that the fictional death of Adonais as it has been
described is quite inconsistent with the actual death of Keats
provokes the curse directed at the previously unmentioned
reviewer with which the stanza ends:

> the curse of Cain
> Light on his head who pierced thy innocent breast,
> And scared the angel soul that was its earthly guest. (151–3)

Shelley's poem begins to progress in the manner of *Lycidas*. An
awareness of the incompatibility of the conventional fiction with
the actual fact provides the dynamic which forces the poem
forwards, just as Milton's poem displays the discrepancy between the conventional decking of the hearse with flowers, the
'false surmise', and the actual situation of King's body, to create
the emotional pressure which will hurl his poem towards

heaven. But at this stage in Shelley's poem, the discrepancy forces him not into paradise, but into a cul-de-sac. In the poem's first movement Shelley tried through metaphor to reconcile his demand for a humanly significant world with the fact of Keats's death. He failed. In its second movement, he attempted to subjugate the fact to artifice, to write a poem invulnerable to intransigent reality, because it refused to contact that reality. But the facts refused to be dismissed so summarily; they rose up and shattered the fiction. In the poem's third movement, stanzas XVIII to XXI, he attempts to achieve a stable attitude to death by accepting that man lives in a world which does not respond to his feelings. He attempts to conclude his poem by rejecting the pastoral notion of harmony between man and nature as a fiction. All this is signalled in the first two lines of stanza XVIII: 'Ah, woe is me! Winter is come and gone,/But grief returns with the revolving year . . .' (154–5). In stanza XVI, Shelley had imagined the returning Spring displaying her grief by behaving like Autumn. In this stanza he rejects the conceit as a fiction. Nature will joyously renew itself paying no heed to human pain. Shelley's mature stylistic assurance is very evident in these two lines. He moves easily away from the extravagantly mannered conceits of the preceding movement, into a style that engages and expresses human experience.

There is a development within this movement of the poem. It begins by expressing a dislocation between human emotion, and the world outside, but progressively human emotion is subjugated to the natural order. The poem's second movement attempted to win an artificial assurance in the face of death, the third movement attempts to gain a naturalistic assurance. Shelley's returning grief is disregarded as soon as it is mentioned, and the remaining seven lines of stanza XVIII, and the whole of stanza XIX constitute a hymn to the re-emergence of life, to the 'quickening life' bursting from the earth's heart. The end of the reptiles' winter hibernation becomes, through one of the long negative epithets that Shelley uses so well, a joyous liberation from constricting confinement: 'And the green lizard, and the golden snake,/Like unimprisoned flames, out of their trance awake' (161–2).

In stanza XIX this *joie de vivre* is said to infuse 'All baser things': man is isolated from it, but in stanza XX it is felt even by Adonais's corpse, which

Exhales itself in flowers of gentle breath;
Like incarnations of the stars, when splendour
Is changed to fragrance... (171–5)

This simile, beautifully accomplished ('like in-carnations of the stars'), later becomes a means by which the poem develops away from naturalism. To praise the worldly, vegetation, Shelley compares it with what is outside this world, to praise the transient he compares it with the eternal. But the implications of that procedure are not yet realised. Adonais's corpse has become manure for flowers, and it feeds 'the merry worm'. Despite his death, his body still plays a part within the great lifecycle of nature. This perception gives Shelley a new, naturalistic assurance. He can conclude, 'Nought we know dies'.

It is typical of the whole poem that a phrase which marks the resolution of one problem should itself become the basis of another. This is achieved simply by transferring the attention from the object to the subject of the sentence, from 'nought' to 'we', from the phenomenon known to the consciousness, the knower. It is no consolation to realise that the flesh will be manure for flowers since the consciousness will not be preserved. The mind will be sunk 'in a most cold repose'. This, the last phrase of stanza XX, is a distorted imitation of an idea Shelley had formerly expressed as a wish: 'surely he takes his fill/Of deep and liquid rest, forgetful of all ill' (62–3). But from the poem's new naturalistic perspective, the mind's tranquillity is no longer its rest, but its annihilation. The wish has come true, but only to reveal itself as something not to be desired.

In the first stanza of this movement, Shelley exclaimed, 'Woe is me!' This exclamation was a response to his inability to shake off his grief, a response to the lack of coincidence between his sadness and the joy of nature. In stanza XXI, the last stanza of the movement, Shelley utters the same exclamation, but now he is unhappy because he knows that time will cure his grief, that human emotions, like natural seasons, are transient, not permanent:

Alas! that all we loved of him should be
But for our grief, as if it had not been,
And grief itself be mortal! Woe is me! (181–3)

All things in nature are mutable. If man is subject to nature, then human feelings are mutable. The seasonal cycle becomes a pointless repetition. The knowledge that man is subject to it, leaves him empty of purpose, his life insignificant, his questions unanswered: 'Whence are we, and why are we? of what scene/The actors or spectators?' (184–5). Shelley is experimenting with a naturalistic notion of human life and death. From that perspective no answers to these questions are possible. He sums up in the remaining lines of the stanza:

> Great and mean
> Meet massed in death, who lends what life must borrow.
> As long as skies are blue, and fields are green,
> Evenings must usher night, night urge the morrow,
> Month follow month with woe, and year wake year to
> sorrow. (185–9)

In a sense, these lines are the most important in the whole poem, for only if the reader reacts to them as Shelley would have him will the continuation of the poem be satisfying. They are utterly drab. Shelley strives after maximum predictability. He introduces a rhyme word 'borrow' which leaves no doubt in the mind of any reader of English poetry which two words will rhyme with it. The stanza ends with three lines each of which contains one half-line of minimal interest followed by another almost entirely predicted by the first. In these lines Shelley reaches the only conclusion he finds possible granted that man's consciousness ends with life. They work to persuade the reader that such a conclusion is not, and cannot be, a proper ending for the poem. They work to enlist the reader as the poet's accomplice in the poem's continuation.

The poem's machinery, Urania, Adonais's Muse, and the various personifications, were absent from the poem's third movement, necessarily absent, because in that movement Shelley viewed death from a naturalistic perspective. As a means of escaping from the naturalistic cul-de-sac they are reintroduced. In stanza XXII Misery, Dreams and Echoes all address Urania, just as the poet addressed her in the poem's first movement. Shelley has moved back to square one. But in the opening stanzas of the poem, Urania was the mute recipient of the poet's directions. He told her to cry, to stop crying, to 'weep again'. Only one action was ascribed to her, 'She sat'. When she reappears in the poem she is again hectored. Misery tells her to 'Wake' and 'rise', and expects 'tears and sighs' from her, and then the Dreams and Echoes form a deputation demanding that she arise: 'Swift as a thought by the snake memory stung/From her ambrosial rest the fading Splendour sprung' (197–8). At last, she is active; she is the subject of an energetic verb. She goes in search of Adonais, and her journey is a painful pilgrimage; the souls of her feet are 'wounded', her 'soft Form' is torn by 'barbed tongues' and sharp thoughts. Finally, in stanza XXV, she speaks, breaking the passive silence she has maintained for so long. This is the sign that she has been granted an independent existence:

> 'Leave me not wild and drear and comfortless,
> As silent lightning leaves the starless night!
> Leave me not!' cried Urania: her distress
> Roused Death: Death rose and smiled, and met her vain caress.
>
> (222–5)

Urania imagines Adonais to be alive, reaches out to embrace him, but instead embraces Death. A practical joke is played on her like that played on the Dream, who washed Adonais's legs 'as if embalming them'. Our reaction to it is so different because of the contrasting verbal context. In Urania's speech Shelley allows a graceless rhetorical imbalance. After the second appearance of the phrase 'Leave me not', he frustrates the reader's expectation of a complement that will complete the balance between the two phrases. When the phrase reappears the word 'not' negates the verb, rather than its complement; it is stressed, whereas before it was unstressed. The style, instead of being directed by the need to create graceful rhetorical patterns, is directed by the need to express emotion. Urania reappears in order to displace Adonais as the focus of the reader's sympathy. It is a technique similar in effect to the displacement of the person mourned by the mourner at the critical moment of Christian versions of pastoral elegy.

At this point a close inspection of stanza XXIII is necessary:

> She rose like an autumnal Night, that springs
> Out of the East, and follows wild and drear
> The golden Day, which, on eternal wings.

Even as a ghost abandoning a bier,
Had left the Earth a corpse. (199–203)

Urania rising to go in search of Adonais is compared to an
'autumnal Night'. The simile integrates this movement of the
poem, with the naturalistic movement that preceded it. But she
is a night which follows a day that has not ceased to exist, but has
left the Earth 'on eternal wings'. The adjective introduces
a notion incompatible with the naturalistic notion of time expressed in the preceding movements. There month followed
month. Times were consecutive, so that two times could not
coexist. Urania, when she is compared to a night that goes in
search of the day she has ended, speaks for the poem in her
impulse to escape from depressing naturalistic notions of time.
The night goes in search of a day that has left the earth 'on eternal
wings'; Urania goes in search of Adonais. This is the first
suggestion within the poem that any supernatural afterlife is
postulated for Adonais. The suggestion is introduced casually, as
if it were an incidental byproduct of Shelley's development of the
simile, rather than a considered statement of belief. It is
characteristic of Shelley's technique in this poem that ideas are
introduced as if unconsciously. The apparent unconsciousness
with which they are presented is understood as a guarantee of
their fidelity to human nature.

Both the developments that I have noticed, the intrusion into a
simile of the idea of immortality, and the growth of Urania into a
character capable of acting as the focus of the reader's sympathy,
prepare us to receive the crucial lines of this passage. They are
spoken by Urania to Adonais's corpse:

I would give
All that I am to be as thou now art!
But I am chained to Time, and cannot thence depart! (232–4)

Urania's mistake in embracing Death rather than Adonais
becomes not a grim joke but an allegory of her now-recognised
desire to die. Not by a rational argument, but by following what
we may term the logic of the emotions, the poem has turned full
circle. Shelley began by attempting to confront the fact of death,
but the problem has now become the pain of life. The poem
began in an attempt to describe death in a manner that made

death tolerable. In the poem's naturalistic movement this was achieved: death became a 'cold repose', uninviting, but unappalling. But death in becoming bearable made life intolerable, a succession of meaningless months and years. The new problem raised by the poem is how to find a manner of describing death that makes life tolerable. In the description of the procession of mourners that arrives to pay homage to Adonais, this problem becomes dominant.

The description of a procession of mourners is a conventional theme in pastoral elegy; it can be paralleled in Theocritus's first idyll, in eclogue X, and in *Lycidas*.[13] But again Shelley disconcertingly unites the conventional and the personal. Not only are the mourners contemporary poets in pastoral disguise – Byron as the 'Pilgrim of Eternity', Tom Moore as Ireland's 'sweetest lyrist', and Leigh Hunt as a 'softer voice' –, but the procession is dominated by the notorious self-portrait, Shelley dressed as Dionysius,[14] and self-described as a 'pardlike Spirit beautiful and swift'. A violent fusion of the personal and the formal controls the style of the passage. Asked by Urania to identify himself, the strange Shelleyan mourner:

> with a sudden hand
> Made bare his branded and ensanguined brow,
> Which was like Cain's or Christ's – oh! that it should be so!
> (304–6)

The effect of self-melodramatisation is countered, until the last phrase, by the formality of expression. The brow is branded, like Cain's, and ensanguined, like Christ's pricked by the crown of thorns. The rigorously formal construction of the sentence fits oddly with the reader's sense of it as an uncontrolled emotional outburst.

The critical defenders of this passage demand that it be understood within its context; they claim that it is tightly integrated with the rest of the poem, and their case can be powerfully argued,[15] and yet the tendency to extract these stanzas either like a Victorian Shelleyan in homage to the seraphic spirit that inhabits the body of Shelley's verse, or like a new critic as a demonstration of the self-indulgent, self-pitying narcissism that mars his work, remains for most readers a temptation hard to resist. It may help to recall an analogous critical debate, that concerning Peter's diatribe against time-

serving clergymen in *Lycidas*. Strenuous and successful attempts
have been made to build this passage into the thematic development of the poem, and yet does there not remain some truth in
Ransom's observation that the passage is 'angry, violent', and
fits oddly with the formality of other parts of the poem?

In *Lycidas*, and in more extreme form in *Adonais*, there is a
conflict between conventionality and personality. Many passages in *Adonais* exist on both a personal and a formal level, and
the two levels are strangely unreconciled. In the self-portrait
both levels of the poem ought to obtrude themselves forcibly on
the reader's consciousness. He ought to recognise both the
embarrassing nakedness of the self-exposure and the formality of
the Dionysian disguise. It is no part of the critic's duty to choose
between these reactions. He must accept both. Unresolved
conflict is suggested within the style of the self-portrait:

>   he, as I guess,
> Had gazed on Nature's naked loveliness,
> Actaeon-like, and now he fled astray
> With feeble steps o'er the world's wilderness,
> And his own thoughts, along that rugged way,
> Pursued, like raging hounds, their father and their prey.
>
> A pardlike Spirit beautiful and swift –
> A Love in desolation masked; – a Power
> Girt round with weakness; – it can scarce uplift
> The weight of the superincumbent hour;
> It is a dying lamp, a falling shower,
> A breaking billow; – even whilst we speak
> Is it not broken? (274–86)

The comparison between the pursuit of Actaeon by his dogs and
the pursuit of Shelley by his own thoughts is developed in a
complex sentence in which the various correspondences are
rigorously pursued. There is a certain formal muscularity in the
working out of the simile. In the following stanza we are offered
a series of related images without any attempt to articulate
logically their relationships. A strong syntax is replaced by a
series of phrases linked weakly by apposition. The contrast
reflects the theme of the description. Shelley describes himself as
'a Power/Girt round with weakness'; he comprehends both

strength and frailty. He walks the world with 'feeble steps', yet his inner life, though self-destructive, is powerful; his thoughts are like 'raging hounds'. In stanza XXXIII he holds a spear that shakes in his weak grasp, but the vibration betrays the power of his 'ever-beating heart'. He combines physical weakness, and spiritual strength; more precisely, a spiritual strength that reveals itself in this world as weakness. The contrast within the passage between a strong and a weak syntax, between rigorously pursued and weakly aggregated similes, expresses the same paradox. But more than that the contrast epitomises the dislocation between a strong, formal structure, and a much more tenuous sequence of mental movements, that infuses the whole poem. In the self-portrait this conflict achieves its most powerful expression. Shelley mimes the impersonality of the classical elegist by dressing up as Dionysius, but at the same time gives vent to the self-pity through which he identifies with Keats, and reveals the pressure that drives the poem forward as his own thirst for immortality.

Within the self-portrait the elegist compares himself with Cain and Christ, the murderer and the victim. The comparison seems to be a particularly disturbing example of the kind of paradoxical definition of the poet and poetry favoured by the Romantics. But both Cain and Christ were rejected by their societies; both, in Blake's terms, were members of the devil's party. Cain, Christ, Shelley and Keats now represent the whole spectrum of social misfits for whom life is pain. The transference of attention from the injustice of death to the injustice of life is complete, and it is signalled by the curse on the reviewer in stanza XXXVII: 'Live thou whose infamy is not thy fame!' Shelley wishes him alive. In line 151, Shelley had wished on the reviewer 'the curse of Cain', but at that point he seemed unaware of the inconsistency between such a curse and grief for the death of Adonais. The notion that death might be preferable to life becomes more explicit in Urania's exclamation of grief:

> I would give
> All that I am to be as now thou art!
> But I am chained to Time, and cannot thence depart! (232–4)

By the end of the poem the elegist has committed himself to death, even suicide, and the progression has been driven to its final conclusion. Again we meet the poem's central problem. Is the poem an expression of the truth and beauty of a pre-existent belief in immortality, or do subjective pressures control the poem's development, because the elegist is in a situation in which only through a surrender to subjectivity can he find consolation for the pain which affronts the conscious mind living in an indifferent world? On the answer depends the reader's understanding of the poem's final movement. If he accepts the first suggestion then, in the final stanzas, Shelley satisfyingly completes the intricate patterns of the poem's symbolisms. If he accepts the second, then in these last stanzas Shelley tries on different notions of immortality like a woman trying on new hats, and for the same reason: he is looking for one that fits and that looks pretty. It is this second suggestion that I shall develop.

Consider stanza XXXVIII. The poem has arrived at the position that we should be thankful that Keats has escaped in death the calumny to which he was subject while alive, but Shelley is still sceptical of immortality: 'He wakes or sleeps with the enduring dead'. The reader is still asked to believe only that the dead endure by virtue of their earthly fame, even though as early as stanza VII the notion that Keats's life, if his poetry proved of lasting value, might be considered fulfilled seemed absurd. The famous win only 'a grave among the eternal'. But stanza XXXVIII continues, and makes more extravagant claims:

> Thou canst not soar where he is sitting now. –
> Dust to the dust! but the pure spirit shall flow
> Back to the burning fountain whence it came,
> A portion of the Eternal, which must glow
> Through time and change, unquenchably the same,
> Whilst thy cold embers choke the sordid hearth of shame.
> (337–42)

The development is impelled by the need to distinguish 'he', Adonais, from 'thou', the reviewer. In a world where good and evil, talent and mediocrity, are confused, it is emotionally necessary to postulate an afterlife that will sort them out. The verb forms of the stanza indicate such a pressure: the pure spirit 'shall flow', the Eternal 'must glow'. 'Shall' is not just a future

tense; it indicates an exercise of the will. 'Must' suggests not only
that the Eternal has no choice in the matter of whether or not to
glow, but that it must be so, Shelley's feelings demand that it
should be so.

Stanza XXXIX expresses the new belief through the conventional paradoxes of Christian Platonism:

> Peace, peace! he is not dead, he both not sleep –
> He hath awakened from the dream of life . . .

Shelley, like Milton, and unlike those Christian elegists who
remember this important item of doctrine only as their poems
draw near to the conclusion, has exposed the pressures that force
him towards this belief. But at this point in *Lycidas* Milton can
splendidly invoke the Christian heaven; Shelley, deprived of
theological support, must construct the heaven to which he may
consign Keats, and he must construct it out of a vacuum. In
stanza XL life is described as 'unrest': death negates the negative
of life. This is all that can confidently be deduced by the living of
an afterlife. It is vacuous. Once again the poem has reached a
conclusion which, it attempts to persuade the reader, is unsatisfactory. Again the reader is asked to comply with the poem's
continuance, to become the poet's accomplice as he searches for a
more positive description of immortality.

Just as Shelley escaped from the cul-de-sac that he reached in
stanza XXII, by reinvoking Urania, so he escapes from this
conclusion by returning to the conventions of pastoral elegy. He
reverts to the pastoral notion that nature sympathises with
human emotions, and tells forests, flowers, fountains, etc. to
cease mourning, and join him in a celebration of death. This
prepares for the first definition of immortality announced at the
beginning of stanza XLII: 'He is made one with Nature . . .'. In
the following stanza this notion is developed:

> He is a portion of the loveliness
> Which once he made more lovely: he doth bear
> His part, while the one Spirit's plastic stress
> Sweeps through the dull dense world, compelling there,
> All new successions to the forms they wear;
> Torturing th' unwilling dross that checks its flight
> To its own likeness, as each mass may bear;

And bursting in its beauty and its might
From trees and beasts and men into the Heaven's light.
                                                    (379–87)

This recalls stanza XIX. The plastic stress is similar in its action
to Spring. But the joy of Spring was delusive: it revived only
'baser things'. Adonais's mind, the 'intense atom', did not share
in the regeneration. In this stanza 'he' is a part of the vital activity
described: Adonais is the subject of both sentences. And yet even
now he is only 'a portion of the loveliness/Which once he made
more lovely'. The active creativity of Keats's life, 'made', is
contrasted with his neutral existence, 'is', after death. The plastic
stress is a creative force, and its activity in moulding the world, in
so far as its materials allow, to its own likeness, parallels the
activity of the idealist poet struggling to adapt language so that it
will express the pictures of his mind, and yet the conjunction that
associates Adonais with this activity, 'while', fails to unify him
with it. The stanza offers little encouragement to the reader to
imagine Adonais participating in the exciting struggle in which
the stress is described as engaged. The notion that the individual's life after death consists in being subsumed in an
impersonal life-force, no matter how excitingly described, is
shown to be unsatisfactory. The elegist is forced onwards to
contemplate, in the following stanzas, the notion of individual
immortality. Chatterton, Sidney and Lucan, the 'inheritors of
unfulfilled renown' are introduced as the representatives of those
'whose name on Earth is dark', but who have found 'dazzling
immortality' after death. Immortality is disentangled from
worldly fame, which was contingent on chance. It is available
even to those unknown on Earth. Their invitation to Adonais to
join them, and his assumption of his role as the 'Vesper of our
throng', a role which seems to include both individual existence
and the impersonal immortality of becoming a part of nature,
brings the poem to yet another conclusion.

Adonais has been successfully removed to a safe Heaven, 'Far
in the Unapparent'. This suggests the last resolution that the
poem must attempt; having dismissed the notion that Adonais is
a part of 'the one Spirit's plastic stress', and rehoused him in a
star, Shelley must reforge a relationship between the eternal
world in which Adonais has taken his place, and the world in
which we live. Stanza XLVIII returns to the world from the

esoteric paradise among the stars. Rome is the world. It is described as a huge paradox, 'the Paradise/The grave, the city, and the wilderness'. The paradoxical nature of the whole city is epitomised in the description of its English churchyard, in which Keats was buried. Its crumbling walls contrast with 'the keen pyramid' within it, the memorial to Caius Cestius. The pyramid is 'Like flame transformed to marble', but flame is hot, transient and associated with life; marble is cold, enduring and associated with death. The world is a place: 'Where, like an infant's smile, over the dead,/A light of laughing flowers along the grass is spread' (440–1).

In this world life and death are involved incongruously, paradoxically. Stanza LII sorts them out:

> The One remains, the many change and pass;
> Heaven's light forever shines, Earth's shadows fly;
> Life, like a dome of many-coloured glass,
> Stains the white radiance of Eternity,
> Until Death tramples it to fragments. (460–4)

Earl Wasserman finds it strange 'in view of the recurrence of light (sun, star), atmosphere (mist, sky), and color' throughout the poem that this should be 'the passage that was most frequently condemned by New Critics as inorganic and superimposed'. [16] In one way, he is right, and yet Shelley allows the lines to appear as if isolated from their context. He refuses to integrate them with the verbal texture of the preceding and following stanzas. In the poem's final section the stanzas seem to jump away from one another, and the thematic organisation that Wasserman ably describes oddly fails to make itself apparent on the poem's verbal surface.

The stanza expresses the same contrast three times. The first statement is literal, the 'One' contrasts with the 'Many'. In the second statement metaphor is introduced unobtrusively, 'Heaven's light' contrasts with 'Earth's shadows'. But in the third statement of the contrast, the verbal figure, the simile, controls the reader's reaction to it. This structure is typical of the poem. The idea is developed in such a way that the jury is not reason but the emotional reaction to the idea prompted in the reader. Life is 'like a dome of many-coloured glass'. The dome provokes religious and aesthetic awe, but our reaction to it is complicated by the building material. It might suggest the brittle gaiety of the artificial, or a touching fragility, like Christmas tree decorations. The verb 'stains' is influenced both by its subject, and its object, but to contradictory effect. 'Dome' encourages the reader to associate the verb with stained-glass windows, but 'the white radiance' encourages him to think of a disfiguring stain. The stanza's third and fourth lines simply repeat the contrasting elements of the first two lines, reversing their order: the 'dome of many-coloured glass' contrasts with 'the white radiance of Eternity', but the fifth line introduces a new element, 'Death'. Death will trample the glass dome to fragments, an action that we respond to ambivalently, either as joyfully destructive liberation or brutal vandalism. [17]

The poem turned to Rome in order to reconcile the world we live in with the world hereafter. But the paradoxes of the world encouraged in stanza LII an attempt to elucidate the relationship between life and immortality, that left the reader not with a reconciliation between the two, but with a predicament in which he must choose between them. The elegist chooses death: 'No more let life divide what Death can join together'. Stanza LIV appears to offer a retraction. Shelley attempts to reconcile his three notions of immortality: the One which has its being in opposition to the many of this world, the one Spirit's plastic stress which works through this world, and the personal immortality with which Adonais seemed to have been accredited when he joined the 'inheritors of unfulfilled renown', and became 'the Vesper of [their] throng'. The immortal energy is described, like the One, as opposed to the life of this world: 'That Benediction which the eclipsing Curse/Of birth can quench not...' (480–1). But like 'the one Spirit's plastic stress', it is active within this world as a 'sustaining Love' which 'Burns bright or dim, as each are mirrors of/The fire for which all thirst'. Unlike the One or the one Spirit's plastic stress it is personal, described in human terms as a light that smiles, a Beauty, a Benediction, a Love. And yet this stanza does not halt the poem's rush towards death, for the One, though not destroyed when it is born into this world suffers an 'eclipse'. The activity of the one Spirit's plastic stress is limited in this world by its materials; it exists only as it is reflected by man, beast, earth, air and sea. The humanity of the force, like that of Adonais and the Frail form who mourns him, is inhibited by the Curse of earthly life. In

whatever terms it is described the immortal can be perfected only
in death, when it evaporates the mortal as the sun evaporates the
clouds. At the end of the stanza it shines on the poet, 'Consuming
the last clouds of cold mortality'. And so the poem ends in an
excited, almost panic-stricken, voyage, which, like the voyage
of the hero of *Alastor* is a pursuit of death:

> The breath whose might I have invoked in song
> Descends on me; my spirit's bark is driven,
> Far from the shore, far from the trembling throng
> Whose sails were never to the tempest given;
> The massy earth and spherèd skies are riven!
> I am borne darkly, fearfully, afar;
> Whilst, burning through the inmost veil of Heaven,
> The soul of Adonais, like a star,
> Beacons from the abode where the Eternal are. (487–95)

The poem ends by confronting the reader once again with its
central problem. The final couplet of the last stanza echoes the
final couplet of the first. The formal symmetry of the poem is
perfectly achieved, and yet the agitated urgency of the tone
contradicts the notion that a formal pattern has been satisfyingly
completed.

Adonais is made up of three movements. The first, stanzas I to
XXI, represents a series of attempts to confront the fact of
Adonais's death through metaphor, through artifice, and finally
through naturalistic acceptance of death's finality. It ends flatly in
verse that descends to the level of platitude:

> As long as skies are blue, and fields are green,
> Evening must usher night, night urge the morrow,
> Month follow month with woe, and year wake year to
> sorrow. (187–9)

The second movement, stanzas XXII to XL, transfers the
reader's attention from the problem of death to the pain of life. It
ends in the realisation that whatever death is, it is at least an
escape from living pain, and therefore no cause for grief:

> Envy and calumny and hate and pain,
> And that unrest which men miscall delight,
> Can touch him not and torture not again . . . (333–5)

The poem's third movement explores various possibilities of immortality. Having established the life beyond death as preferable to life in this world the poem ends with typically fierce Shelleyan logic: the elegist rejects life, and dashes towards the immortal stars.

To describe the poem in this schematic manner is less than satisfactory, for within each movement there are abrupt transitions, and odd developments, and each movement recollects and develops suggestions that have been let fall earlier in the poem. Shelley exploits the potential of the Spenserian stanza which allows an organisation within the poem that can swing between the two extremes represented by the sonnet sequence and blank verse. Individual stanzas may stand apart from their context assuming something like the autonomy of an independent lyric, or they may form part of a narrative or dramatic movement. The stanzas may develop one from another, or they may jump off from each other, each representing a fresh approach to the problem.

The best explanation of Shelley's technique in *Adonais* is indicated by two quotations from his essays. In the *Essay on Life* he remarks of man, 'Whatever may be his true and final destination there is a spirit within him at enmity with nothingness and dissolution'.[18] In the *Essay on a Future State* he summarises the evidences for a belief in life after death, and concludes: 'They persuade, indeed, only those who desire to be persuaded'.[19] These two recognitions, that belief in life after death is fundamental to human nature, and that there is no logical defence of the belief, determine the technique of the poem. Because man is at enmity with dissolution, the group of poems which dramatise this enmity, Christian pastoral elegies, figure a human truth. All Shelley need do is desentangle the tradition from its dogmatically Christian theology. The recognition that Christian pastoral elegy expresses a human truth becomes a means by which Shelley initiates a *détente* with his literary traditions. The models for his earlier poems had to be handled a good deal more aggressively before they yielded the human truth that Shelley saw disguised within them. The formal and conventional element of *Adonais* represents, then, Shelley's expression of a truth recognised by many other poets, epitomised for him in the Platonic epigram which he prefixed to his poem. They, like him, have demonstrated that a belief in immortality is grounded on the spiritual or emotional rejection of the notion of 'nothingness' that is a distinctive human characteristic.

And yet in the second quotation Shelley considers instinctive belief with an abrasive scepticism absent from the first. The heart's truths, it is suggested, may be exercises in wish-fulfilment. It is to do justice to his scepticism that Shelley introduces into the poem a personality that is disjoined from its formality, so that the poem is both a formal expression of an acknowledged truth, and a poem driven forward by the emotional pressures felt by its speaker. At the centre of the poem is the 'frail Form', who is at once an archetypal pastoral elegist and a violently naked self-portrait, both a generalised portrayal of the poet as an individual condemned to a life of pain because spiritual strength reveals itself in this world as weakness, and an expression of disturbingly personal feelings of paranoia and self-pity. Looked at in one way the belief in immortality is a human truth, looked at in another it is a testimony to human weakness, a belief based on evidences that 'persuade, indeed, only those who desire to be persuaded'. The poem lays bare the motivations that lie behind this belief. In the first movement it approaches with difficulty, and at last reaches, a naturalistic acceptance of death, an acceptance that renders life meaningless, banal. From then on the poem's speaker is engaged in an attempt to rescue himself and his poem from this conclusion. He succeeds, but only by using logically disreputable techniques, by persuading himself to accept as true what he would like to believe. The conclusion of the poem throws down a splendid challenge. If the evidence for immortality is satisfactory, then why 'let life divide what Death can join together'? What prevents all men from following the example of these early Christians who so amused Gibbon, and committing suicide *en masse*?

Adonais is an honest poem about death, honest in the way it lays bare its mechanisms. It is written with an assured competence rare in Romantic poetry. It is both ingenious and intelligent in its handling of conventions. And yet it remains a poem easier to admire than to like, a poem which leaves one uneasy about its achievement. Some of the reasons for this are clear. *Adonais* competes with *Lycidas*, and the contest is, of course, unequal. The myth of Keats's death, the poet 'snuffed out by an article', that Shelley embraces coheres rather too easily with the poem's notion of the poet exiled from, and persecuted by, what is worldly in himself and others. The poem fails in the end to give the kind of satisfaction that comes when an alien reality is contemplated, as when Milton sees King's body 'hurl'd' along the sea bed. Death by tuberculosis is a more serious subject than death by criticism. More fundamental is the disjunction within the poem of its formal and subjective structures. This is a planned effect, and Shelley had precedent for it in *Lycidas*. But in *Lycidas* conflicting pressures are excitingly contained; Shelley intensifies the conflict with the result that it becomes impossible, at any rate for me, to hold the two structures together. The poem falls apart in its attempt to hold together a trust in the truths of human instinct, and a concern to register a sceptical awareness that such a trust may be credulity.

The conflict becomes clearer if we recognise that *Adonais* is succeeded in the nineteenth century not by those poems which still work within the tradition of pastoral elegy, not by Arnold's *Thyrsis* or Hopkins's *The Wreck of the Deutschland*, but by Tennyson's *In Memoriam*. *In Memoriam* is a sequence of lyrics organised more in the manner of a sonnet sequence than of a single elegy. The formality, insistent in *Adonais*, is muted, so that the poem focuses clearly on an individual's struggle with grief. *In Memoriam* develops one aspect of *Adonais* and discards the other. I began my discussion of *Adonais* by distinguishing a use of language that I termed spatial, from a temporal use of language. Tennyson, quite literally, abandons a spatial structure in favour of a development in time. His poem is the diary of his grief; the passing of time, Christmas following Christmas, creates the temporal structure of the poem. *In Memoriam* reveals Tennyson's recognition that the two structures of *Adonais* will not co-here.

I began this chapter by suggesting that *Adonais* begins the final phase of Shelley's work, a phase characterised by a rediscovered harmony with his literary traditions. *Adonais* works with *Lycidas* rather than against it. And yet this statement, though true, is somewhat paradoxical. To be in harmony with Milton is to be in harmony with a predecessor quite as fierce as Shelley in his relations with received literary tradition. It is only in Shelley's last long poem, *The Triumph of Life*, that this rediscovered harmony displays itself fully.

The Triumph of Life

The Triumph of Life is modelled on Petrarch's *Triumphs*, in particular *The Triumph of Love*, a poem that had not exerted an important influence on English literature since the sixteenth century. The choice is even more surprising than the decision to write the elegy to Keats in the form of a pastoral elegy. In the work of Shelley's mature period (*Prometheus Unbound* is the best example) the poet asserts his individuality against the poem's formal and stylistic model, but in this, his last major poem, there is little evidence of aggression. Shelley asserts his individuality most obviously in choosing the tradition within which he will write his poem. He struggles not to free himself from literary history, as in *Prometheus Unbound* where Prometheus's struggle to free himself from his past is reflected in the poet's attempt to free his poem from its models, both victories being signalled in the quasi-independence of Act IV, but finds freedom rather in asserting his ability to write the literary history within which his poem takes its place.

It is useful to compare *The Triumph of Life* with Byron's *Prophecy of Dante*. Byron's poem is a monologue spoken by Dante in exile from his native Florence. Byron chooses that Dante speak from a situation comparable with his own, so that the character who speaks the poem may be an unstable amalgam of Dante and Byron. Byron uses his self-knowledge as a tool with which to understand Dante, and Dante as a tool with which to understand himself. The personal reticence appropriate to the writer of a dramatic monologue is countered by self-assertion. Byron is insubordinate towards his genre with the result that the reader reacts uncertainly to the poem:

> To feel me in the solitude of kings
> Without the power that makes them bear a crown –
> To envy every dove his nest and wings
> Which waft him where the Appenine looks down
> On Arno, till it perches, it may be,
> within my all inexorable town,
> Where yet my boys are, and that fatal she,
> Their mother, the cold partner who hath brought
> Destruction for a dowry – this to see
> And feel, and know without repair, hath taught

A bitter lesson; but it leaves me free:
I have not vilely found, nor basely sought,
They made an Exile – not a slave of me. (Canto I, 166–78)

The sentence moves impulsively, pressed forward by the speaker's emotions which refuse to be shackled by syntactic conventions. It is disconcertingly like some of the sentences spoken by Shelley's madman in *Julian and Maddalo*. The reader is unsure whether to receive it as self-expression or to examine it as a critical exposure of Dante's state of mind. In the terms I used earlier in the book, he is unsure whether the poem implies the existence of a moral language which allows the reader to place an individual utterance within a general perspective, or whether it affirms the presence only of a language of self-love; of whether the poem defines a character or expresses a consciousness. The uncertainty derives from Byron's refusal either to sink into anonymity or to define his relationship with the poem's speaker. An uncertain relationship between the writer and his character is the dramatic analogue of an uncertain relationship between the tenor and vehicle of a metaphor. Both are characteristic Romantic devices.

Uncertainty enters the style of Byron's poem. He writes in terza rima, but his language struggles with his verse form. Contrast this with the assured ease of the terza rima of *The Triumph of Life*, an ease apparent even though all but the first forty lines of the poem exist only in a first draft. Both are poems that it is difficult to read, that leave the reader groping, but Byron engages the reader with his own uncertainties, whereas Shelley's reader grapples with uncertainties that are precisely expressed.

The Divine Comedy and Petrarch's *Triumphs* both represent experience as a series of veils which may be removed one by one by the exercise of rigorous contemplation and with the aid of grace to reveal an absolute and perfect reality. In *The Triumphs* Love, Chastity, Death, Fame and Time are each revealed as mutable, subject to higher powers, and therefore fictitious, but when the last veil is torn aside Eternity is revealed. Dante ascends with Beatrice through the various circles of Paradise, and arrives in the end at that unchanging perfection which is God. In *The Triumph of Life*, too, experience is revealed as a series of veils, but the value of each veil is doubtful, and what it will reveal problematic. The logical world of the Italian poems is replaced by a world that is labyrinthine, in which the distinctions between true and false, good and evil, are doubtful. Hence the poem has provoked critical disputes which centre on a discussion of whether its central symbols and characters, sun, star, and the Shape all light, are emblems of good or evil. The primary effect of Shelley's modification of the Dantescan and Petrarchan tradition that lies behind his poem is to strip it of its metaphysical and ethical certainty.

The narrative shape of *The Triumph of Life* is the key to its meaning. The visionary, the poem's speaker, sinks into a trance in which he sees superimposed on the garden landscape in which he lies a dusty road along which a multitude of people pass pursued by a chariot. Behind the chariot is driven 'a captive multitude'. The visionary wonders about the meaning of this procession, and is answered by what he had taken for 'an old root'. The voice identifies itself as Rousseau, and he is asked by the visionary to tell his own story. One April he had fallen asleep by a river, the murmuring of which induced forgetfulness of his former life. When he awoke he encountered a 'Shape all light'. She offered him a drink, and when his lips touched it there burst on his sight a new vision, the 'cold, bright car', the chariot. Rousseau followed it until he sank by the wayside and assumed his present ghastly, vegetable appearance.

If we compare *The Triumph of Life* with Petrarch's *Triumphs* then it is apparent that Shelley has abandoned a parallel structure in which analogous events follow one another in favour of an involved structure. Petrarch uses parallel structures, for example the parallel between the triumph of Chastity over Love, and the triumph of Death over Chastity, in order to confirm and emphasise distinctions. Within Shelley's involved structure the reader is offered the career of Rousseau as a parallel to the experience of the visionary, but the parallel is incomplete or indefinite, and it blurs rather than clarifies. When dawn broke and the stars were 'laid asleep' the visionary himself lay down. Rousseau was 'laid asleep' in April, which Shelley had considered describing as 'the young year's dwan'.[20] But Rousseau slept, and in his sleep forgot his past life, whereas the visionary experiences a waking dream, and his vision does not bring forgetfulness for it is superimposed on his actual landscape. What is more, whereas the visionary sees only the chariot, Rousseau experiences two visions, first the vision of the Shape all light, and then the vision of the chariot. Shelley suggests a parallel between the two visionaries only to prevent the accommodation one to another of the two men's experiences. Whereas in Dante and Petrarch the technique clarifies, in Shelley it obscures.

The controlling symbols of *The Triumph of Life* are the sun and stars. The poem opens at dawn as the stars fade in the light of the rising sun. This is a sequence that is repeated. As the chariot approaches:

> a cold glare, intenser than the noon,
> But icy cold, obscured with light
> The sun, as he the stars. (77–9)

When the Shape all light appeared to Rousseau she stamped out his sparkling thoughts: 'As Day upon the threshhold of the East/Treads out the lamps of night . . .' (389–90). But when Rousseau's second vision, the chariot, 'burst' on his sight, the Shape herself becomes like a star disappearing in the light of the sun:

> And the fair Shape waned in the coming light
> As veil by veil the silent splendour drops
> From Lucifer, amid the chrysolite
> Of sunrise. (412–15)

The same light may appear successively as like a sun and like a star. This is rather like the sequence in Petrarch's *Triumphs* in which the qualities intervening between Love and Eternity, – Chastity, Death, Fame and Time –,are each described first as a conqueror and then as the conquered. But there is a crucial difference. In Petrarch Chastity conquers Love but is conquered by Death. The three terms are referents: the reader is able to place them within a single, ordered hierarchy. Within Shelley's chariot are two figures, a female occupant described as a 'Shape', and a charioteer described as a 'Shadow'. The dancing lady that Rousseau meets is also called a 'Shape'. Shelley chooses nouns that scarcely exercise a referential function, and as a consequence his poem expresses a relativist world, a world in which phenomena have meaning only in their relations one to another rather than a world in which phenomena relate to one another within a single, coherent order.

In *The Divine Comedy* the stability of Dante's system depends on the reader's acceptance of the reliability of Dante's guides. Virgil is chosen as the guide in the *Inferno* because he is the ancient whose artistic pre-eminence, moral virtue, and peculiar status as a pagan harbinger of Christianity recommend him most forcibly to the reader's trust. The role of Shelley's guide Rousseau is a conflation of the role of Dante's Virgil with that of an inmate of Dante's Hell. This should alert the reader to the fact that Rousseau is chosen precisely because of the ambivalence of the reactions that he provoked, especially amongst those of Shelley's own political persuasion. Mary Wollstonecraft regarded him as a proponent of the inequality of the sexes, and yet was deeply moved by his portrayal of ideal love. Godwin both admired Rousseau and found fault with him in about equal measure. Byron's analysis of Rousseau's character in Canto III of *Childe Harold*, a splendid passage, and a major influence on Shelley's representation of him, is the most striking expression of this ambivalence. Rousseau to Byron was mad or inspired depending on the perspective in which one views his achievement. There is a splendid disjunction as Byron considers each possibility:

> But he was phrensied by disease or woe
> To that worst pitch of all, which wears a reasoning show.

> For then he was inspired, and from him came,
> As from the Pythian's mystic cave of yore,
> Those oracles which set the world in flame,
> Nor ceased to burn till kingdoms were no more . . . (stanzas
> LXXX–LXXXI)

Byron does not articulate the relationship between Rousseau 'phrensied', the victim of private paranoia, and Rousseau 'inspired', the prophet of a new and juster world, for the two are indistinguishable. Shelley chooses Rousseau precisely because of his unreliability, because his value or status was peculiarly undetermined.

The Divine Comedy and Petrarch's *Triumphs* each end with the revelation of an absolute truth; Shelley's fragment ends with an unanswered question: ' "Then, what is life?" I said'. It would be rash to presume that had Shelley completed the poem this absolute scepticism would have been maintained. The example of *Adonais* suggests otherwise. But even in *Adonais* Shelley is careful to build his faith upon a sceptical void. One of his favourite images is of a palace erected on chaos or on water, [21] and it acts as a metaphor for human belief, for Shelley had concluded that all important beliefs, all beliefs that men need to live by, are similarly unsupported. *The Triumph of Life*, as we have it, is Shelley's most beautifully articulated expression of the watery chaos that alone sustains any constructed faith. It may seem that nothing could be more hostile to the ordered, definite worlds of Dante and Petrarch, but one is not conscious when reading *The Triumph of Life* of any fierce rounding on the poem's tradition. The centainties of Dante and Petrarch are dismantled, but the dismantling is achieved quietly, unaggressively.

The difference between Shelley's technique here and the fiercer technique of the earlier poems becomes evident if one examines his handling of the verse form. Shelley uses fewer end-stopped lines than either Dante or Petrarch, and he far less frequently allows syntactic independence to a single stanza. As a result the movement between lines and stanzas in Shelley's poem is far more fluid. Shelley exploits the continuity of terza rima, a verse form in which each stanza is connected by rhyme both with its predecessor and its successor. It is a verse form ideally suited to Shelley's narrative in which one event merges with its successor, and in which value is a doubtful construct imposed on the flux of experience. Shelley releases certain potentialities of terza rima that Dante and Petrarch deliberately resist. Dante's muscular clarity, his concern with definition and order, is, in a sense, imposed against the will of the verse form. Dante, Shelley would have argued, imposed on experience an order, in itself beautiful, but which had no adequate basis in that experience. Dante's and Petrarch's schemes are *a priori* inventions. Shelley, like a good empiricist, allows his verse form to draw the subject matter back within the flux, the indeterminateness, of lived experience. In the madman's speech in *Julian and Maddalo* couplet proprieties shatter when they are subjected to the pressure of passionate speech. In *The Triumph of Life*, on the other hand, Shelley chooses a verse form that allows him to modify his tradition by exploiting the form rather than attacking it. Such criticism of the tradition as there is becomes quiet, in the fullest sense of the word decorous, in contrast to the fierce breaches of decorum that carry Shelley's criticism in poems such as *Julian and Maddalo* and *Prometheus Unbound*.

The poem begins at dawn:

> Swift as a spirit hastening to his task
> Of glory and of good, the Sun sprang forth
> Rejoicing in his splendour, and the mask
> Of darkness fell from the awakened Earth. (1–4)

The sun's energy and power dominate the opening lines: it was an effect for which Shelley had worked hard.[22] Darkness is a deception, a 'mask' removed by the rising sun in whose light power and goodness are united. All nature joins in worshipping the newborn sun. The mountain snows are flaming 'altars'; birdsong is a 'matin lay'; the scent of flowers is 'incense' distributed as the flowers sway, 'swinging their censers'. They are the 'humid flowers' of Milton's Eden that 'breathed their morning incense' as a contribution to the 'silent praise' that ascended to God from every part of the 'earth's great altar'.[23] Shelley's poem opens with a morning hymn. The rising sun is a summons to begin the work of the day:

> And in succession due, did continent,
> Isle, ocean, and all things that in them wear
> The form and character of mortal mould
> Rise as the Sun their father rose, to bear
> Their portion of the toil which he of old
> Took as his own and then imposed on them ... (15–20)

This is the role of the sun in most morning hymns favoured by the Church of England. Bishop Ken responds to the sun's admonition: 'Awake, my soul, and with the sun/Thy daily stage of duty run'. Charles Wesley is filled with a similar determination: 'Forth in Thy Name, O Lord, I go,/My daily labour to pursue'. The rising sun is associated with God in order that the congregation may recognise its duty not to waste a minute of the working day; the worship of God subserves the interests of political economy. Such hymns are a ripe target for Shelleyan parody as he recognised in the pleasant fragment, *The Boat on the Serchio*: 'All rose to do the task He set to each/Who shaped us to his ends and not our own...'. The apparent orthodoxy of the first line is subverted by its heretical successor. The passage is revealed as parody, and the joke is pleasant enough. But the lines from *The Triumph of Life* are more complex, for Shelley fails to define his own attitude towards the orthodox prayer. The Sun is a father who 'imposed' toil on men ; he is the distressingly autocratic father who punished Adam and Eve for their curiosity by condemning them to a life of labour, but he is also the God who took toil 'as his own'; he is the son of man who took upon himself the sins of the world. The Sun is a type of the autocratic God of the Bible, but also of his merciful, self-sacrificing son. The reader is placed carefully in an unstable, indefinite world. Nature is described through Milton's description of Eden, but it includes 'toil', which is precisely the penalty that man suffered on his exile from the garden.

In *The Boat on the Sechio* Lionel and Melchior, pseudonyms of Shelley and his friend Edward Williams, refuse to join the orthodox in praising God and working hard, and choose instead to go on a boating expedition. 'They from the throng of men had stepped aside', and their defection is lightly praised. The speaker of *The Triumph of Life* also defects. When all the rest of creation rises, he lies down. Whereas all other created beings keep time with the daily cycle of the sun, he keeps time with the daily cycle of the stars:

> But I, whom thoughts which must remain untold
> Had kept as wakeful as the stars that gem
> The cone of night, now they were laid asleep,
> Stretched my faint limbs beneath the hoary stem
> Which an old chestnut flung athwart the steep
> Of a green Appenine... (21–6)

The word 'I' functions within any fiction as a signal to the reader inviting his sympathy, and there is also an instinctive sympathy felt for the individual detached from the herd. The reader moves behind the visionary just as he moves behind Rasselas when Johnson remarks: 'Thus they rose in the morning, and lay down at night, pleased with each other, and pleased with themselves, all but Rasselas'. But neither in Johnson nor in Shelley is the reader's instinctive sympathy used to enforce his unqualified approval of the outsider's attitude. Lionel and Melchior are a sprightly pair, but the visionary's limbs are 'faint', and he chooses to lie down under the 'hoary stem' of an 'old' chestnut. His feebleness and his fellow-feeling with the decrepit contrast with the vigour and vitality of all other natural things. When the visionary recounts his dream, it is uncertain whether we should accept it as the sick fancy of a sick mind, or as a true vision available only to the man who stands apart from the herd in prophetic isolation.

The last stanza of the introduction describes natural scenery prettily: 'The birds, the fountains, and the ocean hold/Sweet talk in music through the enamoured air' (38–9). The pathetic fallacy is obtrusive, the picture of the world represented vulnerably fictitious. In his dream the visionary finds himself sitting 'beside a public way/Thick strewn with summer dust'. The real landscape is fanciful in comparison with the visionary landscape, which might represent any road in Shelley's Italy. The final function of the introductory stanzas is to place in doubt the relative status of the two landscapes, the actual and the visionary.

In its opening lines *The Triumph of Life* displays a verbal technique like that which Shelley had used in *The Witch of Atlas*, though deployed more subtly. In both poems the language suggests oppositions and contrasts, but prevents the reader from fixing his attitude towards them. Day and night, community and individuality, reality and vision, are contrasted, but the value to be attached to each member of the contrast remains doubtful, and the terms in which the contrast is understood flicker unstably as the reader progresses through the passage. Similar techniques operate throughout the poem.

Along the dusty road a multitude of people pass, tired and thirsty, but oblivious of the fresh green landscape that the visionary sees around them, intent on pursuing 'their serious folly as of old'. The multitude is pursued by a chariot. Harold Bloom has demonstrated that the chariot is modelled on the divine vehicle recognised by Ezekiel as 'the likeness of the glory of the Lord'.[24] Ezekiel's chariot has four wheels, each of which has four faces, and the rims of the wheels are 'full of eyes'. Shelley's charioteer also has four faces, but all are 'banded'. The eyes that might otherwise 'pierce the sphere/Of all that is, has been, or will be done' are blindfolded. It is clear that Shelley's chariot is either an inversion or a perversion of the orthodox divine vehicle, but it is not clear which. Ought we to concentrate on the divine power of the eyes, or the fact that they are blindfolded? Ought we to focus on the fact that the chariot is 'ill-guided', or note that even when directed by a blindfolded driver it 'passed/With solemn speed majestically on'.

The chariot extinguishes the sun, just as the sun had extinguished the stars. The chariot came 'on the silent storm/Of its own rushing splendour', recalling the sun in the prologue 'Rejoicing in its splendour'. Both the sun and the chariot are obeyed, and both stimulate all they shine upon. But just as it is unclear whether the chariot should be compared or contrasted with Ezekiel's, so it is unclear whether the chariot should be compared or contrasted with the sun. The chariot is supernaturally bright, 'intenser than the noon', which suggests that it functions as an 'intenser' version of the sun in the prologue, but its coming is compared with the rising of the moon, which suggests that it is the sun's antithesis. The ordered beauty of the pious ritual celebrated by all nature 'in succession due' contrasts with the aimless, or apathetic, or violent behaviour of the multitude under the influence of the chariot. But in other respects the influence of the chariot is simply an intensification of the influence of the sun. The sun awakened, the chariot excites; under the influence of its approach the 'throng grew wilder'. The sun 'imposed' toil on men, the chariot enslaves them: a 'captive multitude' follows it.

In *The Triumph of Life* one event follows another and acts as its distorted reflection. Contrast and likeness are both suggested, so that no stable relationship between the two events may be determined. Petrarch's parallel structure becomes a structure in which successive events parody one another, but the parody is of a peculiarly unstable kind, its effect uncertain.

The description that follows, of the lust-crazed young that precede the chariot dancing, until they fall suddenly senseless, and the chariot crushes them, and of the old people who follow the chariot, grotesquely parodying the desires of the young, 'foully disarrayed', and shaking 'their gray hairs in the insulting wind', until they are left behind and consumed by shadows, is Shelley's version of the traditional dance of death. It is powerfully written, but not problematic. All are in thrall to the chariot, 'All but the sacred few', 'they of Athens and Jerusalem'. Two paths of salvation are outlined. Those are spared:

> who could not tame
> Their spirits to the Conqueror, but as soon

As they had touched the world with living flame
Fled back like eagles to their native noon . . . (128–31)

Those also who 'put aside the diadem/Of earthly thrones or gems'. Athens and Jerusalem are chosen as the two origins of Western culture, the Hellenic and the Hebraic, the one representing an escape from worldliness through philosophic contemplation, the typical figure being Socrates, the other through religion, the typical figure being Christ. The lines describe a human aspiration different from either the seer's role as passive spectator of human misery or the multitude's frenzied participation in life, and they introduce an absolute light, the 'native noon', quite different from the flickering, relative lights that dominate the rest of the poem. But the lines spin a thread that is not picked up in the poem as we have it.

Rousseau is introduced metamorphosed into 'an old root', and he identifies various individuals among the 'mighty captives' chained to the chariot. He guides the visionary as Virgil guides Dante, but he is an inmate of the Hell he describes. The sweet humility of Virgil is supplanted in Rousseau by a proud bitterness. His is a voice out of the *Inferno*; its closest analogues are the voices of Guido and Farinata. When Rousseau speaks a bitter awareness of his own degradation is combined with a fierce self-assertion. He recognises the pre-eminence of 'the great bards of old', who were the masters not the victims of the passions of which they sang:

See the great bards of old, who inly quelled
The passions which they sang, as by their strain
May well be known, for their soft melody
Tempers its own contagion to the vein
Of those who are infected with it . . . (274–8)

But as the passage proceeds the compliment is attacked by the disease metaphor through which it is expressed. The tribute to Homeric impersonality is distorted into a suggestion of deceit, the invisible progress of an infectious disease, and at the last Rousseau dismisses classicism, and makes a proud statement of his own ethic of sincerity: 'I/Have suffered what I wrote, or viler pain'. The sentence is both a confession of inferiority, and a boast.

Rousseau's odd kind of self-despising self-assertion controls his relationship with the visionary, so that even when responding helpfully to the visionary's questions, his tone is taunting. He promises to tell the visionary how he had submitted to the chariot's influence:

> If thirst of knowledge shall not then abate,
> Follow it thou even to the night, but I
> Am weary. (194–6)

The visionary responds to Rousseau's fierce cynicism by attempting a grand gesture, by representing himself as a man above the world, grown bored by watching the grim procession of those whom life has conquered:

>   'Let them pass,'
> I cried, 'the world and its mysterious doom
> Is not so much more glorious than it was
> That I desire to worship those who drew
> New figures on its false and fragile glass
> As the old faded.' 243–8)

He dismisses the world of mortality rather as Shelley in *Adonais* dismissed life as 'a dome of many-coloured glass', but his formulation of the thought lacks the residual appreciation of the beauty of what is dismissed that preserves the honesty of the simile in *Adonais*. The comparison helps to expose the visionary's boast as a rhetorical gesture. Rousseau brushes it aside:

>   Figures ever new
> Rise on the bubble, paint them how you may;
> We have but thrown, as those before us threw,
> Our shadows on it ere it passed away. (248–51)

He rejects the visionary's pronoun, 'those', in favour of 'you' and 'we'. The visionary suggested that man's desire to paint the glass of life was a ridiculous vanity. Rousseau responds by changing the metaphor; the figures are 'shadows' that we cast whether we will or no. Rousseau punctures the speaker's self-assertion, but self-assertion is the quality that he is himself only too ready to display: 'I/Am one of those who have created, even/If it be but a world of agony'.

The interplay between Rousseau and the visionary is powerfully dramatic. The dramatic technique is another method by
which Shelley preserves the fluidity of the poem, a method by
which Rousseau is prevented from fulfilling the Virgilian role of
trustworthy guide, and the visionary from fulfilling the Dantescan role of grateful student progressively initiated into the truth.
It is a means by which Shelley maintains the questionmark as the
sign dominating the punctuation of the poem.

The visionary asks Rousseau another series of questions:
' "Whence camest thou and whither goest thou?/How did thy
course begin," I said, "and why?" ' (296–7). In response
Rousseau tells his own story, a partial parallel to the visionary's
own experience, a distorted reflection of the kind that dominates
the poem. Rousseau went to sleep by a river, the murmur of
which brought forgetfulness of all things: 'All pleasure and all
pain, all hate and love'. The line carefully preserves the neutral
value of amnesia, and so do the exempla that follow. Lulled by
the river a mother would forget the death of her only child, a
king his deposition. Maternal love and the lust for power would
both equally be forgotten. Rousseau has no notion what his life
had been before that sleep, but he wakes from it trailing
Wordsworthian clouds of glory:

> I arose, and for a space
> The scene of woods and waters seemed to keep,
> Though it was now broad day, a gentle trace
> Of light diviner than the common Sun
> Sheds on the common Earth . . . (335–9)

Rousseau seems to scorn 'the common Sun' in comparison with
a star-like 'light diviner', but immediately he turns to describe
with awe the sunlight diffusing itself though an 'orient cavern'.
He speaks of 'the bright omnipresence of morning', and the sun
performs the characteristically divine office of transforming the
merely natural into the precious, grassy tracks into 'paths of
emerald fire'.

When the 'Shape all light' appears she is closely associated with
the sun:

> there stood
> Amid the sun, as he amid the blaze

Of his own glory, on the vibrating
Floor of the fountain, paved with flashing rays,
A Shape all light, which with one hand did fling
Dew on the Earth, as if she were the dawn... (348–53)

Notice the reappearance of the reflexive construction, 'Amid the
sun, as he amid the blaze/Of his own glory', which was used to
describe the sun in the prologue, 'Rejoicing in his splendour',
and also the chariot, 'on the silent storm/Of its own rushing
splendour'. The Shape stands on the water of the well from
which the sun's image is reflected 'radiantly intense'. The chariot
shone with a light 'intenser than the noon'. The transference of
the reader's attention from the rising of the sun to the Shape all
light seems to parallel the supplanting of the sun in the prologue
by the 'intenser' light of the chariot. And yet the Shape all light
also acts as a powerful contrast with the chariot. When she moves
she glides along a river; the chariot rolled along a dusty road. The
chariot moved weightily, crushing all it passed over; the Shape
moves so lightly that her feet 'broke not the mirror of [the
river's] billow'. The Shape is 'all light'; the chariot's occupant sat
beneath 'a dun and faint ethereal gloom'.

That the appearance of the Shape all light parallels the
appearance of the chariot seems only to be a means by which
Shelley enforces the contrast between them. But then Rousseau
describes the effect produced by her dancing:

And still her feet, no less than the sweet tune
To which they moved, seemed as they moved, to blot
The thoughts of him who gazed on them; and soon
All that was, seemed as if it had been not,
And all the gazer's mind was strewn beneath
Her feet like embers, and she, thought by thought,
Trampled its sparks into the dust of death,
As Day upon the threshhold of the east
Treads out the lamps of night... (382–90)

There is a delicate movement here from a description of the
hypnotic power of her dance to a suggestion of its destructive-
ness. One by one she trampled the thoughts of Rousseau's mind
into 'the dust of death', and in doing so she achieves the same
effect that the visionary had witnessed performed by the chariot.

The chariot crushed the young people it juggernauted into the dust of the road, and it left the old trailing behind it until they sank 'to the dust' from which they had been created. The Shape all light is like and unlike the chariot just as the chariot itself was like and unlike the sun.[25]

To Rousseau, watching the Shape dance, 'All that was seemed as if it had been not'. In him the dance induces amnesia, just as the murmur of the river had done. Wordsworth had suggested that 'our birth is but a sleep and a forgetting', but Shelley translates Wordsworth's stable Platonic scheme into a labyrinth of successive forgettings.

The Shape offers Rousseau a cup filled with nepenthe, the drink of forgetfulness. The action is radically ambivalent for Shelley refuses to place it within either of the two traditions within which it might belong. The drink might confer knowledge of a high mystery. For Christians the type of such a drink is the communion cup. On the other hand, the cup that the Shape offers might be a cup like Circe's containing a liquor that degrades its drinker. A third tradition plays with this ambivalence. In Southey's *The Curse of Kehama*, Shelley's favourite poem in his youth, Kehama demands to drink from a cup which he imagines will bring him immortality:

> He did not know the holy mystery
> Of that divinest cup, that as the lips
> Which touch it, even such its quality,
> Good or malignant... (XXIV, 214–17)

The Shape offers Rousseau the cup in response to his demand that she tell him 'whence I came, and where I am, and why ...'. Again the questions that dominate the poem are asked, and again no answer is supplied. Rousseau touches the cup with his lips, and his brain becomes 'as sand'. Immediately a new vision bursts on his sight, the chariot.

As the chariot approaches, the Shape all light, that had stood 'amid the Sun, as he amid the blaze/Of his own glory', dissolves into a star:

> And the fair Shape waned in the coming light
> As veil by veil the silent splendour drops
> From Lucifer, amid the chrysolite
> Of sunrise... (412–15)

And as the light fades its value seems at last to be fixed. Rousseau describes it as:

> A light from Heaven whose half-extinguished beam
> Through the sick day in which we wake to weep
> Glimmers, for ever sought, for ever lost... (429–31)

Deprived of the Shape Rousseau joined the multitude; he 'was swept' into the crowd, and he 'plunged' into 'the thickest billow of that living storm'. To the last he represents himself both as passive victim and as active hero.

The Triumph of Life is a fragment; as we have it, it is a sequence of carefully constructed uncertainties. Both the sun and the night as they are described in the prologue are ambivalent. The sun performed a 'task/Of glory and of good', but it also 'imposed' toil on man. The night was a 'mask/Of darkness', but it was also 'gemmed' by stars. The visionary's refusal to join all nature in welcoming the sun was an assertion of the poet's individuality, an unhappy acceptance of what distinguishes the selfconscious man ('thoughts which must remain untold') from the rest of creation, and also an alliance with the decrepit, the 'hoary stem' of an 'old chestnut', rather than the vital in the world. The visionary turns his back on the sun, and sees in a waking dream the triumph of the chariot. We may conclude that his individuality preserves him from the fate of the multitude doomed to follow the chariot, or we may think that in rejecting life, in allying himself with the stars rather than the sun, the visionary has doomed himself to see life as a pointless progress from nowhere to nowhere ruled over by a blindfolded god. The chariot itself may be an inversion of the divine chariots of Ezekiel and Dante, in much the same way that in *The Faerie Queene* the pageant of Lucifera is an inversion of a divine pageant, or it may rather be a truly divine chariot, the divinity of which is, for the time, distorted; it might be possible to remove the blindfolds from the charioteer. The chariot might be the antithesis of the sun in the prologue, it is like the moon, or it might be an 'intenser' reflection, a caricature, of the sun. When Rousseau introduces himself to the visionary new problems arise. The visionary had seemed immune from the influence of the chariot by virtue of his 'thoughts', his selfconsciousness, and his individuality. Rousseau has both these qualities, and yet in him they seem the cause of his conquest by the chariot. Rousseau's vision of the chariot is preceded by a series of events each of which is ambivalent. The river by which he sleeps erases his memory, but it is doubtful whether this is a curse or a blessing. The 'Shape all light' flickers between being an ideal beauty and a Circean temptress. When Rousseau joins the procession he was 'swept', but he also 'plunged' into its midst. The 'sacred few', the only individuals that the visionary notes are absent from the multitude of the chariot's followers, reacted to life entirely negatively. One group died young, the other 'put aside' all worldly ambitions. Their rejection of life is not self-evidently more admirable than Rousseau's active involvement in it. Among the chariot's followers are individuals that Shelley despised, but also some, like Plato, whom he enthusiastically admired. What is one to make of all this?

The crucial nouns of the poem are 'shape', 'shadow', 'figure'. This is no accident. Shelley carefully chooses nouns in which the referential function is reduced to a minimum. *The Triumph of Life* is the clearest possible exemplification of Bentham's dictum that a sentence is not a collection of names but a proposition; that meaning resides in the proposition rather than as an aggregate of the meanings of the individual words of which the proposition is composed. It is only by concentrating on the syntax of the poem that a limited meaning will emerge.

The recurring metaphor of the poem is a sun's extinction of a star. The poem opens at dawn, as the stars fade. Then the chariot 'obscured with light/The sun as he the stars'. On awakening from his sleep by the river Rousseau was conscious of a 'light diviner' that did not long survive the light of the common sun. Associated with this sun is the 'Shape all light', but on the approach of the chariot she becomes herself a star, and fades like Lucifer at twilight. The same light may be successively like a sun and like a star. This is a warning that the values in which the poem deals are not absolute but relative. As the 'Shape all light' disappears she becomes for Rousseau:

A light from Heaven whose half-extinguished beam
Through the sick day in which we wake to weep
Glimmers, for ever sought, for ever lost . . . (429–31)

The Shape achieves a stable value by disappearing, and this is the process that Shelley's poem repeatedly represents. When Rousseau awoke from his sleep by the river, he imagined his life before that sleep to have been 'heaven'. As the sun rose in the prologue, night, which had before been a 'mask/Of darkness', became 'gemmed' by stars. Stars may appropriately represent human ideals, but only because man is a daytime creature. The ideal is defined by its absence: it can exist only when it is 'unseen'. The 'Shape all light' when she is visible is thoroughly ambivalent; as she disappears she becomes for Rousseau a 'light from Heaven'.

In *The Triumph of Life* lights become ideal when they disappear, but they are also beautiful in their approach. The sun's rising in the prologue is strikingly beautiful, but as the prologue continues counter-suggestions appear. The same process is enacted in the description of the 'Shape all light', and is repeated in Rousseau's description of the chariot's approach. The brightness of the chariot is at first magnificent:

A moving arch of victory, the vermilion
And green and azure plumes of Iris had
Built high over the wind-winged pavilion,
And underneath etherial glory clad
The wilderness . . . (439–43)

Only afterwards does Rousseau note the chariot's pathetic worshippers and the 'captives fettered' to it. Visions are beautiful in their approach and in their disappearance, and this Shelley thought of as man's predicament: 'We look before and after,/And pine for what is not . . .'. Ideals are located in the past and the future; they are reactions against one's present predicament. When he awoke from his sleep by the river Rousseau did not know:

whether my life had been before that sleep
The Heaven which I imagine, or a Hell
Like this harsh world in which I wake to weep . . . (332–4)

He did not know, and yet he imagined it to be Heaven in reaction against his present Hell. Similarly starlight is an ideal because it is unseen throughout 'the sick day in which we wake to weep'.

This explains Shelley's techniques within the poem. It explains why the values of the various lights flicker. Value is a perception, a quality bestowed by the percipient rather than inherent in the perceived. An ideal is an imaginary construct that has its existence in both the past and the future because they too are imaginary constructs. But it is nonetheless powerful for that. For Rousseau the 'Shape all light', once she has disappeared, becomes a controlling dream that shapes his notion of life, a light which 'Although unseen' (Shelley would correct Rousseau's 'although' to 'because')

> is felt by one who hopes
> That his day's path may end as he began it
> In that star's smile.

An ideal can give satisfying aesthetic shape to what otherwise would appear merely the shapeless linear progress of the chariot. It can make life fulfil the demand Coleridge made of art: it can make 'those events which in real or imagined History move on in a *straight* line, assume to our understanding a *circular* motion'. And it can do so precisely because it is imaginary.

Ideals exist only in the absence of what is idealised. They are apprehended by the imagination. They exist therefore only in the individual's apprehension of them. And yet *The Triumph of Life* conducts a massive attack on the notion of individuality. A characteristic verbal device of the poem merges the many with the one. When the visionary first describes the multitude moving along the dusty road, he refers to 'a great stream/Of people', 'one of the multitude', 'One of the million leaves of summer's bier', and notes that 'Old age and youth, manhood and infancy,/Mixed in one mighty torrent did appear'. The unit is sometimes the crowd, sometimes the individual amongst the crowd. The point is that there is no difference between them. The one among the many is not effectively different from the many formed into one. Rousseau points out many individuals among the chariot's captives; he distinguishes them, but he emphasises their sameness: 'But all like bubbles on an eddying flood/Fell into the same track at last...' (458–9). The effect of this repeated pattern is quite different from the effect of similar patterns in, say, Act IV of *Prometheus Unbound*. When the Earth insists that we speak of 'Man, oh not men! a chain of linked thought', he is celebrating human community, the recognition that individual human minds are each a portion of the one mind. In *The Triumph of Life* the device works rather as Pope uses it in *The Dunciad*: 'lo! one vast egg produces human race', 'One Trill shall harmonize joy, grief, and rage', 'We bring to one dead level ev'ry mind'. This theme reaches its climax in the poem's last episode. The chariot's followers exhale shadows which at first seem 'Each like himself and like each other'. But they are 'distorted', differentiated, by the 'car's creative ray'. Instead of the many falling into the one track, the one becomes various. But the reversal is ironic. The different shapes of the shadows are random, insignificant, 'Obscure clouds moulded by the casual air'. Individuality of appearance which may seem only an external emblem of a more personal individuality, becomes an idle joke, a whimsical moulding of identical shadows. The car's 'creative ray' is a grim parody of divine creativity (compare the 'uncreating word' of Pope's goddess of Dulness). Value or the ideal is, then, a perception of the individual, and individuality is a sick joke.

The poem ends with its bitterest twist, and yet the way is open for a characteristically Shelleyan development. The uniformity that the poem describes as rendering human life banal, meaningless, might be reinterpreted in the light of Shelley's 'intellectual philosophy'. The revelation that the distinctions between men are arbitrary might become a cause not for despair but for celebration. An ideal is the imaginary construct of the individual, but the notion of individuality is a fiction. The ideal therefore is a perception common to man, a thought that has existence within the 'one mind'. Similarly, the ideal is established only in the absence of what is idealised. It has its existence in the past and the future, because past time and future time are themselves imaginary constructs. The poem, as we have it, stresses the delusory nature of the ideal, but the realisation that the past and the future are fictions frees the way for an attack on the tyranny of temporal series. The stars shone in the night that is past, and will shine in the night that is to come, but, the poem reminds us, they shine still, although unseen, 'Through the sick day in which we wake to weep'. But to imagine such developments is to indulge in speculative criticism.

Leavis's description of *The Triumph of Life* is reasonably accurate:

The poem itself is a drifting phantasmagoria – bewildering

and bewildered. Vision opens into vision, dream unfolds within dream, and the visionary perspectives... shift elusively and are lost.

Its value as a poem depends very much on how far its reader is prepared to accept and be satisfied with its labyrinthine inconclusiveness. The activity of most of the poem's admiring critics suggests that they are no more satisfied with such a state of affairs than Leavis[26], and yet perhaps a precisely expressed bewilderment, an elegantly articulated scepticism, is not a gift that we should scorn.

6 Shelley's Development

The preceding chapters have offered an account of Shelley's development. Poems like *Alastor* and *Laon and Cythna* exist loosely within particular traditions of poetry, but their meaning, their central activity, is not integrated with their form. The intelligence that they reveal is a subtle one, but it is an intelligence that works underneath the poem rather than an intelligence that reveals itself through the poem.

In the poems of Shelley's maturity, word and thing, aesthetics and ethics, are reconciled, though somewhat paradoxically. Shelley's politics and ethics remain aggressive, but the aggression reveals itself through rather than beneath the poem's form. The poems tend to attack the traditions to which they belong, so that the radical poet's dissatisfaction with existing modes of thought is revealed through the language of his poem. Shelley admits still to 'a passion for reforming the world', but the distinctive characteristic of the mature poetry is that the passion for reforming the world is unified with, and expressed through, a passion for reforming poetry. This phase of Shelley's work is characterised by an exciting, precarious fierceness, precarious because in wrestling with the likes of Aeschylus and Milton, Shelley is rather in the situation of Jacob wrestling with God.

The third and final phase of Shelley's development is prefigured in *Adonais* and fully developed in *The Triumph of Life*. It is characterised by an eccentrically individual, even anachronistic, choice of literary models. The poet finds freedom from literary history in asserting his ability to write the literary history within which he places his poem. The result is a new stylistic assurance, an autumnal sobriety not evident in Shelley's earlier poems. Much of the energy of the earlier poetry is lost, but so too is the precariousness.

A description of Shelley's development in these general terms serves little purpose. It is in the examination of particular poems that the generalities have their basis. In the body of this book,

therefore, the need to give due attention to the individual poem
has been given precedence over the thesis. But in this final
chapter I shall clarify the development that I have described
through a discussion of three short poems, *Hymn to Intellectual
Beauty*, *Ode to the West Wind*, and *With a Guitar, to Jane* – one
poem of Shelley's youth, one of his maturity, and one from his
final phase.

Hymn to Intellectual Beauty

Hymn to Intellectual Beauty is not a hymn, but an ode. It is
conventional eighteenth-century practice to give the title 'hymn'
to any poem in which the quality addressed is awarded divine or
celestial characteristics. Parnell wrote a *Hymn to Contentment*,
Thomson a *Hymn on Solitude*, Akenside a *Hymn to Cheerfulness*
and a *Hymn to Science*. The lighthearted ascription of divine status
to an abstract quality is distinguished very clearly from the
earnest hymn which celebrates God. There is no confusing
Thomson's manner in his *Hymn on Solitude* with the serious
sublime of his *Hymn to God's Power*.

Romantic poets characteristically refuse such clear distinctions
between poetic figures and expressions of belief. Their tendency
to locate divinity in the human mind necessarily obscures the
distinction that Thomson makes so easily. In Southey's *Hymn to
the Penates*, for example, the Penates enter the poem as a
traditional figure expressing Southey's reverence for domesticity; they end it as an expression of his sense that at home he is
watched over by the ghosts of those he has loved who are now
dead. Whether he ascribes to the ghosts' actual existence, or
whether they function simply as metaphors for emotional
longings remains deliberately doubtful. In Wordsworth's *Immortality Ode* the seriousness with which Wordsworth entertains the
notion of pre-existence is both genuinely problematic and
unimportant; problematic because Wordsworth fails to follow
Thomson in expressing his attitude to the belief asserted in the
poem through his tone, unimportant because the kind of belief
that he demands has its basis not in theology, but in psychology.
The truth that Wordsworth claims for it, and for him it is the
most important kind of truth, is truth to human experience.

Shelley's hymn is obviously influenced by Wordsworth's ode.

The Spirit to which he refers in the poem's title as Intellectual Beauty is an intimation of immortality. He prays: 'Depart not – lest the grave should be,/Like life and fear, a dark reality' (47–8). It is a Spirit that illumines, occasionally and inconstantly, human experience, so that the chaotic world in which we live appears during these moments beautiful and significant. On its occasional descents it 'Gives grace and truth to life's unquiet dream'.

Shelley's Hymn, like other Romantic odes, refuses to determine with any precision the kind of belief in this Spirit that is required of the reader. Shelley refuses to choose between a Spirit who is a means of describing those moments in experience when the world we live in seems transformed, and a Spirit who is literally a transcendental power that occasionally visits human life. But whereas Southey and Wordsworth sidestep the problem of belief, Shelley encounters it directly. He asks why the Spirit he addresses is inconstant in its visitations, and replies sceptically:

No voice from some sublimer world hath ever
    To sage or poet these responses given –
    Therefore the names of Demon, Ghost, and Heaven,
Remain the records of their vain endeavour,
Frail spells – whose uttered charm might not avail to sever,
    From all we hear, and all we see
    Doubt, chance, and mutability. (25–31)

In other words, theological systems impose a certainty, a stability on the world that has no basis in the reality of human experience, which is an experience of uncertainty, of flux. His Spirit is apparently distinguished from such 'Frail spells' by being itself 'inconstant' and a 'mystery', and therefore compatible with the facts of experience. 'Intellectual Beauty', it seems, is presented as a hypothesis better founded than, say, God, but still a hypothesis. The reader is not required to assent to the transcendental existence of the Spirit, but only to its appropriateness as a means of describing the common experience of life.

This seems to be confirmed by the opening lines of stanza IV: 'Love, Hope, and Self-esteem, like clouds depart/And come, for some uncertain moments lent'. The status of Intellectual Beauty seems to be reduced to that of a personification, like Love, Hope and Self-esteem. The eighteenth-century technique seems to act as a reminder that Shelley expects us to take the divinity of Intellectual Beauty not much more seriously than Akenside expected his reader to take the divinity of 'Cheerfulness'. But the stanza continues:

Men were immortal and omnipotent,
Didst thou, unknown and awful as thou art,
Keep with thy glorious train firm state within his heart.
(39–41)

These lines convey a quite different claim; they are meaningless if addressed to a personification, significant only if they are addressed to a God. If we refer back to the stanza's opening lines then we may reinterpret 'Love, Hope, and Self-esteem', understand them not as eighteenth-century personifications, but as a Shelleyan version of that trinity of virtues, Faith, Hope and Charity, which, through association with the Father, the Son and the Holy Ghost, has accrued for Christians a quasi-divine status quite different from that awarded by Akenside to Cheerfulness. A poet like Thomson wrote two kinds of hymn, but carefully distinguished the tone and the vocabulary appropriate to each. Shelley chooses to conflate them.

It might be argued that this is exactly what Wordsworth, too, accomplishes in the *Immortality Ode*, but there are two crucial differences. Shelley raises the problem of belief that Wordsworth either sidesteps or refuses as meaningless. And Shelley uses a vocabulary that forces the reader to make decisions about the status of the Spirit addressed. I have already suggested that such a problem occurs in the phrase 'Love, Hope, and Self-esteem'. It is perhaps more easily identified in the phrase 'thy glorious train'. A 'train' is a conventional item in the vocabulary of eighteenth-century odes. Thomson's *Solitude* has a train composed of 'Innocence', 'Religion', and 'Liberty'. But God also has a train; he is surrounded by his angels. It is a word appropriate to either of the kinds of hymn that Thomson wrote, but he would certainly have indentified in each kind of hymn the way in which the word was used. Shelley may have been attempting to fuse these two kinds of hymn, but the effect is rather confusion.

The problems raised by Shelley's poem become more extreme in its autobiographical section, stanzas V and VI. He describes how, as a boy, he had visited churchyards, and tried, without success, to raise ghosts. He was 'musing deeply on the lot of life', when: 'Sudden, thy shadow fell on me;/I shrieked, and clasped my hands in ecstasy!' It is clear that Shelley chooses to describe this experience in the language of religious conversion, or of prophetic rapture. This is a common enough technique among Romantic poets. Compare Southey's recollection of his feelings on first leaving home in *Hymn to the Penates*:

I can remember the first grief I felt,
And the first painful smile that clothed my front
With feelings not its own: sadly at night
I sat me down beside a stranger's hearth;
And when the lingering hour of rest was come,
First wet with tears my pillow. (40–45)

The repetition of the word 'first' suggests that the experience has a kinship with the religious – it is a revelation – but Southey chooses a language that maintains close links with the more ordinary human experience of homesickness. This is necessary, because for him the divinity of the Penates is a notion that receives its support from the reality of the human experience that it expresses. Similarly, Wordsworth's use of the notion of pre-existence is sustained by his ability to describe, and the reader's to recognise, the child's experience of living in a world not his own. Shelley, on the other hand, chooses a vocabulary, 'shriek', 'clasp', 'ecstasy', that expresses a lack of contact with the normally human.

The problem is that the divinity of Intellectual Beauty, like the divinity of the Penates, and like Wordsworth's notion that the soul before birth lives in heaven, can be supported only by a demonstration that it expresses a human truth. Southey and Wordsworth achieve this, Shelley does not. His shriek is, as it were, unlocated. It does no good to compare Shelley's lines with similar exclamations by St Theresa or any other visionary whose experiences take place within an established theology. St Theresa is free to express the otherworldliness of her experience because the existence of her God is not at issue. She has no need therefore to ground her experience on the experiences of common human nature. What is more, the Gothic environment of Shelley's lines, visits to graveyards and attempts to raise the dead, place his shriek in an uncomfortable limbo between the shriek of the ecstatic prophet and the shriek of the fluttering heroine of a novel by Mrs Radcliffe.

Shelley suggests that the Spirit he addresses may, in some unspecified manner, accomplish the overthrow of tyranny. He calls the ghosts of his past to witness that:

> never joy illumed my brow
> Unlinked with hope that thou wouldst free
> This world from its dark slavery . . . (68–70)

Thomson places Liberty in the train of Solitude. He does not need to argue in favour of this conjunction; it is enough that the reader recognise that Solitude and Liberty are both admirable and that he feel them to be congruent. Southey's case is different. When he suggests that if man would only show proper reverence for 'Household deities', then 'all mankind' would be united 'in the equal brotherhood of love', one might wish that he had traced more cogently how a love of domesticity can be expected to accomplish this end. Shelley, too, establishes no necessary connection between the Spirit he addresses and the freeing of the world from 'its dark slavery', but the poem fails to make clear whether this omission is the result of a pictorial imagination, like Thomson's, that places Solitude and Liberty together because such a juxtaposition seems aesthetically appropriate; or whether the omission is the result of a weak mind, like Southey's; or whether it is an expression of Shelley's scepticism. If we agree to read this poem through our knowledge of Shelley's other poems, then it becomes clear that the third effect is the one intended. That Mont Blanc has a voice 'to repeal/Large codes of fraud and woe' is a similarly unsupported assertion, and *Mont Blanc* makes obvious use of sceptical modes of thought. But my point is that *Hymn to Intellectual Beauty* fails to provide a context that makes this possibility any more acceptable than the other possibilities that I have described.

The last stanza of Shelley's Hymn imitates, successfully but too obviously, the final stanza of the *Immortality Ode*. Shelley, like Wordsworth, accepts that the Spirit that visited him in his youth will no longer offer him the same intensity of experience. Like Wordsworth he finds consolation in the calmness of maturity, and in the recognition that his life is still controlled by his youthful experience:

The day becomes more solemn and serene
  When noon is past – there is a harmony
  In autumn, and a lustre in its sky,
Which through the summer is not heard or seen,
As if it could not be, as if it had not been!
  Thus let thy power, which like the truth
  Of nature on my passive youth
Descended, to my onward life supply
  Its calm – to one who worships thee,
  And every form containing thee,
  Whom, Spirit fair, thy spells did bind
To fear himself, and love all human kind. (73–84)

The first ten lines of Shelley's stanza are a superior pastiche of
Wordsworth. Compare the following lines from the *Immortality
Ode* (197–9):

The Clouds that gather round the setting sun
Do take a sober colouring from an eye
That hath kept watch o'er man's mortality . . .

But the final declamatory couplet of Shelley's poem is quite at
odds with Wordsworth's meditative conclusion: 'To me the
meanest flower that blows can give/Thoughts that do often lie
too deep for tears' (203–4). The moral of Shelley's poem is
ringing, declamatory, like the ending of an eighteenth-century
ode rather than a Romantic ode.

What Shelley is trying to accomplish in *Hymn to Intellectual
Beauty* is reasonably clear. The poem is an address to a deity who
is designed to be consistent with Shelley's scepticism, and who is
related antagonistically to the Christian God. When he asks why
his Spirit is inconstant, and why it allows the existence of evil, he
concludes: 'No voice from some sublimer world hath ever/To
sage or poet these responses given . . .' (25–6). He chooses a
word out of Christian ritual, 'responses', in order to assault
Christian claims that man is the recipient of a divine revelation.
The lesson that his Spirit teaches man, 'To fear himself, and love
all human kind', in its substitution of 'himself' for 'God',
similarly challenges Christian orthodoxy. He asserts a connection between the Spirit he worships and the overthrow of the
world's tyrannies to counter the association he imagined to exist

between the Christian God and oppressive governments.

But it is hard to believe that the poem's religious language consistently works on the level of parody. When he recalls his youthful experience of conversion, 'Sudden, thy shadow fell on me;/I shrieked, and clasped my hands in ecstasy', he borrows subversively the language of Christian mysticism, but to what effect? Shelley becomes the hierophant of Intellectual Beauty in opposition to the prophets of the Christian God, but it is far from clear how seriously his prophetic role is to be taken. The poem fails to establish the value of its deity by deriving it from a convincingly imagined human experience. Shelley's God remains a rhetorical device rather than an embodied emotion, so that Shelley becomes the prophet of a rhetorical figure, a role that the reader is expected to regard with an unacceptable gravity. One meets the same problem later in the nineteenth century in poems by Swinburne like *Dolores* and *Hertha*.

The poem contains three languages; a religious language borrowed from orthodox Christianity, a declamatory language borrowed from the eighteenth-century ode, and a language borrowed from Wordsworth. It is easy to see why these three languages are chosen. The religious language becomes the means through which Shelley establishes the antagonism between his hymn, and a Christian hymn. Through the language of the eighteenth-century ode Shelley expresses his scepticism, his awareness that the ascription of divinity to Intellectual Beauty may be no more than a rhetorical device. Through the poem's Wordsworthian language he suggests the basis of religious conviction in human experience. But the poem does not reconcile these languages; they remain at odds with one another, and are even mutually destructive. *Hymn to Intellectual Beauty* is a poem that reveals its poet's failure to create a language and a form that express his theme. In this, it is symptomatic of the failure of almost all of Shelley's early poems.

Ode to the West Wind

F. R. Leavis's suggestion that stanza II of *Ode to the West Wind* reveals a poet concerned to extract emotional capital from a description of clouds rushing across the sky which bears no precise relationship to any actual skyscape has prompted a number of

learned rebuttals.[1] The question at issue is Leavis's charge that
Shelley has only a 'weak grasp upon the actual', that the imagery
of his poetry is only loosely related to the phenomena of the real
world. This is a substantial issue, one that deserves critical
attention, and the debate has produced interesting results. But it
is time now to state that the presumed audience of the poem is
not confined to those expert in meteorology, that the poem's
natural description is not its end, but its means.

The crucial activity of the poem is its simultaneous suggestion
of rigid order and violent, uncontrolled energy. The rigidity of
its formal construction has often been remarked. The first stanza
concerns leaves and seeds, the second clouds, the third waves.
The arena of the first stanza is the earth, of the second the sky, of
the third the sea. The fourth stanza introduces the poet, and binds
together the first three stanzas:

> If I were a dead leaf thou mightest bear;
> If I were a swift cloud to fly with thee;
> A wave to pant beneath thy power . . . (43–5)

This seems to summarise the contents of the poem thus far. But
the poem's first stanza concerned seeds as well as leaves, and the
fourth stanza interrupts, rather than marks the completion of,
the poem's elemental scheme. The first stanza concerned earth,
the second air, the third water. The poem is resolved only in its
fifth stanza when the poet's words are described as 'Ashes and
sparks' from 'an unextinguished hearth', and when the description of his thoughts merges dead leaves with germinating seeds:
the thoughts will be driven 'over the universe/Like withered
leaves to quicken a new birth!'

Francis Berry notes that the structure of the poem exactly
imitates that of the conventional prayer;[2] its first three stanzas
describe the power and attributes of the spirit addressed, its
fourth confesses the unworthiness of the supplicant, its fifth
makes a petition and asks that it be granted.

The structure of Shelley's poem is, then, both conventional
and solidly architectural. It is a structure designed in opposition
to the poem's subject, the formless, 'uncontrollable' west wind.
But to say this is to make modification immediately necessary,
for any reading experience of the poem is likely to include a sense
of interpenetration between the poem's subject and its form

which is at least as strong, if not stronger, than an awareness of the contrast that I have described. The reader who claims to like the poem because he can hear the wind in it is not obviously deluded. The poem does not express a simple contrast between itself and its subject, but rather a contrast within itself between rigid order and uncontrollable energy.

As we might expect of the mature Shelley this contrast is reflected in the poem's verse form. Each of the five stanzas contains fourteen lines, each ends with a couplet. Shelley's stanza is, as has often been noted, a version of the sonnet.[3] But the poem is written in terza rima, the onrush of which is halted at the end of each stanza by a couplet. The vaulting momentum of terza rima contrasts with the self-contained structure of the sonnet. Shelley, addressing the wind, describes the autumn night as 'the dome of a vast sepulchre' which will be 'Vaulted with all thy congregated might'. The reference to the dome enforces the architectural sense of the word 'Vaulted', and yet if we consider the action of a wind rushing against a dome, then the other, gymnastic sense of the word intrudes. It is a poem that attempts to hold together the contradictory notions of explosive energy and containment, a paradox that Shelley achieves in the pun on 'Vaulted', in a phrase like 'congregated might', but also in the poem's simultaneous use of two apparently antithetical verse forms, terza rima and the sonnet.

Shelley's ode is addressed to the west wind, to Zephyr or Favonius. Zephyr begins his literary career in Hesiod as a violent wind, though a wind that brings fair weather, but by the eighteenth century zephyrs had come to denote soothing spring breezes. For Pope a zephyr is a light breeze in the description of which only soft sounds are appropriate: 'Soft is the strain when Zephyr gently blows,/And the smooth strain in smoother numbers flows...'.[4] Shelley, too, addressing Miss Sophia Stacey, claimed that her thoughts 'like zephyrs in the billow/ Make thy gentle soul their pillow'.[5] Zephyr, the west wind, is emasculated in eighteenth-century poetic diction. It suffered the same fate as the word 'gale' which so far lost its violence that Thomson could claim that 'every gale is peace'. Shelley, then, in recreating the west wind as a violent tempest, rounds on his immediate literary tradition. His wind is created in dramatic opposition to the zephyrs that had soothed the slumber of many an eighteenth-century swain.

The word 'zephyr' puzzled etymologists, some of whom derived it from *zophos*, darkness, others from zoaphoros, life-bearing. In eighteenth-century poetry the word has no contact with either of these etymologies. Gray associates zephyrs with 'the clear blue sky',[6] and, far from invigorating, they lull; Shelley in his weaker mood associated them easily with pillows. Shelley reforges the links between his Zephyr and the word's etymologies. His west wind drives dark stormclouds across the sky, and it is literally 'life-bearing', it carries 'winged seeds'. Shelley returns to the literary and etymological origins of the zephyr, but the effect of this is to mark a violent break with his immediate literary inheritance.

Shelley's Zephyr is an autumn wind, 'the breath of Autumn's being'. The first line of Shelley's poem breaks the very strong literary tradition that associated the west wind with the spring.[7] Of course, Shelley had the best of authorities for his defiance of the convention. The west wind dominates the Florentine autumn. One of the effects he gains is to suggest a fresh and vital contact with the actual by creating his wind in dramatic opposition to the lulling, spring zephyr that had become a conventional poetic prop. But another effect is equally, if not more, important. Shelley begins the poem in defiance of a strong literary convention, the association of the west wind with the spring. He marks this defiance by reminding his reader in the first stanza of the conventional west wind, the autumnal wind's sister, 'Thine azure sister of the Spring'. The same association exists between the two winds that exists between Laon and Cythna, his sister and his other self. The momentum that dominates Shelley's poem, the drive of autumn towards spring, is analogous to the journeys made by several Shelleyan lovers in pursuit of a union with the ideal self that they love, but in *Ode to the West Wind* the journey becomes urgent rather than dreamlike as in *Alastor*, or vaguely discursive as in *Laon and Cythna*. One of the ways in which Shelley creates this momentum is to begin his poem in abrupt defiance of a strong literary convention, so that the drive of autumn towards Spring, the momentum demanding the transformation of the violent west wind into his 'azure sister', is powered by the reader's demand that his conventional expectations be gratified, that 'the breath of Autumn's being' become the wind of Gray's spring: 'Cool Zephyrs through the clear blue sky/Their gathered fragrance fling'.

In Shelley's ode order and energy clash. The total structure of the poem is firm, even rigid, rather like the strong structures that Keats favoured in his odes, but the effects gained by the two poets are quite different. Keats's odes have a slow, ritualistic movement; Shelley's ode gives an impression of barely restrained wildness. Keats seems to officiate, Shelley to participate. The three sections of Shelley's poem, corresponding to the three parts of a prayer, are each dominated by a single grammatical construction. The first three stanzas are dominated by the vocative, the address to the wind, the fourth stanza by the conditional of hopeless aspiration, the last by the imperative, by demand. The speaker lives through the various stages of the poem, implicated in them. The strong construction of a Keats ode is reflected in the poet's assured mastery of his subject, but the speaker within Shelley's poem struggles for control over his subject matter. Keats's assured mastery is refused in favour of a precarious energy.

Examine the last stanza of Keats's *Ode to Psyche*:

Yes, I will be thy priest, and build a fane
In some untrodden region of my mind,
Where branchèd thoughts, new grown with pleasant pain,
Instead of pines shall murmur in the wind:
Far, far around shall *those* dark-cluster'd trees
Fledge the wild-ridged mountains steep by steep;
And *there* by zephyrs, streams, and birds, and bees,
The moss-lain Dryads shall be lull'd to sleep;
And in the midst of *this* wide quietness
A rosy sanctuary will I dress
With the wreath'd trellis of a working brain,
With buds, and bells, and stars without a name,
With all the gardener Fancy e'er could feign,
Who breeding flowers, will never breed the same:
And *there* shall be for thee all soft delight
    That shadowy thought can win,
A bright torch, and a casement ope at night,
    To let the warm Love in! (50–67)

In the riches of this stanza it may seem perverse to direct the reader to the italicised words; *where, those, there, this*, and yet they are important. They are syntactic pointers insisting that each of the stanza's clauses refers back, directly or indirectly, to the phrase 'some untrodden region of my mind'. They impose on the stanza a reassuringly firm structure within which linguistic daring, 'branchèd thoughts', coexists harmoniously with conventionality, those 'zephyrs', and which supplies an adequate protection to the poem's splendidly vulnerable last line. Keats's syntactic security is a reflection, and one of the causes, of a mature assurance of manner that conciliates the reader.

Keats's syntax presents his diction and his theme to the reader, Shelley's syntax is an aspect of the experience that the poem expresses, inseparable from the materials that it organises. Take the second address to the wind in the poem's first stanza:

> O thou,
> Who chariotest to their dark wintry bed
> The winged seeds, where they lie cold and low,
> Each like a corpse within its grave, until
> Thine azure sister of the Spring shall blow
> Her clarion o'er the dreaming earth, and fill
> (Driving sweet buds like flocks to feed in air)
> With living hues and odours plain and hill . . . (5–12)

This is a reasonably firm sentence; it describes the west wind in its aspect as 'preserver', and therefore firm order is appropriate. But it is quite unlike Keats's sentence. Notice, for example, that in the phrase 'their dark wintry bed', the pronoun has no antecedent: it refers forward to the 'wingèd seeds'. The clauses generate one another avoiding backward reference. Keats was unembarrassed by the inappropriateness of describing a future action, 'I will be thy priest', through a syntax that is organised by the backward reference of its individual members. He uses a syntax that presents an experience to the reader, but is not itself implicated in that experience. Shelley, on the other hand, devises a syntax that in itself expresses the forward momentum of the seasonal cycle. That the sentence is the product of some thought is clear if we compare it with an early treatment of the same theme (from *Laon and Cythna*):

> The blasts of Autumn drive the wingèd seeds
> Over the earth, – next come the snows, and rain,
> And frosts, and storms, which dreary Winter leads

Out of his Scythian cave, a savage train;
Behold! Spring sweeps over the world again,
Shedding soft dews from her etherial wings;
Flowers on the mountains, fruits over the plain,
And music on the waves and woods she flings,
And love on all that lives, and calm on lifeless things. (3649–57)

This is, of course, a poor exercise in the manner of Thomson, but notice the inept connectives, 'next come', and 'Behold'. The seasons follow one another like different groups in a pageant. The sentence quite fails to express how the seasons are bound together as different stages of a single natural process. It is a merit of the sentence from *Ode to the West Wind* that the firm, onward-moving rhythm of its syntax expresses the harmonious process of the seasonal cycle.

That this is a merit will, I suspect, be conceded readily enough. More problematic are those sentences that describe the wind in its aspect as 'destroyer'. The poem begins:

O wild West Wind, thou breath of Autumn's being,
Thou from whose unseen presence, the leaves dead
Are driven, like ghosts from an enchanter fleeing,
Yellow, and black, and pale, and hectic red,
Pestilence-stricken multitudes . . . (1–5)

The lines contain three addresses to the wind. Compare the opening lines of Keats's *Ode on a Grecian Urn*:

Thou still unravish'd bride of quietness,
Thou foster-child of silence and slow time,
Sylvan historian . . .

Each address personifies the urn, but the three comparisons are carefully distinguished – the bride, the child, the historian. One is conscious that the figures are judiciously, even analytically chosen. Shelley's three addresses to the wind are far less carefully distinguished, and unlike Keats he puts in doubt the figurative status of his expressions. Words like 'breath' and 'presence' are border-posts between the literal and the figurative. 'Breath' may be a literal description of the wind blowing, but the phrase 'breath of Autumn's being', suggests rather that the word is a subdued pun, a translation of the Latin *spiritus* or the Greek *pneuma*. 'Presence' suggests the actuality of the wind, but also a divine or kingly presence. Shelley, as Leavis remarks, tends to confuse the tenor and vehicle of his metaphors. When the leaves are compared to ghosts fleeing from an enchanter, and to 'Pestilence-stricken multitudes' the figurative status of the expression seems clear. But in a celebrated simile, Virgil, followed by Milton, had compared the dead with leaves.[8] Shelley inverts the simile, but the reader is conscious still of its original form. The references to the leaves as ghosts and as 'Pestilence-stricken multitudes' are separated by a line that is most easily understood as a literal description of their colour: 'Yellow, and black, and pale, and hectic red'. But 'hectic' is a disease word, 'pale' refers more usually to sickly faces than leaves. The line might just as easily list the symptoms of various diseases; it refers unstably both to the leaves and to the plague-ridden multitudes with which they are compared. The inversion of adjective and noun in the phrase 'the leaves dead/Are driven' has a similar effect. The inversion reminds the reader than the word 'dead' may also function as a noun. The phrase can be read as a compressed simile, as if a stroke seprarated 'leaves' and 'dead', or as if 'dead' were a sudden substitution for leaves. The lines work strenuously to confuse the literal and the figurative, so strenuously that it would be difficult to maintain that the effect was the result of carelessness rather than premedi-tation. The confusion is relevant to the poem in that Shelley wishes to present his wind as a symbol of apocalyptic change, and to suggest that this association is natural, rather than willed. But it is surely also true that he wishes his language to reflect the turmoil that is the result of the wind's activity. Notice that when the wind is described as a preserver, the similes are lucidly articulated: 'Driving sweet buds like flocks to feed in air'.

The reader should respond to the potential confusion of the lines, in order to appreciate the somewhat fragile order that Shelley successfully imposes on them. Similar effects are achieved throughout the first three stanzas:

Thou on whose stream, mid the steep sky's commotion,
Loose clouds like earth's decaying leaves are shed,
Shook from the tangled boughs of Heaven and Ocean,

Angels of rain and lightning: there are spread
On the blue surface of thine aëry surge . . . (15–19)

Notice how syntactic order is precariously maintained by
punctuation alone. The phrase, 'Angels of rain and lightning', is
in apposition to the phrase 'loose clouds'. The clouds are 'angels'
or 'messengers' of the approaching storm. But a strong exercise
of the will is needed, when reading the lines, not to end the clause
beginning 'on whose stream' with the word 'Ocean', so that the
'Angels' become the subject of the verb 'are spread'. The colon is
the one defence against the anarchic energy of Shelley's sentence.
A reading of the ode engages the reader in the poem's central
activity, the attempt to impose on the 'uncontrollable' energy of
the wind the human order of language. The reader imposes order
on Shelley's sentence by reading it correctly, but is made aware
that this is a precarious, threatened achievement. Compare these
lines from the poem's fifth stanza: 'Scatter, as from an unextinguished hearth/Ashes and sparks, my words among mankind!
(66–7). Both parts of the simile are objects of the same verb,
'Scatter'. It is the same device that Keats used in the final stanza of
Ode to Psyche: 'Where branchèd thoughts, new grown with
pleasant pain,/Instead of pines shall murmur in the wind . . .'
(52–3). Here 'branchèd thoughts' and 'pines' are joint subjects of
the same verb, 'shall murmur'. But notice that Keats uses the
phrase, 'Instead of', to secure a clear distinction between
'thoughts' and 'pines'. Shelley, on the other hand, tempts the
reader to misread his sentence, tempts him to pause at the end of
the line ending the simile after the word 'hearth'. He works to
engage the reader in the attempt to control the uncontrollable.
    In the examples I have given syntax wins precarious victories
over the wind's energy. But sometimes syntax is defeated:

            Thou
For whose path the Atlantic's level powers
Cleave themselves into chasms, while far below
The sea-blooms and the oozy woods which wear
The sapless foliage of the ocean, know
Thy voice, and suddenly grow gray with fear,
And tremble and despoil themselves: oh, hear! (36–42)

The wind defeats the Atlantic's 'level powers', piling up large waves, but then Shelley turns to the sea bed, 'while far below'. The conjunction 'while' links simultaneous actions, but when used in the middle of a sentence it also creates an expectation that the action of the second clause will contrast with that of the first, an expectation that Shelley strengthens by the phrase 'far below'. The reader expects the sea's 'sapless foliage' to be immune from the wind's destructive power. The expectation holds for two lines, until it is threatened by the ominously biblical phrase, 'know/Thy voice', and finally collapses in the lines that follow. Shelley's syntax suggests limits to the wind's destructive power, but the wind refuses to conform to them.

Shelley attempts to impose a syntax on the wind, the wind seeks to escape from the poet's syntactic confines. Energy struggles with order. The struggle embodies the human attempt to order the violent power of nature, and also the struggle between two perceptions of the wind, the wind as a violent, anarchic energy, and the wind as a necessary constituent of the stable, harmonious order of the seasonal cycle. In the first three stanzas the struggle is unresolved. Each stanza consists of two addresses to the wind, each of which is followed by a complex description of the wind's attributes:

> Thou dirge
> Of the dying year, to which this closing night
> Will be the dome of a vast sepulchre,
> Vaulted with all thy congregated might
> Of vapours, from whose solid atmosphere
> Black rain, and fire, and hail will burst: oh, hear! (23–28)

Shelley's awe of the wind's power seems to have distracted him from the need to provide his sentence with a main verb. The final words of the stanza, 'oh, hear!', seem to be a desperate plea for the wind's attention syntactically unrelated to the stanza they end. In fact, 'hear' is the main verb on which the sequence of subordinate clauses of which the entire stanza is composed depends. Each of the first three stanzas is a tangle of subordinate clauses which become a sentence only in the stanza's last word, its main clause, 'hear!' And yet that same word acts as a refrain, and the refrain in most poems is syntactically unrelated to the stanza it ends. In so far as we react to the word as a refrain, the wind has defeated the poet's attempt to impose on it a syntactic order. In so far as we recognise it as the stanza's main verb, the poet has succeeded in imposing grammar on the wind.

Stanza IV describes and expresses Shelley's awareness of weakness. Formally, the stanza is integrated with the whole poem; the supplicant's confession of his unworthiness is a conventional item in the prayer. But when a Christian confesses that he is the most miserable of sinners, unworthy to address God, his prostration, though it may be passionately enacted, is impersonal. Shelley borrows the formal structure of the prayer, but he cannot similarly borrow the emotional ritualism of Christianity. As a consequence his prostration is also a breakdown. The stanza expresses an imaginative failure in the face of the wind.

The stanza uses a borrowed vocabulary, borrowed from the Psalms, the Book of Job, and most obviously from *Childe Harold* (IV, X, 7–8): 'The thorns which I have reap'd are of the tree/I planted, – they have torn me, – and I bleed . . .'. But it would be quite wrong to argue that the borrowings create an impersonal language that saves the stanza from an embarrassingly personal reference.

The stanza fails, but the reader ought to be aware that its failure is accomplished; it is an achieved failure. Shelley signals it by an abrupt change of the rhythm. Instead of a strong movement from line to line, and from clause to clause, the stanza jerks from one phrase to another. Instead of an unchecked forward movement, the poet looks back, both at the first three stanzas of his poem ('Oh, lift me as a wave, a leaf, a cloud'), and at his own childhood ('if even/I were as in my boyhood'). The poem collapses from prophecy into nostalgia, and once again form and theme are unified; the poet looks back at his past poem and looks back at his past life. Imaginative failure is suggested by a different kind of metaphor. In the first three stanzas the wind achieved metaphorical status through the power with which it was presented, but now metaphors are weakly explained, 'the thorns of life'. Formally Shelley signals his awareness that the stanza fails by its omission of fire. The first stanza concerned earth, the second air, the third water: not until the fifth do we meet fire, the 'unextinguished hearth'. The fourth stanza is a hiatus in the poem's symmetry. The stanza represents Shelley's verse at its most precarious, for if it succeeds, it succeeds in failing.

In the fifth stanza the poem's recovery from this failure is magnificiently achieved. The whole poem expresses a progression from struggle, to collapse, to achieved mastery.[9] The successful completion of this rhythm, which is surely satisfying, is dependent on the failure of the fourth stanza. That the success of one part of a poem must be judged in terms of the function of that part within the whole is a critical commonplace. Stanza IV of *Ode to the West Wind* successfully passes this test, but ought that to result in a revaluation of the merits of the stanza, or a re-examination of the critical principle that sanctions it? Shelley is a poet ready to use any means to secure a desired end. We do not, most of us, admire this procedure in life; ought we to in poetry? Coleridge confronted this problem when considering Wordsworth's method in the *Lyrical Ballads*, and he reacted by revising the commonplace, by arguing that poetry was 'that species of composition' defined by 'proposing to itself such delight from the whole as is compatible with a distinct gratification from each component part'.[10]

At the beginning of the fifth stanza rhythmic units are identified with line units, but as the stanza proceeds they become more confidently expansive. The prayer to the wind becomes less a supplication, more a demand. The poet is at first a 'lyre', a passive instrument played by the wind. By the poem's end the wind is a trumpet: 'Be through my lips to unawakened earth/The trumpet of a prophency!' From being an instrument the poet has become a musician. He assumes the power of the wind: 'Be thou, Spirit fierce/My spirit!' The breath of the wind becomes the poet's own breath; he assumes its spiritual power. In the first stanza the wind was an 'enchanter', but in the final stanza the poet assumes this role; his verse becomes an 'incantation'. In stanza II the cloud driven by the wind rushed on the poet like 'some fierce Maenad'. The poet was Orpheus, but Orpheus at the mercy of a Dionysian power he could not control. During stanza V he reassumes the Orphic power to organise and to direct natural forces by his 'incantation'. He even assumes an Orphic power over death; his 'dead thoughts' will 'quicken a new birth'. The phrase superbly unites the poem as a revolutionary manifesto, the poem as artefact, and the poem as private document. The 'new birth' is the revolutionary change that Shelley anticipates, the poem that he has written, and the baby with which his wife is pregnant.[11]

The poem climaxes in Shelley's assumption of a prophetic

role, but it ends in a question: 'O, Wind,/If Winter comes, can
Spring be far behind?' (69–70). The question bravely attempts to
be rhetorical, but in it affirmation coincides with wistfulness.
The certainty that the seasonal cycle will continue its round, that
nature will be reborn in the spring of 1820, is not matched by a
similar certainty of the imminence of the apocalyptic spring that
Shelley prophesies. The poem's confidence is based insecurely
on a metaphorical confusion to which Shelley must adhere, for it
preseves in him Hope, and 'Hope is a most solemn duty, the
nurse of all other virtues'. [12] *Ode to the West Wind* is, in a sense
other than Shelley intended, a 'congregated might', a grand
peut-être.

The contrast that I have described in the poem between
uncontrolled energy ane rigid order reflects the two aspects of the
wind, 'Destroyer and preserver'. Had Shelley simply accepted
the association between uncontrolled energy and destruction,
and between order and preservation, his poem would have been
built on the antithetical pattern so dear to the eighteenth century.
But Augustan antitheses are supplanted by a Romantic dialectic.
Shelley's terms, 'Destroyer and preserver', recall two of the
Gods of the Hindu trinity, Siva and Visnu. The third, Brahma
the creator, is absent. He emerges in the ode's last stanza as the
synthesis of destruction and preservation, the product of the
battle waged in the poem between energy and order. Creation,
the poem suggests, is the outcome of a strenuous combat
between order, the preserver, and energy, the destroyer. Creation unifies the warring elements that gave it birth. It is
appropriate that *Ode to the West Wind* should be Shelley's most
popular poem, for it presents a metaphor for the aesthetic
practice that characterises the major work of Shelley's maturity.
In a poem like *Prometheus Unbound* Aeschylean drama and
Miltonic blank verse act as preservers against which Shelley must
battle destructively in order to create his poem. The achieved
poem is at once the record and the outcome of this battle.

With a Guitar, to Jane

The final phase of Shelley's work is characterised by a new
assurance. The poet's voice loses its self-assertiveness, and gains
a new impersonality. It may seem unlikely that this development

should be exemplified in one of the late lyrics to Jane Williams. These poems emerge from the claustrophobic, tense atmosphere of the house on the gulf of Spezia that the Shelleys shared with Edward and Jane Williams in the spring of 1822. They record, it seems, real events – Shelley did give Jane a guitar, and this poem no doubt accompanied the gift.

It takes its place within a courtly tradition, characteristic of the sixteenth and early seventeenth centuries, of sending to the mistress a gift accompanied by a poem in which the gift is presented and explained. Turberville wrote a charming lyric 'To His Ring, Given to his Lady, Wherein was Graven This Verse; "My Heart is Yours"'. Donne's fifth elegy accompanies a portrait of the poet given to his mistress. As an example of this tradition, consider Herrick's lyric, 'The Tear Sent to Her From Staines', a poem that purports to accompany a tear, or perhaps a pearl, sent to a cold, demanding mistress.

Herrick sends the tear, but it is the last, he claims, that he will expend in the affair. If the lady continues to demand tears, he admits that he will be forced to pay her in order to keep possession of his 'poor, yet loving heart'. Then he considers his position if she should demand his heart also:

> Say too, she would have this;
> She shall: then my hope is,
>   That when I'm poor
>   And nothing have
>   To send or save,
> I'm sure she'll ask no more.

Herrick builds a stanza that expresses pathos through its broken rhythms, and through its colloquial diffidence. Herbert seems to be the dominant influence, but the reader who recognises this may well be disconcerted by his discovery. Those techniques that Herbert uses to express a serious piety seem trivialised when Herrick puts them at the service of a conventional love lyric.

Herrick's poem pretends to no passionate earnestness; it is, in a sense, a game, but a game played skillfully, and wittily. Take, for example, the poem's title, 'The Tear Sent To Her From Staines'. 'Tears' or 'lacrimae' conventionally denoted poems of complaint or grief, as, for example, Spenser's *Teares of the Muses*. The 'tear' of Herrick's title refers both to his gift, and to his poem. The tear is sent from the town Staines; dropped into the Thames it will flow downriver to where the lady lives, possibly in London. But the title associates 'Staines' with 'tear', so that the word acts as a pun, and the poem's title suggests also the conventional conceit by which the poet-lover claims to have wept the ink from which his poem is written. As Cleveland surprisingly puts it: 'I am no Poet here: my pen's the spout/Where the Rain-water of my eyes runs out . . .'. The title means that Herrick, while at Staines, sent his mistress a tear by letting one drop into the river, but it means also that the poem is a love complaint written in the tears that the lover weeps.

Herrick's poem is addressed to a girl who 'strings [his] tears as pearls'. On its receipt the tear becomes a pearl. Perhaps we should imagine that Herrick in fact sends his mistress a pearl that he chooses to describe as a solidified tear. In any case the conceit is conventional enough, but it is interestingly handled. The obvious point is that the lady is cold, so that when it touches her the tear freezes into a pearl. But there is also a suggestion that the lady is mercenary; she demands tears of the poet, puts a price on them, regarding them as tributes that will 'enrich' her. She demands that Herrick weep for her, because his tears enhance her prestige. She wears them as she might wear jewellery, pearls, to increase her prestige in her own eyes, and in the eyes of others. But the conceit, like the word 'tear' in the poem's title, refers not only to the situation that the poem records, but to the poem itself. Grief, when it is expressed as a poem, achieves definite shape, beauty and permanence; the tear becomes a pearl.

With a Guitar, to Jane is written in the same tradition as Herrick's poem. To quote one of the weaker passages from Shelley's lyric may seem enough to expose this claim as absurd:

> For it had learned all harmonies
> Of the plains and of the skies,
> Of the forests and the mountains,
> And the many-voicèd fountains;
> The clearest echoes of the hills,
> The softest notes of falling rills,
> The melodies of birds and bees,
> The murmuring of summer seas,
> And pattering rain, and breathing dew,
> And airs of evening . . . (65–74)

This seems to be exactly the kind of limp, discursive poeticising into which octosyllabic couplets tempt so many English poets. Shelley's dreadful 'modern eclogue', *Rosalind and Helen* fails to protect itself from this vice by its irregularity, and *Lines Written among the Eugenaean Hills* is not free from it. The verse seems completely to have abandoned muscular control over what is said. Nothing seems further from Herrick's elegant compression, but that notwithstanding *With a Guitar, to Jane* is a witty poem, and witty in a distinctly seventeenth-century manner.

The poem falls very obviously into two parts. In the first Shelley characterises himself as Ariel, and Jane and her husband Edward as Miranda and Ferdinand. The second part of the poem (lines 43–90) describes the history and the attributes of the guitar, Shelley's gift to Jane. The two parts of the poem seem only loosely related, but we should remember that Shakespeare's Ariel was freed by Prospero from imprisonment within a cloven pine. Shelley recalls this incident when he laments that Ariel has been 'Imprisoned for some fault of his/In a body like a grave'. In the second part of the poem the manufacture of the guitar is described; a tree was felled, and its wood carved. The guitar, like Shakespeare's Ariel, had been imprisoned in a tree.

The Tempest links the two parts of Shelley's poem, and it associates Ariel with the present that he gives, the guitar; both suffered imprisonment. But there is a crucial difference between them. The felling of the tree was a death:

> and so this tree, –
> O that such our death may be! –
> Died in sleep, and felt no pain,
> To live in happier form again . . . (53–6)

When the tree is felled, the wood dies, but only that it may 'live in happier form again', freed from its imprisonment within the tree, freed as Shelley's Ariel complains he has not been, from 'a body like a grave'.

Jane is given two presents, a guitar and a poem. The poem explains the history and the qualities of the guitar, but it is also true that the guitar acts as a metaphor explaining the genesis and the distinctive qualities of poetry. Ariel and the guitar both suffer imprisonment; Ariel is confined in 'a body like a grave', the guitar was once imprisoned in a tree. The relationship between Ariel and the man he inhabits should be compared with the relationship between the guitar and the tree. Ariel is the poem's speaker, 'Ariel to Miranda'. He speaks the poem because in writing poetry man is freed from his mortal self: what is immortal within him, and therefore ill-at-ease existing within a mortal body, speaks. The difference between Ariel and the body he inhabits defines the distinction between the poet and the man. The difference between Ariel and the guitar defines the distinction between the poet and his poem. Ariel remains imprisoned. In writing poetry Ariel speaks, finding a limited freedom, but he speaks through Shelley; the poet cannot finally free himself from the man. In *A Defence of Poetry* Shelley claims that even in eternity Dante and Milton are 'enveloped and disguised', the poets still imprisoned within the men. The poem, on the other hand, wins independence from its antecedents. The guitar has been freed from its imprisonment within the tree. The music of the guitar is the product of the tree's experiences – it is presumably during its existence as a tree that the guitar 'learned all harmonies/Of the plains and of the skies' – and yet it is fully independent of the tree. Similarly, the poem expresses the experience of the man who wrote it, but when it is completed the umbilical cord attaching it to the experiences out of which it grew is cut.

The guitar was 'taught' by its maker 'justly to reply/To all who question skilfully'. The music of the guitar is a result of the cooperative enterprise of its maker and its player. The quality of the guitar's music is dependent on the skill of its player just as much as on the skill of its maker. Similarly, the meaning and beauty of a poem are the result of a cooperative enterprise between reader and writer.

The poem's last four lines bring it to a delicately ironic close:

But, sweetly as its answers will
Flatter hands of perfect skill,
It keeps its highest, holiest tone
For our beloved Jane alone.

This is a compliment to Jane's musicianship, and it also suggests that just as the guitar will play most beautifully for Jane, so the poem, though it may be enjoyed by everyone, will mean most to her. But the aesthetic theory that the poem has suggested does not allow that Jane is in any way specially privileged to appreciate the poem, for the poem, like the guitar, has gained independence from its origins. Jane's special relationship with the poet cannot then confer on her any special authority as a reader of the poem. The suggestion that Jane will best enjoy the poem is a compliment as unfounded as the statement that the guitar will reserve 'its highest, holiest tone' for her, or it is a contradiction of the theory that the poem has figured. The poem's last lines are poised delicately between being a gracefully irrational compliment, and a recantation. But the poem can dare to look ironically at itself because it has demonstrated an ingenious sophistication that upholds the notion of the impersonal autonomy of the poem even though, at the last, that notion is playfully doubted.

Shelley writes a poem in order to explain to Jane the history and the attributes of his present to her, the guitar. But the explanation of the guitar becomes a metaphorical explanation of the history and the attributes of the poem, of any poem. The poem explains the guitar, which explains the poem. The witty sophistication with which Shelley handles this conceit suggests that he is writing within the witty conceited tradition that in England was vital in the late sixteenth and early seventeenth centuries. But two questions remain; why should Shelley have chosen to revive this dead tradition, and why should he have thought fit to include within a poem of courtly compliment an aesthetic theory? Why should the poem have such a form, and why should it have such a content? As we answer the two questions, they will resolve into one.

Within the courtly tradition to which Shelley adheres the association between expressions of love and the expression of a literary theory is common. Sidney's, sonnet 'Loving in truth, and fain in verse my love to show' is a well-known example of this association; in fact the whole of *Astrophel and Stella* hinges on it. Shelley's fusion of courtly compliment and literary theory is, therefore, traditional.

With a Guitar, to Jane is a love poem, though restrained in its expression of love, so restrained that even at the poem's end, it speaks only of '*our* beloved Jane'. It is a love poem addressed to the wife of Shelley's close friend, Edward Williams. The seriousness of Shelley's attachment to Jane is not an issue that need be considered. It is enough that the reader is aware of the difficulty of the social situation. As a poet, as Ariel, Shelley is free to write a love poem to Jane, but to love her as a man would be to raise perplexing questions of personal loyalty. As a love poet he can take refuge in the distinction insisted on by Herrick, 'Jocund his music was, but his life was chaste', as a man in love he cannot. The elaborate fictions of the poem – Shelley as Ariel, Jane as Miranda, Edward as Ferdinand – are a means by which Shelley secures the distinction between the man and the poet, between love and love poetry, or, to use Sidney's pun, between faining and feigning. But the fictions are fragile, so that in the poem's last line Miranda is spoken of as 'our belovèd Jane'. The poem contains a theory of poetry that works out the distinctions between the man, the poet and the poem, but it is also written into a social situation in which these distinctions are very much to the point. The theory distinguishes the man from the poet, Shelley from Ariel, and is therefore a defence of the propriety of the poem. But it allows that the man and the poet are incompletely separated – Ariel, the poet, is imprisoned within the body of the man. When in the poem's last line the fictional mistress Miranda, is supplanted by Jane, the poet, as it were, confesses to the man within whom he is imprisoned. But the poem, like the guitar, is able to free itself from its mortal prison. Although the poet may, in the poem's last line, steer dangerously close to impropriety, the poem is safe from the charge. It is fully protected against it by the witty self-consciousness with which the problem is explored. Ariel cannot gain freedom from Shelley, but the guitar can be freed from the tree, the poem can achieve independence from the emotions out of which it grew.

The theory that the poem adumbrates is then prompted by the social situation within which the poem was written, and it is equally true that Shelley's rather surprising choice of literary tradition is prompted in the same way. Love poetry of the late sixteenth and early seventeenth centuries plays with witty self-assurance on the thin line that separates love from poetry. Sidney 'fains' and 'feigns', desires and pretends, and the pun acts as a sign that the activities of the lover and the activities of the poet are wittily reconciled one with the other. In *With a Guitar, to Jane* the literary tradition to which the poem belongs, the literary theory that it expresses, and the social situation out of which it arose explain each other, harmoniously support each other in a manner that is typical of the final phase of Shelley's poetic development. The poet no longer seeks to define himself in opposition to his predecessors. No more does he create a violent autumnal west wind dramatically opposed to the lulling spring zephyrs of the eighteenth century. Instead, he locates a particular literary tradition within which his own poem may quietly take its place. Literary tradition no longer threatens to imprison the poet, because it is no longer seen as monolithic. A poet does not inherit his tradition: he chooses it. The new approach results in the quiet, impersonal self-assurance evident in Shelley's last lyrics and in *The Triumph of Life*, his last major poem.

Notes

Preface

1. Carl Grabo, *A Newton Among Poets* (Chapel Hill, 1935); Peter Butter, *Shelley's Idols of the Cave* (Edinburgh, 1954); Desmond King-Hele, *Shelley: His Thought and Work* (2nd edition, London, 1971); Geoffrey Matthews, 'A Volcano's Voice in Shelley', (*English Literary History*, 24, 1957, pp. 191–228. Peter Butter is especially useful in correcting the interpretative excesses of Grabo. Matthews's article is a model of what this kind of criticism ought to be.
2. Carl Grabo, *The Magic Plant* (Chapel Hill, 1936); C. E. Pulos, *The Deep Truth: A Study of Shelley's Scepticism* (Lincoln, Nebraska, 1962); J. A. Notopolous, *The Platonism of Shelley* (Durham, North Carolina, 1949); N. Rogers, *Shelley at Work* (2nd edition, Oxford, 1967); Earl Wasserman, *Shelley: A Critical Reading* (Baltimore and London, 1971). Grabo, Notopolous and Rogers stress Shelley's debt to Plato and to Neoplatonism. Wasserman follows Pulos in placing Shelley's thought within a tradition of sceptical idealism. I am myself in broad agreement with Pulos and Wasserman.
3. K. N. Cameron, *The Young Shelley: The Genesis of a Radical* (London, 1951), and *Shelley: The Golden Years* (Cambridge, Mass., 1974).
4. Yeats's essays 'The Philosophy of Shelley's Poetry' and '*Prometheus Unbound*' are included in his *Essays and Introductions* (London, 1961); Peter Butter, *Shelley's Idols of the Cave*; N. Rogers, *Shelley at Work*; Harold Bloom, *Shelley's Mythmaking* (New Haven, Conn., 1959); E. B. Hungerford, *The Shores of Darkness* (New York, 1941); Earl Wasserman, *Shelley: A Critical Reading*; Stuart Curran, *Shelley's Annus Mirabilis* (San Marino, 1975).
5. N. I. White, *Shelley* (London, 1947); Richard Holmes, *Shelley: The Pursuit* (London, 1974); Carlos Baker, *Shelley's Major Poetry* (Princeton, 1948); K. N. Cameron, *The Young Shelley* and *Shelley: The Golden Years*; A. M. D. Hughes, *The Nascent Mind of Shelley* (Oxford, 1947); Desmond King-Hele, *Shelley: His Thought and Work*; N. Rogers, *Shelley at Work*; Judith Chernaik, *The Lyrics of Shelley* (Cleveland and London, 1972).
6. It is, of course, untrue that all Shelley's critics lose sight of the individual poem. Wasserman and Curran in particular are not guilty of this. But even when the uniqueness of the individual poem is recognised there is a tendency to concentrate on its inner meaning rather than its surface. Judith Chernaik and Milton Wilson in *Shelley's Later Poetry* (New York, 1959) come closer to the kind of interest that I have in Shelley's poems. Perhaps

Notes

251

the approach that I find most sympathetic is that of Timothy Webb in his
study of Shelley's translations, *The Violet in the Crucible* (Oxford, 1976).
7. *The Complete Poetical Works of Percy Bysshe Shelley*, edited by Neville
Rogers (Oxford, 1975), vol. II. Rogers makes many improvements on
Hutchinson's text, but I have not used his edition consistently for two
reasons. The two final volumes have not yet been published, and Rogers's
editorial methods are so individual that it is unlikely that his text will ever
win general approval.

Chapter 1

1. *Letters of Samuel Taylor Coleridge*, edited by Griggs (Oxford, 1956–71), vol.
I, p. 626.
2. *Biographia Literaria*, edited by Shawcross (Oxford, 1967), p. 11.
3. *Enquiry Concerning Political Justice*, edited by Kramnick (Penguin, 1976), p.
359.
4. *Diversions of Purley* (2nd edition, 1978), p. 31.
5. The first position is that of Lord Monboddo; the second that of Adam
Smith, and, for the most part, Condillac; the third that of Bentham and
Herder. Monboddo states his view in *Of the Origin and Progress of Language*
(Edinburgh, 1773–76). He believes himself to be upholding a conservative
position.
6. Johnson objects to Pope's definition because he believes that wit is located
both in the thought and its expression, but he is far from disagreeing with
Pope's distinction between the two. Johnson's theory of language is
orthodoxly Lockean. See Rackstraw Downes, 'Johnson's Theory of
Language', *Review of English Literature*, III, 1962, pp. 29–41.
7. See the review in *The Literary Gazette*, (9 September 1820).
8. *Oeuvres Philosophiques de Condillac* (Paris, 1947), vol. I, p. 366.
9. *The Works of Jeremy Bentham*, edited by Bowring (Edinburgh, 1843), vol.
VIII, p. 188.
10. *Shelley's Prose: The Trumpet of a Prophecy*, edited by D. L. Clark
(Albuquerque, New Mexico, 1966), p. 295.
11. *The Works of Jeremy Bentham*, vol. II, pp. 253–4.
12. *Prelude*, XI, 1805, pp. 67–73.
13. *Byron's Letters and Journals*, edited by Marchand (London, 1973–), vol.
V, p. 203.
14. *Shelley's Letters: The Letters of Percy Bysshe Shelley*, edited by F. L. Jones
(Oxford, 1964), vol. II, p. 71.
15. *The Works of Jeremy Bentham*, vol. I, p. 49 (footnote).
16. *The Works of Jeremy Bentham*, vol. IX, p. 76.
17. *The Works of Jeremy Bentham*, vol. VII, p. 188.
18. Shelley's preface to *Prometheus Unbound*.
19. *Prelude*, XII, 1805, pp. 264–77.
20. *The Works of Jeremy Bentham*, vol. VIII, pp. 321–2.
21. *An Essay Concerning Humane Understanding* (London, 1690), p. 251.
22. *Wordsworth's Literary Criticism*, edited by Smith (London, 1905), pp. 14–15.
23. *Wordsworth's Literary Criticism*, p. 22.

24. *Wordsworth's Literary Criticism*, p. 129.
25. *Shelley's Prose*, p. 278.
26. Ask any man . . . what relation is expressed by the preposition *of*, and, if he has not before-hand employed his thoughts a good deal upon these subjects, you may safely allow him a week to consider of his answer' (Adam Smith in his *Considerations Concerning the First Formation of Languages*).
27. *The Collected Works of Dugald Stewart*, edited by Hamilton (Edinburgh, 1854–60) vol. V, p. 155.
28. *The Collected Works of Dugald Stewart*, vol. V, p. 155.
29. This might seem to contradict the view of M. H. Abrams in his definitive exposition of Romantic critical theory, *The Mirror and the Lamp*. Abrams argues that neoclassical theory emphasises the relationship between the poem and its reader, whereas Romantic theory emphasises the relationship between the poet and the poem. But the disagreement between us is not so extreme. I suggest only that in neoclassical theory the poet and the reader are very close together: irony, that central Augustan device, demands, for example, that the perspectives of writer and reader coincide. In Romantic theory the three terms poet, poem and reader stand much further apart, and the poets become anxious at their separation.
30. *Wordsworth's Literary Criticism*, p. 36.
31. *Shelley's Prose*, p. 294.
32. *Shelley's Prose*, p. 291.
33. *Shelley's Letters*, vol. I, p. 401.
34. *The Sublime: A study of Critical Theories in 18th Century England* (New York, 1935)
35. *Shelley's Prose*, p. 294.
36. *The Early Letters of William and Dorothy Wordsworth*, edited by de Selincourt (Oxford, 1935), p. 306.
37. *Wordsworth's Literary Criticism*, p. 140.
38. *Shelley's Prose*, p. 287.
39. *Biographia Literaria*, vol. II, pp. 12–13.
40. M. H. Abrams: *The Mirror and the Lamp* (London, 1953), p. 118.
41. *Biographia Literaria*, vol. II, p. 13.
42. *The Works of Peacock*, edited by Brett-Smith and Jones (London, 1934), vol. VIII, p. 22.
43. *Shelley's Prose*, p. 284.
44. *Shelley's Prose*, pp. 289–90.
45. *Shelley's Prose*, p. 282.
46. *Shelley's Prose*, p. 285.
47. *Shelley's Prose*, p. 279.
48. *Shelley's Prose*, p. 280.
49. *Shelley's Prose*, p. 282.
50. The preface to *Hellas*.
51. *Shelley's Prose*, p. 287.
52. A fine example occurs in Shelley's 'Sonnet on the Republic of Benevento':

Man who man would be,
Must rule the empire of himself; in it

Must be supreme, establishing his throne
On vanquished will, quelling the anarchy
Of hopes and fears, being himself alone.

Chapter 2

1. The best discussion of the poem's political background is by K. N. Cameron, *Shelley: The Golden Years* (Cambridge, Mass., 1974), pp. 343–50.
2. *Shelleys Poetical Works*, edited by Thomas Hutchinson, corrected by G. M. Matthews (London, 1970) p. 345.
3. *Shelley's Poetical Works*, p. 389.
4. T. S. Eliot gives *The Witch of Atlas* guarded praise as a 'charming trifle' in *The Use of Poetry and the Use of Criticism* (London, 1944, first published 1933), p. 93 (footnote). Donald Davie, a critic with more respect for charm, sanctions it as urbane in *The Purity of English Diction* (London, 1952), pp. 157–8. *The Mask of Anarchy* is the only one of Shelley's poems that wins F. R. Leavis's admiration (in *Revaluation* (London, 1936), pp. 228–30).
5. 'Uber Realistische Schreibweise', *Schriften zur Literatur and Kunst* (Frankfurt, 1967), vol. II, pp. 162–73.
6. The ballad is translated by John Willett in *Bertolt Brecht, Poems 1913–56* (London, 1976), pp. 409–14.
7. Willett translates:

Spring returned to Germany.
In the ruins you could see
Early green birch buds unfold
Graceful, tentative and bold.

8. Willett translates:

Blood and dirt, elective allies
Winding over hills and vallies
Belched, stank, squittered out their plea:
Freedom and Democracy!

9. *Shelley: The Pursuit* (London, 1974), p. 537.
10. Compare Coleridge's *The Devil's Thoughts*, first published in *The Morning Post*, 6 Sept 1799.
11. *Shelley's Poetical Works*, p. 345.
12. *Shelley: The Golden Years*, p. 347.
13. *The Masque of Anarchy*, edited by Leigh Hunt, pp. VII–VIII.
14. It was Eldon who gave judgement against Shelley when he tried to win custody of his first wife's children. In his memoir of Shelley Peacock remarks that Eldon was the one subject that provoked in Shelley more extreme expressions of horror than his school, Eton. Compare the treatment of Eldon in the *Mask* with 'To the Lord Chancellor' (*Shelley's Poetical Works*, pp. 542–4).

15. *The Masque of Anarchy*, edited by Leigh Hunt, p. V.
16. See K. N. Cameron, *Shelley: The Golden Years*, p. 347.
17. Stuart Curran compares Shelley's poem with Leigh Hunt's masque *The Descent of Liberty*, and argues that Shelley's knowledge of the seventeenth-century masque was derived largely from the 'Account of the Origin and Nature of Masks' that Hunt prefixed to his poem. See Curran's *Shelley's Annus Mirabilis* (San Marino, California, 1975), pp. 187–98. Curran also seems to recognise that Shelley's poem is a reversal of the conventional masque action, but the perception is not developed very clearly.
18. Curran associates the fact that the central character in Shelley's masque is Anarchy with Hunt's rather odd belief that 'lawlessness' is the supreme characteristic of the masque as a genre.
19. Compare Demogorgon in *Prometheus Unbound* (III, i). Jupiter expects the arrival of his son, a Messiah who will stamp out the remaining resistance to his power, just as Milton's Messiah crushed the rebel angels. But Demogorgon, like the Shape in *The Mask of Anarchy*, reveals himself as a member of the Devil's party and reverses the expected action.
20. *Shelley: The Pursuit*, p. 708.
21. See C. E. Robinson, *Shelley and Byron: The Snake and Eagle Wreathed in Fight* (Baltimore and London, 1976), especially pp. 203–20. Robinson provides the best account of the literary relations between the two poets.
22. *Shelley's Letters*, vol. II, p. 198.
23. Compare, for example, *Don Juan* (I, XCI).
24. Compare Dryden's *The Wife of Bath Her Tale*, 1–4.
25. Carl Grabo, *The Meaning of the Witch of Atlas* (Chapel Hill, 1935); G. Wilson Knight, *The Starlit Dome* (London, 1941), pp. 224–34; Harold Bloom, *Shelley's Mythmaking* (New Haven, 1959), pp. 165–204.
26. *Shelley's Mythmaking*, pp. 170–1.
27. *Virgil's Gnat*, 5–8.
28. Mary Shelley records in her journal that in June and July of 1820 Shelley had been reading Fortiguerra's *Il Ricciardetto*. *The Witch of Atlas* was written 14–16 August 1820.
29. I, VI, 16–18.
30. *The Starlit Dome*, p. 224; *Shelley's Mythmaking*, p. 183.
31. *Paradise Lost*, I, 537.
32. *Paradise Lost*, I, 711.
33. *Paradise Lost*, I, 594–9.
34. *Paradise Lost*, II, 1–5.
35. *Paradise Lost*, II, 549.
36. *Peter Bell*, 128–30.
37. Wilson Knight finds in the poem 'the sharp phrase-hardening of Yeats's later style' (*The Starlit Dome*, p. 225), and Harold Bloom agrees (*Shelley's Mythmaking*, pp. 192–3).

Chapter 3

1. *British Moralists, 1650–1800*, edited by D. D. Raphael (Oxford, 1969), vol. II, pp. 55–6.

2. *Shelley's Prose*, pp. 282–3.
3. *Enquiries*, edited by Selby-Bigge (Oxford, 1902), p. 174.
4. *British Moralists, 1650–1800*, p. 79.
5. The whole of *Lara* is a single verse portrait, but my remarks refer in particular to paragraph XVII.
6. *British Moralists, 1650–1800*, p. 80.
7. *British Moralists*, p. 55.
8. *Shelley's Prose*, p. 293.
9. *Byron's Letters and Journals*, edited by Prothero (London, 1898), vol. II, p. 66.
10. *Vindication of the Rights of Women*, edited by Kramnick (Penguin, 1975), p. 168.
11. The most impressive critical reading of *Alastor* is Earl Wasserman's, *Shelley: A Critical Reading* (Baltimore and London, 1971), pp. 11–41. I am much indebted to it. Wasserman realises that the central problem of the poem is whether the career of the poem's hero is set within a context that allows the reader to place it within a critical perspective. He argues that the narrator is a Wordsworthian nature poet, whereas his hero is a poet of the ideal for whom nature is only a shadow obscuring the true god. The two poets have radically different values, and within the poem the two sets of values criticise each other. To the nature poet the ideal poet's rejection of this world is a regrettable and possibly sinful rejection of present good, but to the ideal poet the nature poet's satisfaction with this world would be an infamous denial of all that is divine in man. Wasserman reads the poem as a dialogue, and is able, through this technique, to offer a solution to many of the poem's problems. My disagreement with him is slight, but significant. The plot of the poem makes it impossible to sustain the argument that the poet and his hero are related to one another as two independent characters. The relation of the poet to his hero should be thought of rather as the relation between a poet and his fiction. Eclogue X, within which Gallus is a fiction created by Virgil, is therefore a better guide for the reader of *Alastor* than Shelley's *A Refutation of Deism*, the prose dialogue to which Wasserman compares it.
12. The case for the influence of *Alastor* on *Endymion* was first argued by A. C. Bradley in his *Oxford Lectures on Poetry* (London, 1909), p. 241.
13. The two discussions of the poem that have interested me most are Wilson Knight's in *The Starlit Dome* (London, 1941), pp. 189–97, and K. N. Cameron's in *Shelley: The Golden Years*, pp. 311–41. They have, however, absolutely nothing in common.
14. See *Shelley: The Golden Years*, pp. 311–41 (passim)
15. *Shelley's Letters*, vol. I, p. 564.
16. *Shelley's Letters*, vol. I, p. 411 and 563.
17. In a letter to Godwin Shelley argued that his main talent was 'to apprehend minute and remote distinctions of feeling', and 'to communicate the conceptions which result from considering the moral or the material universe *as a whole*'. He adds, 'Of course I believe these faculties . . . to exist very imperfectly in my own mind'. (*Shelley's Letters*, vol. I, p. 577). In the *Essay on Life* he argues that the individual mind is only an abstraction from what he calls 'the one mind', but again he quickly adds, 'Let it not be

supposed that this doctrine conducts to the monstrous presumption that I, the person who now write and think, am that one mind. I am but a portion of it' (*Shelley's Prose*, p. 174).

18. *Shelley's Poetical Works*, p. 157.
19. In the *Quarterly Review* (April 1819), quoted in *Shelley: The Critical Heritage* (London and Boston, 1975), p. 131.
20. For a different, but not incompatible, account of the poem's structure, see R. H. Haswell, 'Shelley's *The Revolt of Islam* [*Laon and Cythna*]: "The Connexion of its Parts"', *Keats – Shelley Journal*, XXV (1976), pp. 81–102.
21. Most criticism of *Julian and Maddalo* has begun from Byron's remark that the poem records conversation he had with Shelley when Shelley visited him in Venice to discuss arrangements for the upbringing of Allegra, Byron's illegitimate daughter by Clair Clairmont. This has led most critics to assume that Julian represents Shelley, Maddalo Byron, and Maddalo's daughter Allegra. The problem of the poem becomes the identity of the madman. Most argue that he is Shelley in a bad mood, some that he is a depressed Byron, and a few that he is Tasso strayed in from a play on Tasso's madness that Shelley began but never finished. These readings are summarised by C. E. Robinson in *Shelley and Byron: The Snake and Eagle Wreathed in Fight* (Baltimore and London, 1976), pp. 81–104. Robinson himself offers a reading that ingeniously reconciles them all. His ingenuity, however, is surely misplaced, for the poem is explicable in its own terms without recourse to Shelley's biography. Earl Wasserman in *Shelley: A Critical Reading*, pp. 57–83, and G. M. Matthews in '*Julian and Maddalo*: The Draft and the Meaning', *Studia Neophilologica*, 35 (1963), pp. 57–84, both recognise that the biographical problem is irrelevant to the poem, and, as a consequence, offer more satisfactory readings of it. My disagreement with G. M. Matthews is with his assumption that Shelley must approve of Julian because Julian voices some of Shelley's own ideas. My disagreement with Earl Wasserman is that he assumes the poem to be about the ideas that it expresses, whereas I believe it to be a poem about the men that express the ideas, a poem about the *psychology* rather than the *validity* of belief.
22. *Shelley's Letters*, vol. II, p. 196.
23. *Shelley's Letters*, vol. II, p. 108.
24. *Ars Poetica*, 96–8.
25. For an account of the controversy see J. J. Van Rennes, *Bowles, Byron and the Pope Controversy* (Amsterdam, 1927).
26. *Byron's Letters and Journals*, edited by Prothero (London, 1901), vol. V, p. 554.
27. *Institutio Oratoria*, VI, II, 8.
28. *Institutio Oratoria*, VI, II, 18.
29. *Of the Origin and Progress of the English Language* (Edinburgh, 1793–96), vol. III, p. 352.
30. Preface to the edition of 1815.
31. *Institutio Oratoria*, VI, II, 29.
32. *Shelley's Prose*, p. 293.
33. *Prometheus Unbound*, II, iv, 73.

34. See Arnold's essay 'The Study of Poetry' in *Essays in Criticism*, Second series.
35. *Purity of Diction in English Verse* (London, 1952), p. 143.
36. *Shelley's Letters*, vol. II, p. 290.

Chapter 4

1. *Publications of the Modern Languages Association of America*, 40 (1925), pp. 172–84. C. A. Zillman's *Prometheus Unbound: A Variorum Edition* (Seattle, 1959) contains an interesting and comprehensive compendium of previous interpretations. Since then the most interesting discussions have been Harold Bloom's in *Shelley's Mythmaking* (New Haven, 1959), Milton Wilson's in *Shelley's Later Poetry* (New York, 1959), Earl Wasserman's in *Shelley: A Critical Reading* (Baltimore and London, 1971), and Stuart Curran's in *Shelley's Annus Mirabilis* (San Marino, California, 1975).
2. *Shelley's Prose*, p. 291
3. *Shelley and the Unromantics* (London, 1924), p. 202.
4. This, and most of Shelley's borrowings from Aeschylus are traced by Bennet Weaver in his article '*Prometheus Bound* and *Prometheus Unbound*', *Publications of the Modern Language Association of America*, 64 (1949), pp. 115–33.
5. Milton Wilson discusses this similarity in *Shelley's Later Poetry*, pp. 64–6.
6. Stuart Curran explains and emphasises Shelley's use of Zoroastrian mythology, but I believe that he exaggerates its importance and misunderstands its function (see *Shelley's Annus Mirabilis*, pp. 74 86).
7. A. M. D. Hughes compares Panthea's description of Prometheus with Shelley's of Correggio's 'Christ Beatified': 'the lips parted, but scarcely parted, with the breath of intense but regulated passion'. (*Shelley's Letters*, vol. II, pp. 49–50).
8. *Shelley's Prose*, p. 293.
9. *Shelley's Prose*, p. 287.
10. The debt to Virgil was pointed out by Earl Wasserman, *Shelley: A Critical Reading*, pp. 310–13. Wasserman offers the plausible explanation that Virgil's brand of epicureanism has similarities with Shelley's own thought.
11. Compare *Prometheus Bound*, 474–544.
12. *Paradise Lost* II, 666–7, and III, 380.
13. *Mythology and the Romantic Tradition in English Poetry* (New York, 1957), p. 162.
14. *Mythology and the Romantic Tradition in English Poetry*, p. 161.
15. *Shelley's Prose*, p. 293.
16. For an identification of this gas, see Carl Grabo, *A Newton Among Poets* (Chapel Hill, 1935), p. 186.
17. Prometheus's description of the cave recalls Lear's description of the life that he and Cordelia will live in prison. Lear's joy at imagining his imprisonment is a testimony to the power of the human mind to dominate its situation.
18. *Vindication of the Rights of Woman*, edited by Kramnick (Penguin, 1975), p. 261. The significance of Demogorgon has been endlessly discussed. The

fullest account of Demogorgon available to Shelley is Boccaccio's in *De Genealogiae Deorum*. Peacock précised Boccaccio's account in a note to his poem *Rhododaphne*, but Shelley may well have read the Boccaccio himself. Various interpretations of Demogorgon are summarised by L. A. Zillman, *Shelley's Prometheus Unbound: A Variorum Edition*, pp. 313–20. The two most interesting single contributions are by G. M. Matthews, 'A Volcano's Voice in Shelley', *English Literary History*, 24 (1957), pp. 191–228, and Earl Wasserman, *Shelley: A Critical Reading*, pp. 332–8.

19. *Shelley's Prose*, p. 174.
20. *Shelley's Prose*, p. 173.
21. It is evident from this that I accept Earl Wasserman's argument that the theme of the play is the pursuit by the 'one mind' of a knowledge of its own identity. Where I disagree with Wasserman is in his suggestion that Prometheus is the one mind. This seems to me to run counter to the play's plot. Prometheus is only a fragment of the one mind, hence his disappearance from the play.
22. *Lectures on Shakespeare*, edited by Ashe (London, 1890), pp. 188–9.
23. See, for example, Desmond King-Hele, *Shelley: His Life and Work*.
24. See Harold Bloom, *Shelley's Mythmaking*, pp. 143–5, and Carl Grabo, *A Newton Among Poets*, pp. 141–4.
25. *The Use of Poetry and the Use of Criticism* (London, 1944, first published 1933), p. 91.
26. *Shelley's Prose*, p. 287.

Chapter 5

1. *A Variorum Commentary on the Poems of John Milton*, vol. II, edited by A. S. P. Woodhouse and Douglas Bush (New York, 1972), p. 563.
2. The best short survey of this tradition is J. H. Hanford's 'The Pastoral Elegy and Milton's *Lycidas*', *Publications of the Modern Languages Association of America*, 25 (1910), pp. 403–47.
3. *The Pastoral Elegy,*, edited by T. P. Harrison and H. J. Leon (Austin, 1939), p. 263.
4. *A Study of Literature* (Ithaca, 1948), pp. 170–1.
5. *The World's Body* (Washington, 1964, first edition 1938), 'A Poem Nearly Anonymous', pp. 1–28.
6. *Shelley's Letters*, vol. II, p. 294.
7. Compare *Adonais*, 444–7.
8. See I, 65–9.
9. Theocritus, I, 65–7.
10. The original preface is printed by Ingpen and Peck in their edition of Shelley's work.
11. *The Lament for Adonis*, 79–88.
12. *The Lament for Bion*, 37–44 and 86–92.
13. Processions of mourners are described in Theocritus, I, 77–81; *The Lament for Bion* 26–31; Virgil's eclogue X, 19–30; and *Lycidas* 103–31.
14. Dionysius is conventionally represented carrying a *thyrsus* encircled by ivy or vine leaves, and is sometimes represented as a youth rather than as a fat

old man. See Tooke's *Pantheon* (London, 1809), pp. 52–3.
15. For example by Earl Wasserman, *Shelley: A Critical Reading*, p. 502.
16. *Shelley: A Critical Reading*, pp. 485–8.
17. R. H. Fogle offers a similar analysis of these lines in *The Imagery of Keats and Shelley* (Chapel Hill, 1949), pp. 18–19.
18. *Shelley's Prose*, p. 173. Compare the note to a chorus in *Hellas* (Hutchinson, pp. 478–9).
19. *Shelley's Prose*, p. 178.
20. See the footnote to line 311 in G. M. Matthews's edition of the poem.
21. The phrase 'pavilioned upon chaos' occurs in *Hellas*, line 772. In *Laon and Cythna* the temple of the spirit is built on the sea, and in *The Witch of Atlas* the witch's palace is similarly situated.
22. Matthews prints two drafts of the opening lines at the end of his text of the poem.
23. Compare the morning hymn in *Paradise Lost*, V, 153–208.
29. *Shelley's Mythmaking* (New Haven, 1959), pp. 231–6.
25. A. C. Bradley points out that this passage is modelled on Dante's vision of Matilda, 'Notes on *The Triumph of Life*', *Modern Language Review*, 9 (1914), pp. 442–3. But to recognise the model does not help to establish the significance of the Shape any more than a recognition of the source in Ezekiel helps to establish the significance of Shelley's chariot.
26. See F. R. Leavis, *Revaluation* (London, 1936), p. 231. The following discussions of the poem are representative in their variousness: Harold Bloom, *Shelley's Mythmaking*, pp. 220–75; P. H. Butter, 'Sun and Shape in Shelley's *The Triumph of Life*', *Review of English Studies*, n.s. 13 (1962), pp. 40–51; G. M. Matthews 'On Shelley's *The Triumph of Life*', *Studia Neophilologica*, 34 (1966), pp. 104–34; D. H. Reiman, *Shelley's 'The Triumph of Life': A Critical Study* (Urbana, 1965); K. N. Cameron, *Shelley: The Golden Years*, pp. 445–74. All these discussions, except Peter Butter's with which I am most in sympathy, attempt to fix the value of the various characters in the poem. Matthews, for example, insists that the 'Shape all light' is good, Bloom that she is bad. K. N. Cameron is the only critic to argue that Rousseau is right to join the chariot's followers. This view seems perverse, but, as I have suggested, it cannot be dismissed. It gains some support from a passage in Mary Wollstonecraft that strongly recalls *The Triumph of Life*:

Let me now as from an eminence survey the world stripped of all its delusive charms. The clear atmosphere enables me to see each object in its true point of view, while my heart is still. I am calm as the prospect in a morning when the mists, slowly dispersing, silently unveil the beauties of nature, refreshed by rest.

In what light will the world now appear? I rub my eyes and I think, perchance, that I am just awaking from a lively dream.

I see the sons and daughters of men pursuing shadows, and anxiously wasting their powers to feed passions which have no adequate object. . . . After viewing objects in this light it would not be very fanciful to imagine that this world was a stage on which a pantomime is daily performed for the amusement of superior beings. . . . I descend from my height, and mixing with my fellow-creatures feel myself hurried along the common stream.

Nevertheless Wollstonecraft insists that the young person must not stand aside from this pantomime:

> The youth should *act*, for had he the experience of a grey head he would be fitter for death than life . . . . Besides it is not possible to give a young person a just view of life; he must have struggled with his own passions before he can estimate the force of the temptation which betrayed his brother into vice. (*Vindication of the Rights of Woman*, edited by Kramnick, pp. 212–15).

Chapter 6

1. Leavis's charge is made in *Revaluation* (London, 1936), pp. 204–6. It has been very often challenged, for example by Desmond King-Hele, *Shelley: His Thought and Work* (London, 1960), pp. 215–16, and by John Holloway, *Selected Poems of Percy Bysshe Shelley* (London, 1960), p. 139.
2. *Poet's Grammar* (London, 1958), pp. 143–56.
3. For example S. C. Wilcox, 'The Prosodic Structure of the *Ode to the West Wind*' *Notes and Queries* (18 February 1950).
4. *An Essay in Criticism*, pp. 366–7.
5. 'To Sophia', *Shelley's Political Works*, p. 580.
6. *Ode on the Spring*, 9.
7. A tradition originating in Virgil and Ovid; *Georgics*, I, 44, and *Fasti*, 195–212.
8. *Aeneid* VI, 309–10, imitated in *Paradise Lost* I, 301–4. Virgil himself followed Homer, *Iliad* VI, 146.
9. See M. H. Abrams, 'Structure and Style in the Greater Romantic Lyric' in *From Sensibility to Romanticism*, edited by F. W. Hilles and Harold Bloom (New York, 1965).
10. *Biographia Literaria*, edited by Shawcross (Oxford, 1907), vol. II, p. 10.
11. Shelley's son, Percy Florence, was born in November 1819.
12. A phrase of Coleridge's quoted by Shelley. See *Shelley's Letters*, vol. II, p. 125. For the importance that Shelley attached to this precept, see Norman Thurston, 'Shelley and the Duty of Hope', *Keats – Shelley Journal*, XXVI (1977), pp. 22–8.

Index